P9-AQK-003

DISCARDED

Marvell's Allegorical Poetry

Marvell's Allegorical Poetry

BRUCE KING

THE OLEANDER PRESS
NEW YORK · CAMBRIDGE

THE OLEANDER PRESS
17 STANSGATE AVENUE
CAMBRIDGE CB2 2QZ
ENGLAND

THE OLEANDER PRESS
210 FIFTH AVENUE
NEW YORK, N.Y. 10010
U.S.A.

King, Bruce, b.1933
Marvell's allegorical poetry.
1. Marvell, Andrew — Criticism and interpretation
I. Title
821'. 4 PR 3546

ISBN 0-902675-60-5

Printed by
JOHN G ECCLES PRINTERS LTD
INVERNESS

Contents

Books by Bruce King

Dryden's Major Plays

Twentieth Century Interpretations of All for Love

Dryden's Mind and Art

Introduction to Nigerian Literature

Literatures of the World in English

A Celebration of Black and African Writing

Preface

My aim in this book is to offer a reading of Marvell's best-known lyric poems. It may seem a modest goal; however, it is likely that many of my interpretations will be controversial. There is a theory behind my explications: Marvell's imagination was shaped by habits of reading the Bible allegorically and by the influence of biblical allegorisations on devotional and secular literature. I claim that Marvell's lyrics are meant to be read allegorically even when the explicit subject is not religious.

My discussion of the poems is purposely rather one-sided. In the space available it is impossible to discuss the views of other critics, to offer a "practical criticism" of such matters as Marvell's style, imagery, wit, or to trace similarities and differences between Marvell's poems and those of his contemporaries. Basically I have tried to answer the essential question of Marvell criticism. What kind of poet is he? What are the poems about? What view of the world shapes his poetic inspiration? Exactly what are the poems saying?

The first chapter is a discussion of allegory intended for those readers who are unfamiliar with older biblical commentaries and traditional religious symbols. The second chapter explains why I believe Marvell's poems to have parabolic meanings. Succeeding chapters treat of individual poems; I have continually checked my interpretations against the Bible and such basic sources of commentary as Augustine and Bernard. Sometimes I have found that Marvell's images, allusions or puns are obscure and need reference to such commentaries. I have also made use of Matthew Poole's commentary on the Bible, as Poole's patron was General Fairfax, at whose estate Marvell presumably wrote his best poems.

I quote from the King James translation of the Bible, except for a few places where the Douay translation is better suited to my purpose. The many biblical passages to which I refer are meant to illustrate doctrine, themes, traditions and symbols; I do not claim that Marvell necessarily had the same passages in mind. As it would be awkward to write continually of Christian beliefs as if they were exotic myths, I will in the following pages use such phrases as "our hopes of salvation" and "our redemption".

BRUCE KING

All those who are wise in Divine matters, and are interpreters of the mystical revelations . . . prefer incongruous symbols for holy things. (Dionysius the Areopagite)

Distinctions in interpretation of this kind may be made at the will of the reader. (Saint Augustine)

Another interpretation has only just occurred to me. (Saint Bernard)

For the critic there simply exists no substitute for the knowledge of history and literary tradition. (Ralph Ellison)

CHAPTER ONE

The Allegorical Imagination

Marvell's place in English literature rests upon hardly more than a dozen lyrics and two long poems. The lyrics are among the best in English and are in some ways the most puzzling; there is no consensus as to what they are saying, or have as their subject matter. And yet the more we examine such poems as *The Garden* or *The Definition of Love* with the hope of understanding them, the finer they seem. In examining a poet's work in detail we often become bored as the work pales with familiarity. In the case of Marvell the effect is just the opposite. A charming and rather exquisite minor poet on close examination turns out to be a major poet. The poems are richer in imagination, more highly worked in detail, profounder in theme, and more sophisticated in presentation than was at first apparent. A consistency of theme, a central body of subject matter and a personality emerge. Perhaps most important is the kind of imagination which the poems reveal and which has made them possible.

Marvell's world is a world of mirrors in which the divine scheme in its varied aspects is reflected. It is a world of analogy based on the correspondence of all creation within the divine mind which has created the world, whose providence governs it and which sees all time simultaneously. It is Marvell's aim to reflect this divine vision in his poetry. He does not try to present all of it in a long poem as Milton did in *Paradise Lost*; each poem begins with some particular theme, subject or experience and embodies part of the vision. The power of Marvell's poetry is that each of the segments of the totality seems to shine with the light of a harmonious vision. Each poem opens vistas to the imagination. Each poem is a window to eternity. Eternity is not in the poems. Marvell does not attempt to describe the indescribable: his method is to draw upon the associations of an existing body of symbolism which is an expression of Christian belief and which recalls a body of doctrine. The poems are in a sense open rather than closed. They suggest, imply, bring to mind large areas of Christian experience and vision. Marvell's imagination does not need to create a vision in the way that a modern writer needs to organise the phenomena of reality into a myth of order or disorder. Marvell's poetic universe gives expression to centuries of Christian thought and feeling. It is rooted in an understanding of Christian doctrine and in a distinctly Christian view of the created world in relation to eternity.

The essential mode of Marvell's poetry is allegorical. The habits of imagining which govern it developed during centuries of allegorisation of the Bible and the application of allegorisation to other forms of literature. It is allegorical in that its explicit subject matter is not its main concern. The narrative or the feelings expressed refer the mind to spiritual matters which, however, are not explicitly treated in the poem. Christianity inherited from Judaism and from the Alexandrians the seeing of hidden meanings in literary texts. The hidden meaning was the real, or more profound, truth within the work. This was justified on various grounds. The language of both Testaments is often highly metaphorical. Many things described in the Bible are improbable or immoral; they therefore must be read symbolically. Perhaps most important, Christianity adopted from Judaism the habit of seeing the world as prophecy and fulfilment. Each event described in the Bible was part of a divine scheme slowly unfolding from the Creation of the world until the end of time. History has a purpose. The Fall of Adam and Eve would some day be reversed by the coming of a Messiah who destroys the Satanic adversary and restores the faithful to mankind's original happiness. The promise made to Eve in Genesis 3:15 ("And I will put enmity between thee and the woman, and between thy seed and her seed; it shall bruise thy head, and thou shalt bruise his heel") was seen as working its way towards its fulfilment throughout the Old Testament in the covenants God made with Noah and Abraham, in the founding of the Temple in Jerusalem, and in the many prophecies of a Messiah who will redeem Israel from its bondage and rebuild the Temple. Christianity took from Judaism a belief in a divine scheme and applied Old Testament prophecies to itself. The promised "seed" became Christ; Israel became a figure for the Church. The Messianic reign became the expectation of a Second Coming.

Over centuries of biblical exegesis various conventions of allegorisation developed: the Old Testament could be read as an expectation of the coming of Christ; in the events and characters of the Old Testament were types of the biographical details of Christ's life and prophecies of the mysteries which He had come to fulfil; the Bible could be read as referring to the history, life and sacraments of the Church, or as a moral injunction; it could be seen as an allegorisation of the inner life of the Christian or as a prophecy of the future history of mankind.[1] Interpreters made various comments on texts, often looking for the hidden meaning of each word without choosing between the possibilities. While the conventions of allegorisation remained fluid and were never firmly fixed, it was usually agreed that Scripture should be read in three or four senses, four being more common.[2] Durandus says that in Holy Scriptures there are four senses: historical, allegorical, tropological and anagogical. In illustrating four levels of interpretation he offers the standard example of Jerusalem, which is to be understood historically or literally as the earthly city of Jerusalem, allegorically as the Church Militant, tropologically as every faithful soul, and anagogically as the celestial Jerusalem which is our country.[3] Another common way of describing the four levels of interpretation of the Bible is that the literal meaning refers to what has happened, the allegorical alludes to what we should believe in, the moral refers to how we should behave, and the anagogical looks forward to the future, especially as the revelation of our life and glory. While at various times during the history of Christianity primacy has been given to the literal level of the Bible, it has also been believed that the letter of the Bible exists for the sake of its underlying meaning. It was felt that besides the aesthetic pleasure to be derived from the discovery of the underlying truths, the exercise in spiritual interpretation sharpened the mind and was an effective way of teaching. Allegory both concealed truth from the impious and was a means of converting through study.

An important characteristic of biblical interpretation is typology, the belief that the Old Testament prepares for and forecasts the New Testament. Since Christ came to fulfil the law and was the Messiah prophesied in the Old Testament, it is only to be expected that links should be seen between His life and the events, peoples and institutions of the past. The deliverance of the Jews from Egypt looks forward to the Resurrection of Christ and the salvation of the human race from Satan. The sacrifice of the paschal lamb is a prophecy of the Sacrifice of Christ. The temptation of Adam and Eve is recapitulated in the Devil's temptation of the Messiah. Moses and Joshua as leaders of the Jews are types of Christ, the head of the Church. Old Testament events can also be read as foreshadowings of the Church and its sacraments. The sacrifice of the paschal lamb looks forward to the Eucharist; Moses bringing water from the rock typifies the sacrament of baptism; the mysterious manna from Heaven foreshadows the Host, the bread of the Mass. The wandering of the Israelites in their journey to the Promised Land is a figure for the Church Militant.[4]

Allegorisation of the Bible was not restricted to historical and prophetic sections. Since the Bible was a divinely inspired revelation, each section of it could be examined for its hidden meaning. Any book of the Bible could be treated as an extended analogy — saying one thing by way of another — or it could be fragmented into nuggets of divine truth. Canticles (or the Song of Songs) was often treated both ways. It was read as an extended metaphor, interpreted verse by verse, and sometimes certain words were separated from the text for interpretation. Such reading took place in a shifting framework of different but related kinds of significance. The bride might represent the Church, the individual soul, the Virgin Mary; the bridegroom might represent Christ, God, divine love. The Song of Songs might be read as prophetic, as a kind of Apocalypse of the Old Testament. Its details were often allegorised individually as well as within the general allegory. Often phrases from various verses were knit together and further elaborated upon by exegesis of passages from other books of the Bible. Since the love of the bride for the bridegroom could be interpreted as the soul's longing for union with divine love, the allegorisations of Canticles often provided basic metaphors for contemplative literature where the subject is ascent towards communion with the divine. The coming and going of the bridegroom, the ruddiness of his colouring, the blackness of the bride, the bed, the pillar, the apple tree, the concubines, and the various descriptions were given particular meanings with reference to the Church, its sacraments, the life of Christ, the spiritual life of the soul. Despite warnings against excessive and eccentric interpretations, the various meanings accumulated, were handed on from commentator to commentator, were not seen as mutually contradictory, and shaped the response of educated readers over centuries of biblical study. Protestantism did not significantly change allegorical interpretations of the Bible. In attacking scholastic distinctions between levels of interpretation, it made possible less disciplined shifting back and forth between kinds of spiritual meaning. It also tended to apply typology — what was once called the allegorical level — directly to the individual or to contemporary political events.

Allegorisation of the Bible influenced Christian iconography, devotional and theological writing, and the rites of the Church. In devotional literature and sermons allegorisation is even more fanciful than in the biblical commentaries, as the author can knit together various biblical passages without exact care as to their original context. Allegorising became a mode of thinking and feeling which formed the imagination of Christian art. The eventual coming together of classical and Christian art was made possible by reading pagan literature allegorically according to the rules of biblical interpretation.[5] Pagan literature was often seen as containing Christian morals and as prophesying the coming of Christ. Any seeming profanity or blasphemy in the narrative could be explained as having a different allegorical significance. Christian writers soon came to write stories and poems which were apparently secular but which, like pagan literature, could be interpreted allegorically. The narrative became a clothing for other kinds of significance. Such habits of imagining were still alive in the seventeenth century, especially among writers influenced by Spenser. Donne, Herbert, Vaughan and Milton drew heavily from biblical allegorisation. Most of the events in *Paradise Lost*, and the significant patterning of their relationships to each other, are based upon biblical commentaries. Even many eighteenth century novels, such as *Tom Jones* and *Robinson Crusoe*, show traces of the allegorical imagination.

The allegorical imagination is based upon an all-encompassing view of the world and time. History is one great drama beginning with God's Creation of the world, the central action of which is Christ's Incarnation and Passion and the conclusion of which will be the Second Coming and the Last Judgment. Between the events narrated in Genesis and those prophesied in Revelation, the drama of the world's history works its way towards its foreseen conclusion through figures, types, shadows and prophecy. The horizontal chain of events which makes up human history is an unfolding of something eternal, present in the divine mind. The allegorical imagination moves backward and forward through time seeking connections between events; it also moves vertically, attempting to achieve the simultaneity of vision of the divine. The meditative tradition stemming from Augustine through Bonaventura to the seventeenth century poets depends upon similar habits of imagination, a similar view of the world as a sacrament. The mind journeys from the present back into time to recover the divine image within the soul as known to prelapsarian Adam, and ascends upward towards communion with the divine. The ecstasy of the soul in the highest stages of contemplation is a form of knowledge as well as spiritual participation.[6]

The rationale of Christian symbolism is basically the divine scheme as developed in biblical commentary. Christian symbolism has many sources, prominent among which are the rites of the Church; but the logic behind the symbolism is found in the Bible and interpretations of it. The Creation of the world, as seen in allegorisations of the Bible, was sacramental, a sign of the seven ages of man. The world is filled with symbols. The world is emblematic, revealing the divine scheme. Any natural object can be interpreted allegorically, tropologically or anagogically.[7] Water can recall the waters of Creation, the Deluge and baptism. A tree might recall the tree of knowledge in Eden and the cross upon which Christ died, while a boat might bring to mind Noah's ark or the Church. As Augustine said, a sign "causes us to think of something beyond the impression the thing itself makes upon the senses".[8]

If the created world and history (including the future) are two provinces of the allegorical imagination, a third is the human soul in its relation to God. God's love created the world and keeps it in motion while all creation aspires towards union with God; bonds of love keep the world together in mutual sympathy. Man, however, who has free will, fell into temptation and sinned; since the Fall his soul has been attracted to carnal things and does not naturally love God. God's love expressed through the Sacrifice of Christ and through grace gave man the ability to love God once more. The central drama of life is whether we love God or whether we repeat Adam's Fall by loving ourselves and things of this world. Key words to describe the two conditions are charity and cupidity. Augustine defines charity as the motion of the soul towards the enjoyment of God for His own sake. Cupidity is the motion of the soul towards the enjoyment of oneself, one's neighbour or things for the sake of something other than God; cupidity corrupts the soul and results in vice and crime.[9] The central situation often found in Christian literature, whether Milton's *Maske* or Marvell's lyrics, allegorises the conflict between charity and cupidity. Whether the soul chooses one or the other will determine its salvation, its hopes of ascending to a vision of the divine, and its future. The drama is often seen as a parallel to Adam's Fall or Christ's success in overcoming Satan's temptations. The soul can fall with Adam into corruption, it can sin and remain bound to the material world; it can overcome temptations of the flesh and spirit, live virtuously and regain Paradise.

Marvell's father was a minister. Marvell would have studied biblical commentaries in school and university, would have heard allegorical interpretation used in sermons, and would have been aware of the symbolism of the Mass and that contained in various hymns and the vestments and objects of the Church. With other educated readers of the past he would have taken allegory and typology in his stride. The Bibles he used were glossed and filled with commentaries. He would have seen allegorically inspired pictures and emblems on the walls of churches, shops, taverns and the tapestries hanging in great halls. He would have read emblem-books and devotional literature. He would have possessed a common tradition of Christian doctrine and symbol which nourished his imagination. He could not have lived through the Interregnum without hearing discussion of the Bible and its application to the age around him. His poem, *The First Anniversary of the Government under O.C.*, is filled with typology. The growth of Protestantism and non-conformity sharpened awareness of the problems of biblical interpretation and the meaning of Christian symbolism and Church ritual.

The poems of Marvell's which are most successful, and which I describe as shaped by the allegorical imagination, are usually believed to have been written when he was a tutor in the Fairfax household. Lord Fairfax was the commander of the army on the Parliamentary side in the Civil War who retired as a result of disagreements of principle with Cromwell. In *Upon Appleton House* Marvell implies that given the choice between power and virtue Fairfax chose to govern his appetites rather than govern others. His life is seen as an imitation of Christ, and his tending of his estates as a return to Paradise. Even if we allow for a certain hyperbole in Marvell's praise of his patron, Fairfax appears to have been a man of unusual spiritual concerns. He was highly educated and translated from Latin a history of the Church. He translated the Hermetical books from French. He wrote metrical versions of the Psalms, Canticles and other books of the Bible. He wrote religious hymns and poetry on themes of retirement and solitude. Among the 650 pages of his poetry in the Bodleian Library, over 550 pages are religious verse or translations from the Bible. Even his secular poetry is often on ethical and moral themes.[10] His library contained polyglot Bibles, biblical commentaries including Jerome's works, Wyckliffe's Bible, and the works of various allegorical writers, including Gower. He knew and patronised Matthew Poole, who wrote a commentary on the Bible and made a synopsis of commentaries.

It seems likely that Marvell's most important poems were either written while at Nun Appleton House or shortly afterwards. The poems could only have been written by someone immersed in a study of the Bible and whose imagination was thoroughly soaked in biblical commentary and devotional literature. It is widely agreed that the poems which are presumed to have been written after Marvell left the Fairfaxes show a falling off of creative power. The poems presumably of the Nun Appleton period are great poems, among the best in the English language. The poems written afterwards are those of a minor poet. A logical explanation for this difference would seem to be found in the years Marvell spent at Nun Appleton, helping Fairfax with his translations of the Bible and his poetry, and in the moral and spiritual education of Fairfax's daughter. Great pains were taken with Mary Fairfax's religious education, and it is known that Fairfax, his wife and Mary regularly took notes on the sermons they heard.[11] Marvell was constantly engrossed in religious and poetic matters and his own poetic imagination formed the habit of apprehending allegorically.

CHAPTER TWO

Marvell and Allegory

Opinion about Marvell's poetry has shifted radically during this century. Marvell formerly appeared to be a charming minor poet, who had no particular view of life and whose work did not reveal any profundity of thought or feeling. Closer attention to his poetry has revealed a major poet who now seems obscure and difficult. His lyrics, although charming, now seem puzzling, even impenetrable. They appear to be parabolic and to suggest something more profound than what is explicitly being said. My claim is that Marvell's best poems are religious and allegorical. The influence of Christian allegory on Marvell's imagination can be seen in his habit of speaking obliquely, of bringing to mind several ideas at once, and of using words as symbols which recall profound matters. His poems are woven from biblical words, biblical phrases, allusions to biblical events, Christian symbols, and other means of bringing to mind Christian doctrine. The poems are allegorical in that they refer the mind to spiritual matters even when their subject is not explicitly religious. Even the persuasion in *To his Coy Mistress* to make the most of time is attempted in images which, ironically for the speaker's purpose, recall the Christian scheme of history.

A few of Marvell's poems are explicitly on religious subjects. They surprise us with their difficulty; they require us to concentrate on the significance of words and symbols if we wish to understand what is being said. Meditative poetry focuses our minds on religious truths; but Marvell's meditative poetry is allegorical, bringing to mind a wider body of associations than we expect. Rather than speaking directly to us, it indirectly recalls doctrine through symbols, allusions and riddles. Marvell's poems on secular topics are also religious allegories; here we must see the narrative as shadowing or figurative of biblical events, prophecies, or kinds of Christian experience.

Some of Marvell's poems — such as *The Nymph complaining for the death of her Faun*, *The Garden*, *Bermudas*, and *The Picture of little T.C. in a Prospect of Flowers* — could be interpreted according to four levels of meaning, on analogy to traditional biblical interpretation. We need not, however, define allegory by the implied simultaneous presence of three or four levels of reference within a literary text. We can see the influence of allegorical habits of reading and imagining whenever something is said by way of something else, whenever the narrative suggests analogies to biblical events or prophecies, or whenever what is being said demands that we recall a larger body of ideas or doctrines. Allegory is what is hidden, it is the gospel pearl that is not to be cast before the swine, the wheat that is to be separated from the chaff. Even irony was traditionally regarded as a form of allegory, since it is a way of speaking indirectly and a way in which sacred mysteries could be kept from the eyes of the uninitiated.

How do we know when one of Marvell's poems is allegorical? All art is based upon conventions of perceiving significance. We can try to explain why we perceive meaning in an art object, but our explanation is bound to be a simplification of the many impressions which have determined our response. In the case of Marvell, our impression of there being something further to what is being said is often created by the emphasis given to various biblical and religious words. "Hope", "adore", "Soul", "Praise", "exalt", "justice", "bless", "Gifts", "virtues", "grace", "presume", "Glories", "retreat" and "Image" start the imagination seeking further dimensions. Sometimes the words and phrases Marvell chooses specifically recall the Bible or Christian doctrine: "Flood", "Eternity", "Heaven", "Fall", "eternal Spring", "Gospels Pearl", "holy", "Heaven's eye", "Virtue's Grave" or "our hopes". A large body of doctrine is brought to mind by Pleasure's greeting to the Resolved Soul:

Welcome the Creations Guest
Lord of Earth, and Heavens Heir.[1]

The rhyme "recall"/"fall" also serves to set the Soul-Pleasure debate within a larger context. The Soul is "that thing Divine" being created in God's image; Pleasure is a "Tempter". Many words and phrases seem charged with religious significance: "annihilate" in *The Garden* brings to mind the future destruction of the created world. The green grass, upon which the speaker lies or falls so often in Marvell's poems, recalls the many passages in the Bible where flesh is described as grass which will wither and die. Our difficulty in comprehending what is meant by "Magnanimous Despair", or why Hope is described as "feeble" in *The Definition of Love,* causes us to think clearly about the Christian meanings of despair and hope and the nature of the soul.

Scenes which bring to mind biblical events, and phrases which echo the Bible, are common in Marvell's poetry. The first four lines of the *Dialogue between the Resolved Soul and Created Pleasure* echo Ephesians 6:16-17:

Courage my Soul, now learn to wield
The weight of thine immortal Shield.
Close on thy Head thy Helmet bright.
Ballance thy Sword against the Fight.

The soul in *On a Drop of Dew*, in "recollecting its own Light" and "Remembring still its former height", brings to mind the first chapter of Genesis when man was created in God's image. The "he" whose praises are sung in *Bermudas* and who leads the voyagers through a "watry Maze" and helps them to escape from the "Prelat's rage" is God. He brought the Israelites out of Egypt and led them through the wilderness of the Red Sea. Once we recognise this allusion, the Bermudas seem analogous to the Promised Land and the voyagers are seen as the Church Militant journeying towards its eventual triumph at the end of time. *A Dialogue between the Soul and Body* begins:

O Who shall, from this Dungeon, raise
A Soul inslav'd so many wayes?

It recalls "O wretched man that I am! who shall deliver me from the body of this death?" (Romans 7:24) and almost demands the answer "I thank God through Jesus Christ our Lord. So then with the mind I myself serve the law of God; but with the flesh the law of sin" (Romans 7:25). Stanza eight of *The Garden* directly alludes to "And the LORD God said, *It is* not good that the man should be alone; I will make him an help meet for him" (Genesis 2:18); it demands that we see the mystical experience of the previous stanza as a similitude of man's first Paradise:

Such was that happy Garden-state,
While Man there walk'd without a Mate:
After a Place so pure, and sweet,
What other Help could yet be meet!

In stanza seven of *Damon the Mower* the shepherd and his flock recall the many places in the New Testament where Christ is the shepherd and the faithful are His flock. Pursuing the analogy further we discover that the Mower with his scythe, who although he does not have flocks is richer in hay (withered grass), is a figure for death, time, mutability and the Devil. In *The Nymph complaining for the death of her Faun*, "Their Stain/ . . . dy'd in such a Purple Grain" recalls the purple robe in which Christ was mockingly dressed before His Crucifixion. "Though they should wash their guilty hands/In this warm life blood"[2] recalls Matthew 27: 24-25, where Pilate washes his hands saying "I am innocent of the blood of this just person", and is answered by all the people saying: "His blood *be* on us, and on our children". Through the use of such biblical allusions, the death of the Faun brings to mind the death of Christ.

Marvell's poetry includes many descriptions which have their biblical analogies. In *The Mower to the Glo-Worms*, the glo-worms recall the pillar of fire leading the Israelites in their wanderings through the Red Sea.

Ye Glo-worms, whose officious Flame
To wandring Mowers shows the way,
That in the Night have lost their aim,
And after foolish Fires do stray.

The speaker in *To his Coy Mistress* who cannot make the sun stand still ironically brings to mind Joshua who could. T.C. in her garden naming the flowers brings to mind Adam naming the animals. In *Bermudas* "He cast . . . The Gospels Pearl upon our Coast" recalls Matthew 7:6: "Give not that which is holy unto the dogs, neither cast ye your pearls before swine". We are also reminded of Jonah, the prophet cast into the sea and then on to dry land to preach God's word. Since Jonah is traditionally seen as a type of Christ and is so referred to in the New Testament, the casting of the Gospel's pearl in *Bermudas* should bring to mind both Jonah and Christ. The same typology symbolically linking Jonah, Christ, and the Church can be seen in the second stanza of *The Unfortunate Lover* who "e're brought forth, was cast away" and is eventually born upon a rock.

The biblical allusions Marvell uses are meant to carry their traditional interpretations. Often books of the Bible, such as Canticles, have a long history of allegorisation, and such significances are carried over into Marvell's poems. Nature courting T.C. with fruits and flowers, and the various fruits and flowers pressing themselves upon the speaker in *The Garden* incorporate the traditional allegorisation of Ecclesiasticus 24:26 as Christ offering His love to man: "Come over to me, all ye that desire me; and be filled with my fruits". The fruit tree in *The Garden* upon whose branches the speaker's soul ascends is reminiscent of the apple tree of Canticles 2:3, usually allegorised as the Saviour and associated with the tree of life in Eden and the heavenly Paradise (Revelation 22:2). That the root of the fruit tree is mentioned is probably an allusion to the prophecy of the coming of Christ in Isaiah 11:1: "And there shall come forth a rod out of the stem of Jesse, and a Branch shall grow out of his roots".

In *The Nymph complaining for the death of her Faun* the echoes of Canticles are so frequent as to require us to see within Marvell's poem the usual allegorisations of the Song of Songs. The Nymph has a garden filled with roses and lilies recalling "A garden inclosed *is* my sister, *my* spouse" (Canticles 4:12), which is usually taken to stand for the Church and for the Virgin Mary; it also brings to mind "I *am* the rose of Sharon, *and* the lily of the valleys" (Canticles 2:1). The Nymph feeds the Faun with milk and sugar, recalling "I have eaten my honeycomb with my honey; I have drunk my wine with my milk" (Canticles 5:1). The skipping feet of the Faun challenging the Nymph to a race and trotting as on four winds recall "The voice of my beloved! behold, he cometh leaping upon the mountains, skipping upon the hills" (Canticles 2:8). Each of the verses and images in Canticles has traditional meanings to which the poem implicitly directs us.

If we need to study the commentaries on Canticles by Origen or Bernard to establish Marvell's meaning, such a response presumably is intended. Allegorical poetry is not the expression of unique feelings and emotions; the responses aroused by the poetry are those traditional to a common body of belief. To lament and die over the death of a fawn would be absurd; but to lament recalling the death of Christ and to look forward to Heaven is an appropriate response to Marvell's poem.

There are many images and phrases in Marvell's poetry which press our minds towards an allegorical reading. In *The Nymph complaining for the death of her Faun* we read: "if my simple Pray'rs may yet/Prevail with Heaven"; "Heavens King / Keeps register of every thing: / And nothing may we use in vain"; "There is not such another in / The World, to offer for their Sin"; and "to bless / Its self in me". In *The Garden* analogy is created by "Your sacred Plants, if here below, / Only among the Plants will grow". In *Musicks Empire* there are references to the Book of Numbers in "Progeny of numbers", to Moses and David in "Mosaique of the Air", and a reference to man's duty to praise God in "Heavens Hallelujahs raise". In the Mower poems, "Luxurious Man, to bring his Vice in use, / Did after him the World seduce".[3] In *The Definition of Love* "Magnanimous Despair alone / Could show me so divine a thing". In *Bermudas*, God "Apples plants of such a price / No Tree could ever bear them twice", no doubt an allusion both to Christ the tree of life and to the apple eaten by Adam and Eve.

Marvell often points to the allegorical mode of his poetry. His poetic universe is a place for meditation and contemplation. It consists of figures, symbols and examples. The analogy between the development of music and the Creation of the world as a sacrament foreshadowing its future history is established with an outrageous pun on cymbal / symbol: "First was the World as one great Cymbal made".[4] The Nymph, in having a statue made for the dead Faun, suggests the figurative nature of the poem in "For I would have thine Image be / White as I can, though not as Thee".[5] The Mower sees his hopes in the meadows and grass "as in a Glass",[6] bringing to mind "For now we see through a glass, darkly" (I Corinthians 13:12) and the meditative use of the Book of Creatures as a mirror or speculum. The moral and eschatological dimensions of *The Picture of little T.C.* are suggested by "Do quickly make th' Example Yours" and "Nip in the blossome all our hopes and Thee". In *The Mower to the Glo-Worms* the nightingales study and meditate by the natural lights of the worms. The glo-worms "presage the Grasses Fall". *Damon the Mower* ends with "For Death thou are a Mower too". The figurative nature of *The Mower against Gardens* is suggested by "But howsoe'er the Figures do excel". In *Damon the Mower* the unusual heats which "the Sun could never raise", and "Which made the Dog, and makes the Sun" can only be supernatural and symbolic. The significance of the Mower's death is suggested by "While I lay trodden under feet"[7] recalling Genesis 3:15: "It shall bruise thy head, and thou shalt bruise his heel". In *The Garden* "this Dial new" keeps before the reader the analogy established earlier in the poem, between Adam's contemplative enjoyment in Eden and the speaker's contemplation in the garden.

Since allegory presumes that the world as we know it is but a shadow of the ultimate reality in the divine mind, it tends to view the here-and-now-ness of the world as part of a larger scheme. Scenes and events are symbolic figures or types pointing forward, backward, above, below, or serving as moral examples. The presence of allegory in Marvell is often revealed by an unusual concentration on the moment as a symbolic event, or else by dislocations of time and space suggestive of the simultaneity of all time as viewed by God. Concentration on the symbolic moment can be seen in the beginning of the *Dialogue between the Resolved Soul and Created Pleasure*: "Courage my Soul, *now* learn to wield"; "*Welcome* the Creations Guest". In the last stanza of *To his Coy Mistress* "now" is repeated three times. In *The Unfortunate Lover* Christ's atoning Sacrifice is suggested by "And *now*, when angry Heaven wou'd / Behold a spectacle of Blood". The symbolic importance of Charles I's death in *An Horatian Ode* is suggested by "This was that memorable Hour". Time is continually alluded to in the poems, whether directly as in "Had we but World enough, and Time"[8] "they kept the time"[9] and the Resolved Soul's "I sup above and cannot stay";[10] or indirectly as in the many allusions to withering grass, hay and flowers: "But most procure / That Violets may a longer Age endure"[11] The effect is to make our mind recall the Christian view of time stretching forth from the Creation through the Incarnation to the Last Judgment, during which individuals are tested and either fall with Adam or are saved in Christ. Our time is measured against eternity.

The dislocations of time and space in Marvell's poems contribute towards suggesting that the subject is the fulfilment of prophecy, or a shadow of divine realities. In *Bermudas* the tenses are confusing, and it is difficult to know exactly when the events described took place, whether they are now taking place or whether they will take place. The singers describe a land which presumably they have not yet seen. While still on their journey they sing of it as if they had already reached their destination. They also speak of the future beyond the end of their journey. Though the singers "row'd along" the "he", who is presumably God, "led us through the watry Maze", "lands us", "gave us", "sends" and "hangs". The poem ends with "Thus sung they", while they are still rowing. The speaker, who at the beginning of the poem is describing an event which is taking place, at the end of the poem seems to see, from some higher point of view, a chain of events which are simultaneously taking place and have already taken place.

The Nymph complaining for the death of her Faun is filled with shifts in tense which have the effect of moving backward and forward in time, so that the death of the Faun is seen as a climactic moment of a larger drama. The troopers "riding", "have shot", "it will dye"; "Thou neer didst alive", "nor cou'd / Thy death yet"; "I will Joyn my Tears", "Their Stain / Is dy'd". After the shifts in tense in the first stanza the poem moves backward in time to events before the shooting of the Faun, focuses on the Faun dying and then looks forward to the future. "Unconstant *Sylvio*, when yet / I had not found him", "Thenceforth", "I have a Garden", "I see it faint: / And dye", "I in a golden Vial will", "Now my sweet Faun is vanish'd", "I / Will but bespeak thy Grave, and dye". Though a sequence of events can be pieced together from the poem, the presentation dissolves the normal horizontal movement of time into a fluid symbolic world where there is little action and much evocation. One is reminded of medieval paintings where symbolic scenes, related by typology or as prophecy and fulfilment, are set alongside each other. The disruption of normal syntactical patterns in the first stanza of the poem prevents us from having any expectations of realistic action. Consequently our imagination focuses on the allegory rather than on such questions as what the Nymph could have done between the shooting and death of the Faun.

In *The Garden* similar dislocations of time and space occur. We move from "have I found thee here" to "I sought you then", "if here below", "Mean while". "Here", "There", "till prepar'd", "such was", "there walk'd", "'twas beyond", "this Dial", "Where", "be reckon'd". We move backward and forward in time from the present, move from the physical world into the mind, and ascend to mystical illumination. At the end of the poem the speaker is reflecting upon his experience.

While it might be possible to straighten out the sequence of tenses in *Damon the Mower* and *The Mower's Song*, it would be a thankless task. The narrative frame of *Damon the Mower* and the refrain in *The Mower's Song* add to our confusion as to exactly what is taking place at a particular moment. The most important event seems to have been in the past "when *Juliana* came", and yet the concluding stanzas of the last poem of the sequence, *The Mower's Song*, end with "For *Juliana* comes". The Mower's revenge and death will take place in the future. Such fluidity of time is appropriate to an allegory where death's dominion over the world of flesh is foreseen as being brought to an end. The second stanza of *The Unfortunate Lover* so completely disrupts our normal expectations of cause and effect that the events described hardly have any literal meaning and each word seems to demand that we focus upon it for allegorical possibilities. The Lover is presumably floating on the seas before he is even born and is described as "e're brought forth, was cast away".

A reader familiar with habits of allegorical reading will understand that Marvell's poetry is often about the life of the soul and is influenced by devotional practice. It recalls the past history of man as found in the Bible, and it is prophetic, looking forward to the future. We should not look for one symbolic meaning for each image; rather we should let our minds, under the guidance of the poetry, recall a body of ideas with which we are supposedly familiar. We may read a stanza in the "good" sense, as recalling our hopes for salvation, or we may read it in the contrary sense as referring to evil. Both extremes are possible and are inherent within the images Marvell uses. The "green Thought in a green Shade",[12] while appropriate to the moment, suggests the kind of contemplative knowledge familiar to Adam before the Fall; if the fruit tree recalls Christ then the green thought includes our hopes of salvation, under the shadow or shade of Christ's mercy which protects us from the hot sun of justice. Our reading is open-ended although governed by traditional meanings of symbols and the kinds of levels of interpretation found in Christian allegory. We need not choose, in *The Nymph complaining for the death of her Faun*, between seeing the Faun's death as recalling the Crucifixion or as an allusion to the execution of Charles I: it probably alludes to both. We may need to turn to a book on Christian symbolism or older biblical glosses to understand the meaning of the bell and chain attached to the Faun. But even they are likely to offer multiple interpretations, each of which may be appropriate to the poetic context. It could be argued that such multiplicity of reference is a sign of the poet's art. The best Renaissance poets, like some twentieth century critics, prized ambiguity as a means of creating imaginative depth. George Herbert's *Prayer* is an obvious example of a poem that directly demands from the reader a continually expanding imaginative response.

In *The Unfortunate Lover*, "Thus while they famish him, and feast, / He both consumed and increast" is open to varied interpretations, each of which is appropriate to the ambiguous focus of the poem. As a literal statement the lines do not make much sense, although they are metaphorically meaningful as a statement of the extreme alternative emotions the lover is undergoing. The lines become significant, however, if we think of them as referring to Christ's taking on the physical and emotional sufferings of humanity, if we remember the history of the Israelites and the Church, and if we see "consumed" and "increast" as recalling the Eucharist. In stanza seven of the same poem the lover's skin is torn into strips; here we may remember the flagellation and the wounds on the Cross. "A Lover drest / In his own Blood does relish best" is an allusion to the Eucharist, bringing to mind both the relationship of the Last Supper to Christ's Sacrifice and the typology of the Old Testament paschal lamb.

Marvell's lyric poetry often recalls the divine scheme as set forth in the Bible and Christian doctrine. In *The Coronet*, weaving a garland leads the speaker to recall the serpent in Eden tempting Eve through pride; he is also led to recall the full extent of Christ's glory. The Nymph knows that the Faun's death will eventually do the troopers some good. In *The Definition of Love* both Genesis and Revelation are recalled, through allusions to the Fall, and to the coming together of the heavens and the earth at the end of time:

Unless the giddy Heaven fall,
And Earth some new Convulsion tear;
And, us to joyn, the World should all
Be cramp'd into a *Planisphere*.

In *The Unfortunate Lover* we are reminded of prophecies of the coming of Christ, and there is an allusion to the Last Days: "the Fun'ral of the World".

In Marvell's poetry the created world and time are seen as symbolic. Nature and history are mirrors reflecting the divine. Through contemplation the mind can recollect the divine image within itself and ascend towards a knowledge of God. *On A Drop of Dew* uses the dew as an emblem for the soul's desire to remain uncorrupted by the temptations of this world. It recalls the soul's divine nature and its desire to ascend to God. T.C. reforming the errors of the spring brings to mind the eternal springtime of Eden, the Fall, and the unchanging garden promised in Revelation. Our hopes for T.C.'s future are a figure for mankind's hopes at the end of time. The bond of love which separates yet unites the speaker with the love object, in *The Definition of Love*, is the whole of God's creation and is in itself divine love.

Music, as in *Musicks Empire*, reminds us of the harmony of the divine scheme. The assurance of what will be met in the journey to the Bermudas is only possible to those whose view of the world and time is based upon a scheme of history transcending the individual moment. It is an assurance based upon divine providence, as revealed in the Bible and as elaborated upon in biblical commentaries. Such an assurance, requiring a simultaneous apprehension of the meaning of all time and all creation, can only be given poetic form by a writer whose imagination works with allegorical symbolism.

When we look through the first edition of Marvell's poetry we notice a semblance of an arrangement. The arrangement is not perfect. It is difficult to see how *Tom May's Death* and *The Match* fit in. It is not even certain that the arrangement is Marvell's. But whoever put the lyrics in their present order seems to have been guided both by subject matter and by an awareness of the kind of response required. As we read through the collection the lyrics tend to become increasingly deeper in their allegory, while their overt subject matter gives increasingly less indication of what is being figured. The arrangement of the poems guides the reader's imagination progressively from the literal to the allegorical, from the overtly religious to the implicitly religious.

The English poems begin with one of Marvell's main themes: the Resolved Soul's temptation by Created Pleasure. The *Dialogue* brings to mind Adam's Fall, Christ's overcoming the temptations of Satan, and the soul's need to imitate Christ's purity and humility if it is to ascend to its heavenly home. *On a Drop of Dew* shows us that the whole world is an emblem of such themes, and that the promise of redemption is part of divine providence and mercy. The concluding four lines of the poem explicitly make use of a well-known typology in which the biblical manna of Exodus is prophetic of Christ's Incarnation and man's eventual restoration. *The Coronet* also brings to mind Christ's role in the economy of redemption — a theme later recalled in *The Definition of Love*. Throughout the poems time is contrasted to eternity, the misuse of God's creation is contrasted to its proper use. *Eyes and Tears* makes similar distinctions between the correct and incorrect use of eyes and tears; it also reminds us of the place of penitential tears as the offerings God requires of man in contrast to Old Testament sacrifices: "The Incense was to Heaven dear, / Not as a Perfume, but a Tear".

Within the arrangement of the poems *Bermudas* marks a transition between the explicitly religious lyrics and those poems which either treat secular love ironically or which clothe their allegory in apparently secular narrative. *On a Drop of Dew* and *The Coronet* are meditations upon emblems often found in devotional literature. They are allegorical only in the sense that they require us to recall the doctrine behind their imagery and to see that many things are being said obliquely and through allusion. *Bermudas*, while recognisably a religious poem, does not draw its subject matter from the Bible, theology or devotional literature. The voyage of some pilgrims to the New World is not necessarily a religious subject. It could be treated as heroic, political, or in other ways. Except that the journey takes place to escape religious persecution, there is nothing intrinsically sacred about it. Its religious allegory results from Marvell's imagination seeing within the subject matter such symbolic possibilities as the Church's voyage through the world of time, and the application of the Exodus typology to contemporary events. If the poem recalls Paradise, various biblical events and prophecies, it is because Marvell has created from his material something symbolic and allegorical, on analogy to the way the literal text of the Bible is read as metaphorical and allegorical.

Clorinda and Damon says that pastoral poetry — and implicitly all poetry — must change with the coming of Christ. What "once had been enticing things" (notice the implications of "enticing") have been superseded since "great *Pan*" came bringing "Words that transcend". If we remember the chorus of *Clorinda and Damon*, it is easier to understand the kind of imagination found in the Mower poems, *Musicks Empire* or *The Garden*:

Of Pan *the flowry Pastures sing,*
Caves eccho, and the Fountains ring.
Sing then while he doth us inspire;
For all the World is our Pan's *Quire!*[13]

The use of secular subject matter as an allegory which recalls religious doctrine and history is carried further in *The Nymph complaining for the death of her Faun*, where a girl's love of her pet brings to mind the life and death of Christ. After *The Nymph complaining for the death of her Faun* there follows a group of poems on love, some of which are complex allegories on the nature of Christian love, others of which are on secular love and gain their full ironic force when seen in contrast. The irony of *To his Coy Mistress*, for example, is intensified if the speaker's claim that sexuality is the only means to conquer time is seen in contrast to Christ's atoning Sacrifice as recalled in *The Unfortunate Lover* or in contrast to the divine love paradoxically presented in *The Definition of Love.* While I do not claim that all the love poems, including *Young Love* and *The Match*, are meant to have a significance within a larger thematic structure, it does seem that some attempt has been made to bring together poems on love and time so that they can be seen in relation to each other. Next follows the Mower sequence where the pastoral love lyric is used to allegorise the divine scheme. Finally the lyric poems are rounded off with two of

Marvell's most deeply imagined allegories — *Musicks Empire* and *The Garden* — in which the Creation is recalled and seen as a sacrament of man's future redemption.

If I am correct in reading the apparently secular poems as religious allegories, it would seem that the order in which Marvell's lyrics were first printed shows the remains of a planned sequence. As with many Renaissance collections — various love sonnet sequences, Spenser's *Faerie Queene,* Herbert's *The Temple,* Traherne's *Centuries* — the progression is often devious and by association or contrast rather than straightforward and linear. Such fluidity of movement within a complexly unified work shows that the authors are the descendants of both Petrarch's labyrinth ways and the medieval allegorists.

CHAPTER THREE

On a Drop of Dew

And this is the will of him that sent me, that every one which seeth the Son, and believeth on him, may have everlasting life: and I will raise him up at the last day. The Jews then murmured at him, because he said, I am the bread which came down from heaven. (John 6:40-41)

On a Drop of Dew is a meditation upon an emblem. A drop of dew is used as a focus for reflections about the soul and the significance of the manna upon which the Israelites fed. In seeing analogies between the natural world, the soul and the biblical manna, the reader recalls the significance of the Creation and divine goodness. Throughout the poem images of circles and roundness point towards God's perfection as seen in the created world and the soul. The dew is "Round", a "Globe", and is divided from the "Sphear". The soul has "circling thoughts": "So the World excluding round". All creation is an emblem of its Creator. All God's creation wishes to return to Him. The circle motif is reflected in the pattern of generation, descent and return in which the drop of dew, soul, and manna participate. Images of cyclical process can be seen in the various states of water mentioned in the poem: "destil", "congeal'd", "dissolving". God is seen in created things (dew), man (soul) and history (manna). Just as God creates the waters which ascend to Heaven, so He creates the soul which will ascend, and the world which will some day pass away and be replaced by a new creation. All the world, including man's soul, is shown participating in a divine scheme of redemption of which the central event is Christ's Sacrifice.

The poem begins with apparent simplicity, depicting the emblem within its setting:

See how the Orient Dew,
Shed from the Bosom of the Morn
    Into the blowing Roses.

The situation is similar to that found in *A Dialogue between the Resolved Soul and Created Pleasure*, and *The Picture of little T.C.*:

new born innocence faced by temptations. The virginal is tested by the ripe pleasure of the material world ("blowing Roses"). Marvell ascribes to the drop of dew an awareness analogous to human feelings. Just as the Resolved Soul, conscious of its hopes of Heaven, can reject Created Pleasures, so the drop of dew is:

Yet careless of its Mansion new;
For the clear Region where 'twas born
Round in its self incloses.

Marvell imagines the surface of the dew enclosing "its self" from the outside world, like an anchorite. Later he will draw an implied comparison between the drop of dew and the human mind shutting out the distractions of the world to rediscover the divine image within itself. The drop of dew, in terms of its own physical experience, performs similarly to the mind remembering and recollecting:

And in its little Globes Extent
Frames as it can its native Element.

Marvell transfers many of the characteristics of the contemplative soul to the emblem. The rationale of the soul's preparation "to ascend" is partially stated through the description of the dew. Since Marvell does not suggest at all points a parallel between the dew and the soul, it is sometimes thought there is confusion in the logic of the poem. What critics are noticing is Marvell's art rather than confusion. The strategy allows Marvell to compress his presentation of the soul's progression, to imply the soul's differences from the drop of dew, and to avoid describing the higher stages of mystical experience for which the soul has prepared itself.

The usual pattern of mystical experience is purgation, purification and illumination, reaching its climax in union or communion. Marvell does not show the soul actually achieving communion; but the drop of dew achieves something similar when the sun exhales "it back again". The drop of dew purges itself from the passions of the world ("the purple flow'r") and purifies itself ("Scarce" touches); in reflecting the light of day ("Shines") it is a similitude for the soul's illumination while remembering "its former height":

How it the purple flow'r does slight,
Scarce touching where it lyes,
But gazing back upon the Skies,
Shines with a mournful Light;
Like its own Tear,
Because so long divided from the Sphear.
Restless it roules and unsecure,
Trembling lest it grow impure:
Till the warm Sun pitty it's Pain,
And to the Skies exhale it back again.

Marvell is careful to avoid crossing the boundary between the emblem and what it recalls. The dew "Frames as it can", it is "like". It is "so long divided" from the "clear Region" of the crystalline "Sphear", not from God. The dew is "Like its own Tear" because it is tear shaped, and because it is an emblem for the penitential tears of the soul. The sphere refers the mind to the purity and immutability of the outer regions of the sky near Heaven, and the dew's longing to return to the skies is an emblem of the soul's desire for purity and permanence.[1] By its own nature the dew shows that all creation is "Restless", "roules", and lacks repose ("unsecure"); all creation, in love with its Maker, is "ready to ascend". The drop of dew, all created things, the soul, and mankind throughout history share in the same process. Time begins with the Creation of the world, but the creation longs for eternity, even at the cost of its physical destruction. Marvell's imagination continually anticipates itself; images and themes found at the beginning of the poem are only fully explicable in terms of allusions and symbols which occur later. The analogy drawn between the drop of dew and the soul is a sign of something larger and more inclusive. The drop of dew is a sign of a divinely generated process seen throughout history.

> So the Soul, that Drop, that Ray
> Of the clear Fountain of Eternal Day,
> Could it within the humane flow'r be seen,
> Remembring still its former height,
> Shuns the sweat leaves and blossoms green;
> And, recollecting its own Light,
> Does, in its pure and circling thoughts, express
> The greater Heaven in an Heaven less.

If the drop of dew provides a model of conduct for the soul, the soul is capable of a wider range of experiences. Throughout the description of the soul we are reminded of what Christian doctrine has traditionally said of the nature of man's soul. It is a drop or ray "Of the clear Fountain of Eternal Day", being created in the divine image and having within it the divine light:

> For God, who commanded the light to shine out of darkness, hath shined in our hearts, to *give* the light of knowledge of the glory of God in the face of Jesus Christ. (II Corinthians 4:6)
>
> *That* was the true Light, which lighteth every man that cometh into the world. (John 1:9)

God is both a fountain from which flows the world's spiritual light, and the light of Eternal Day in contrast to the changeable light of the world of time. The soul is illuminated by divine light and created by God, so it can be spoken of as a drop or ray of Eternal Day.

"Could it within the humane flow'r be seen" offers a parallel to the "blowing Roses" of line three. The relationship of the soul to the body is similar to that of the dew and roses, being temporary; the soul is housed in the body "Remembring still its former height". Its "former height" is not an allusion to the pre-existent soul of Neo-Platonism. The poem is directly in the tradition of Christian contemplation, as represented by Augustine and Bonaventura.[2] To remember is to find in the memory. The "former height" is the state of happiness known to prelapsarian Adam, enjoying the pleasures of Paradise, contemplating God directly through His creatures, before the divine image within the self became dim through the distractions of carnality.

Is the soul's "former height" the original condition of mankind as experienced by Adam, or the innocence of a new born child? In the tenth book of the *Confessions*, the classic Christian statement of how the image of God is rediscovered within the mind, Augustine is uncertain whether we were all once individually happy, or whether our notions of happiness derive from prelapsarian Adam.[3] While Marvell's poems retrace the divine image in man to "that happy Garden-state",[4] his Resolved Souls begin their "golden daies"[5] innocent and virginal, although, like the drop of dew, faced by the temptations of Created Pleasure. If "former height" can be interpreted as recalling man's first innocence and the innocence of the new born soul, it can also be seen as looking forward to God's judgment at the last days of the world. The soul shunning the "sweat leaves and blossoms green" not only resists temptations, it avoids the distractions of the temporal world. Sweet leaves outside the "humane flow'r" are worldly pleasures. "Blossoms green" are buds, and may be an image for sexual indulgence.

After seeing the drop of dew as an emblem of the soul's longing for union with the divine, we trace the movements of the mind in the act of contemplation. The mind must purge itself of sensual distractions to recover the divine image within itself; contracting itself from the world, it regains and is illuminated by its original knowledge and ascends towards communion with God. The journey takes place within the mind and has two directions. The mind looks backward in time to recover its former knowledge of God, as experienced by Adam contemplating the garden of Paradise; the mind moves upward from the material world, to a knowledge of itself, and towards communion with God.

The soul "recollecting its own Light" pulls itself together, avoids the distractions offered by images within the mind of temporal things, and recovers its original knowledge of its immortal nature. "Recollecting" is an active process of the mind, an assembling and thinking upon knowledge already present within the memory which has been lying scattered and unheeded.[6] It is at this stage that the contemplative mind banishes all images and thoughts of external things, abstracts itself from the bodily senses, and finds the image of God within the soul.[7]

In the moment of illumination the mind gazing upon the divine image of the soul "does, in its pure and circling thoughts, express / The greater Heaven in an Heaven less". The thoughts are pure because uncorrupted by any attractions of the world. They are circling because they are thoughts of God. The image is traditional. God is a circle, since a circle is the most perfect geometric figure, having no beginning or end. Circling thoughts occur in contemplation when the mind ascends towards God by reforming itself in the image of God within itself. Ficino says the soul seems to move in a circle when it turns to God.[8] Donne says "God is a circle".[9] Throughout the Middle Ages and Renaissance it was common to think of the rational soul as a circle. The soul's thoughts "express", in the sense of being an image of, "The greater Heaven in an Heaven less". The mind is less than Heaven, but has been reformed in the image of the greater Heaven, having found God within itself.

Why Heaven? Partly as an expression of the contentment involved; the mind views the divine image within itself like the soul in Heaven gazing upon God. But also because in this stage of contemplation, Bonaventura says, "the soul, entering into itself, enters into the heavenly Jerusalem, where, considering the orders of the angels, it sees God in them, Who living in them causes all their operations".[10] We need not follow Bonaventura's analogy between the nine orders of angels and the nine steps of the soul's hierarchy to understand that the greater Heaven expressed by the soul is prophetic of the soul's heavenly life after death.

The soul in the act of contemplation is next described as:

In how coy a Figure wound,
Every way it turns away:
So the World excluding round,
Yet receiving in the Day.

"Coy" has the sense of modest, and is used here to suggest the chaste nature of the soul. Continence and the avoidance of temptations are necessary if it is to remain gazing upon its inner light. The soul is like a "Figure wound", being a perfect circle turning around the image of God, the still point within it. It excludes the world around it, while receiving the light of God, the Eternal Day. It is a figure in the sense of shadow or analogy: "*which are* the figures of the true" (Hebrews 9:24).

The soul in mystical contemplation of the image of God within itself is

Dark beneath, but bright above:
Here disdaining, there in Love.

The soul being circular is round like the earth with the sun shining down, illuminating the upper hemisphere while the lower hemisphere remains in the dark. But how can the light be inside the mind and yet above it? Augustine's *Confessions* offer us a similar paradox. Augustine says that having entered into the depths of his soul, he saw the light that never changes casting its rays over his mind. "It shone above my mind, but not in the way that oil floats above water or the sun hangs over the earth. It was above me because it was itself the Light that made me, and I was below because I was made by it. All who know the truth know this Light, and all who know this Light know eternity. It is the Light that charity knows"[11]

The immortal soul, weighed down by the mortal body, occupies an intermediate place between the eternal light of God and the darkness of the world of sense. Its resolution and will towards communion with God are shown by "Here disdaining, there in Love". The soul now lives in the world of time, but it desires to enjoy eternal life in God. The opposition "Here" and "there" refers to eternity in contrast to the world of time. The contrast between the eternal "there" and present "here" is a favourite polarity of Augustine ("Here we hope, there we shall enjoy"[12]) and has behind it: "For here have we no continuing city, but we seek one to come" (Hebrews 13:14). The contrast "disdaining" and "Love" shows a right relationship of the will to God. Love of God, or of God through His creation, is the main commandment of the New Testament.

The soul has now progressed in its contemplation to the point where it is:

How loose and easie hence to go:
How girt and ready to ascend.
Moving but on a point below,
It all about does upwards bend.

The soul's state of looseness, easiness and readiness is different from that of remembering and recollection. Having located the divine image within itself, it replaces anxiety by faith, hope and charity; certainty has replaced fear. The mind is at the dividing point between illumination and communion, between contemplating God within the self and experiencing those higher states of mystical rapture which are so often metaphorically described as a kind of death, since the mystic loses his sense of being when in communion with universal Being. In Bonaventura contemplation of the divine unity or Being is the fifth stage in the ladder of mystical ascent, and begins the ascent towards the final, seventh stage where the mind experiences repose and the affections are elevated into God.

Marvell alludes to such ascent by showing the looseness, easiness and readiness of the soul, and expects his readers to recognise just what stage of contemplation has been reached. Marvell does not say that the soul has ascended. It is rather stretched or extended "upwards" towards God. Marvell uses traditional metaphors to describe the soul's spiritual progress. It is upright, erect, fixed on God, "Moving but on a point below".[13] Bending "upwards" is a technical term for the soul's state of vision. If it looked downwards its vision would be upon earthly matters.

If the soul has not ascended to God or achieved actual communion, it is because such an experience is impossible to the soul weighed down by the body. Marvell's poems speak of illumination, which elevates and prepares the soul for its heavenly rewards. The soul does not actually experience the joys of eternity while alive, it obtains a knowledge of the heavenly joys awaiting it after the body's death. Marvell is specific. The soul, unlike the drop of dew, does not experience liquefaction (a term sometimes used to describe the higher states of rapture or mystical death). The drop of dew serves as an emblem for how the soul will "ascend" by being exhaled back to the skies. The soul must remain an exile from the heavenly kingdom until it actually goes from this life to the next. "Go" is an allusion to the soul's departure from the body at death, a subject which interested the scholastic mind.[14] What has been described, then, is the soul's contemplation of God through itself as a preparation for the final communion to be experienced after death.

The last four lines of *On a Drop of Dew* require a knowledge of conventions of allegory if they are to be understood:

> Such did the Manna's sacred Dew destil;
> White, and intire, though congeal'd and chill.
> Congeal'd on Earth: but does, dissolving, run
> Into the Glories of th' Almighty Sun.

The poem's logical structure ("See . . . the Dew . . . So the Soul . . . Such did the Manna") is revealing; the emblematic function of the dew and the process of the soul's spiritual progress are explicitly foreshadowed by the sacred dew: "Such *did* the Manna's sacred Dew destil". The tenses point to the distinction. The soul can act as it does in the present, because the "Manna's sacred Dew" was distilled in the past. Marvell's syntax, we notice, points forward and backward, to the soul and to the manna. It will be necessary to return to the problem of syntax presently. For the moment, the problem is the relationship of manna to the soul's contemplative progress. What is the significance of the manna? The "Manna's sacred Dew" occurs in Exodus, after the Israelites escape from Egypt, pass through the Red Sea and find themselves in the "wilderness of Sin" (Exodus 16:1). They murmur that they are famished and dying of hunger. "Then said the LORD unto Moses, Behold, I will rain bread from heaven" (16:4). In the morning God sends manna for bread: "in the morning the dew lay round about the host. And when the dew that lay was gone up . . . *there lay* . . . manna" (Exodus 16:13-15). "And the children of Israel did eat manna forty years, until they came . . . unto the borders of the land of Canaan" (16:35), the Promised Land.

Marvell closely follows the biblical account of the bringing of manna. The sacred dew brings it ("did . . . destil"); it is "white" ("it *was* like coriander seed, white" [Exodus 16:31]); "congeal'd and chill" ("as the hoar frost on the ground" [16:14]); and dissolves ("when the sun waxed hot, it melted" [16:21]). It runs into "the Glories of th' Almighty Sun" ("And in the morning, then ye shall see the glory of the LORD" [16:7]).

In the Gospel of John the manna is seen as a type of Christ's flesh, and as a prophecy of the Eucharist:

> Our fathers did eat manna in the desert; as it is written, He gave them bread from heaven to eat. Then Jesus said unto them, Verily, verily, I say unto you, Moses gave you not that bread from heaven; but my Father giveth you the true bread from heaven. For the bread of God is he which cometh down from heaven, and giveth life unto the world . . . I am the bread of life; he that cometh to me shall never hunger; and he that believeth on me shall never thirst. (John 6:31-35)

The manna of Exodus, which is used for bread, is thus a shadow of Christ, the true bread of eternal life, Who came down from Heaven to give His life to this world. Bonaventura specifically equates the contemplative soul's journey with the crossing of the Red Sea and the tasting of the hidden manna. Those who contemplate Christ as the mediator of God and man make

> a passover — that is, the phase or passage [Exod. 12, 11] with Him — that he may pass over the Red Sea by the staff of the cross from Egypt into the Desert, where he may taste the hidden manna and with Christ may rest in the tomb as if outwardly dead, yet knowing, as far as possible in our earthly condition what was said on the cross to the thief cleaving to Christ: "Today thou shalt be with me in Paradise".[15]

The manna here is associated with spiritual regeneration. The soul dies to things of this world, and by tasting the manna is reborn through Christ, Who is Himself the hidden manna.

Just as Christ's Sacrifice is necessary for man's salvation so contemplation of God is only possible through Christ. Bonaventura says "one cannot enter into the heavenly Jerusalem through contemplation unless one enter through the blood of the Lamb as through a gate".[16] Not only is it necessary to have faith in Christ for contemplation, but contemplation leads us to understand that we cannot see God's image in our mind without Christ's grace. Bonaventura says that when someone has fallen he must remain prostrate unless given a helping hand; the soul could not raise itself above the senses to an intuition of itself unless Truth, in the human form of Christ, had made Himself into a ladder, "repairing the first ladder which was broken in Adam".[17] When fallen Adam lost man's original gift of directly contemplating God, Christ's mediation was necessary if man were to rise above his senses to illumination. It is only because of the coming of Christ that the soul is "Here disdaining, there in Love".

We can now see that the manna in Marvell's poem recalls the role of Christ in the economy of man's redemption. He is white or pure, His Gospel is one or entire, and He has taken on the flesh of humanity ("congeal'd and chill"). He, dissolving, dies, and ascends to the Glory of God: "I ascend unto my Father" (John 20:17). The process, or stages, of Christ's life is symbolised throughout the creation. It is shown in a drop of dew and in the life of the soul. It is shown emblematically and sacramentally in the world:

So the World excluding round,
Yet receiving in the Day.
Dark beneath, but bright above:
Here disdaining, there in Love.
How loose and easie hence to go:
How girt and ready to ascend.
Moving but on a point below,
It all about does upwards bend.

Marvell sometimes uses ambiguous syntax to create double meanings. Such manipulation of syntax is a form of wit, similar to a pun.[18] The above lines can be read on their own as referring to the world, rather than to what the soul excludes. The world is also an emblem of the desire for purity and of the longing "to ascend".

If my reading is correct, all creation is a sign of Christ's saving manna. We can study or contemplate Christ's role in the economy of redemption through the Book of Nature (the drop of dew), the Bible (the manna), and through the Book of the Self (the soul). And if we reflect upon the history of the world we see it also as a sign, offering an analogy to the Incarnation, life, Sacrifice and Ascension of Christ. The world is not only pictorially or emblematically "round", like the drop of dew or the soul, it also is created, falls, loves its Maker, and will someday dissolve or pass away (Revelation 21:1) to the glory of God.

It is now necessary to ask about the "sacred Dew" which distilled the manna. In Exodus the dew covers the ground and the manna is hidden within it. Our best guide to Marvell's meaning is the Bible. In Deuteronomy 32:2 dew, rain, and doctrine are linked: "My doctrine shall drop as the rain, my speech shall distil as the dew". In Psalm 110:3 dew is a sign of the presence of God's revivifying spirit: "Thou hast the dew of thy youth". This is followed by God saying to David: "Thou *art* a priest for ever after the order of Melchizedek" (Psalm 110:4). Melchizedek is a type of Christ. In Hosea 14:5 God's promises to Israel are "dew": "I will be as the dew unto Israel". Again the verses which follow speak of reviving ("they shall revive *as* the corn") and contain images usually associated with Christ (branches of the Lebanon tree, shade, vine, wine). Commenting upon Isaac blessing Jacob with the dew of Heaven (Genesis 27:28,39), Augustine says "the dew of heaven is His divine doctrine".[19] Donne says the dew is the words from the lips of preachers, the balm of Gilead, a portion of the Saviour's blood, and washes away sins.[20] George Herbert also uses dew as a figure for scripture,[21] while the famous Catholic emblem book, *Partheneia Sacra*, refers to dew as the "Word"; "The Divine generation of the Sonne, which is begotten of the Father by the way of Understanding; from whence as from a fruitful clowd, distils the Divine *Deaw* of the Word: *Let my word flow like deaw*".[22]

If the typology requires us to see the Divine Word ("Dew") begetting Christ ("Manna"), there is a secondary significance in the passage which parallels the "pitty" which the sun felt for the drop of dew in the first half of the poem. Dew is sometimes an emblem of mercy, while hail is a sign of God's corrective punishments. Thomas Traherne, meditating upon God's goodness as seen in the Second Day's Creation, says, "He is the Father of Rain, and hath begotten the Drops of the Dew. He causeth it to come to his Land, whether for Correction, or for Mercy; for with God is terrible Majesty."[23] The dew of "Correction" is hail. Marvell's pattern of "congeal'd and chill" followed by "dissolving . . . Into the Glories of th' Almighty Sun" brings to mind a distinction between the Old and New Law. No doubt such associations are intended, especially if we keep the previous "pitty" or mercy of the sun in mind.

On a Drop of Dew does not have the kind of theme that can be expressed in a sentence. We might say it is about God's goodness as shown in the created world, in the soul, and as revealed in the Bible. We could say that the poem is about love: the love for God that is demonstrated by both creatures and the soul; the love for man that is revealed by the Creation, and the divine grace that makes our love possible. But even this will not fully describe the poem, since it is also about the will and effort necessary for purgation, illumination and communion. It portrays a universe "Restless" and "unsecure", which is active even when apparently static, because it is the world of time, in contrast to the repose of Heaven and Eternal Day. It is a world of process in which the dew, its native element (water), tears (water) and the congealed manna are seen as similar to the soul, which is a drop of the divine fountain. The sun, the soul's own light, the light of day, flow from, and wish to return to, the Eternal Day of the Almighty Sun. While the natural world is an emblem of such process and transformation, man must turn his will actively towards God. If the corrupting temptations of the world of time are to be overcome, and heavenly repose is to be gained, it is necessary actively to turn the mind from the world towards God ("shuns", "excludes", "disdains", "remembers", "recollects"), by way of contemplation, especially by contemplation of Christ, the hidden manna, Whose Sacrifice makes the recovery of the divine image within the soul possible to fallen mankind. It is only because the sacred dew distils the saving manna that man and the world can be rescued from the dominion of time; it is only through Christ's Sacrifice that man can discover God's love. *On a Drop of Dew* is a contemplation on the divine scheme as revealed in the Bible, as seen in the Book of Creatures, and as known within the soul. The allegory recalls the coming and death of Christ, which makes salvation possible. The poem appropriately concludes with the "Glories of th' Almighty Sun".

CHAPTER FOUR

Bermudas

> *They shall inherit the land for ever, the branch of my planting, the work of my hands, that I may be glorified. A little one shall become a thousand, and a small one a strong nation: I the LORD will hasten it in his time.* (Isaiah 60:21-22)

The allegorical mode of *Bermudas* is signalled by the way the narrative dissolves into timeless events without any clear sequence. Although we respond to the poem as a unified work of art, it is impossible to say what is taking place or when it occurs. Are the voyagers on their way to the Bermudas, or have they already discovered it? Why do they appear to be singing as if they were already there, about a place to which they are still voyaging? Marvell's vagueness as to the actual setting of the poem is reflected in the sequence of tenses. My point can perhaps best be illustrated by: "From a small Boat, that row'd along, / The listning Winds receiv'd this Song. / 'What should we do but sing his Praise / That led us . . . He lands us . . . He gave us . . . And sends' . . . Thus sung they". Time, space and perspective are dislocated in *Bermudas* as a means of focusing upon symbols.

The first four lines establish what little setting and plot there are in the poem. Somewhere in the Atlantic a small boat is sailing to the Bermudas. The voyagers are singing. The central portion of the poem consists of the song and describes what the island to which they are journeying will be like. The last four lines of the poem say that the song you have read is what the voyagers sang on their journey. There is no real narrative development in the poem, there are no major events or incidents and no characters. Development takes place through the juxtaposition of symbols rather than narrative action.

In *Bermudas* the crossing of the Puritans to the New World is used as an image of the Church journeying through the ocean of time and space, carrying the faithful towards their triumph at the end of time.

It is a continuing journey, recapitulated throughout history by various figures and types of the Church. God says to Abraham "Get thee out of thy country . . . unto a land that I will shew thee: and I will make of thee a great nation" (Genesis 12:1-2). God then promises "Unto thy seed will I give this land" (Genesis 12:7). The subduing of the earth is a prophecy of the Church's mission. The contemporary manifestation, for Marvell, of the remnant of the faithful fulfilling their destiny throughout time, is the voyage of the Pilgrims to the New World.[1] The "Gospels Pearl" must be spread to all nations before the Second Coming.

Faith in the promise of redemption lies at the heart of *Bermudas.* Christ is the head of the Church, the helmsman of the ship of salvation. He leads the faithful towards their eventual glory. The faith of Abraham in God's promises, and the faith of the Israelites journeying to the Promised Land, are types of those whose faith is in Christ (Hebrews 11:8-14). It is because the voyagers in Marvell's poem have faith in the purpose and eventual fulfilment of their journey that they can, while sailing, sing praises of a land they have not seen.

Bermudas is a song of praise for God's promises and goodness in the past, present, and future. The island is described in imagery recalling the Creation, Paradise, Solomon's Temple, and the heavenly Jerusalem. The varied associations brought to mind might be described as follows: the Creation was a sign of God's goodness; the various works of the Creation are prophetic of future events, such as the story of the Israelites, the coming of Christ, the progress of the Church, and the restoration of man to his heavenly Paradise.

Where the remote *Bermudas* ride
In th' Oceans bosome unespy'd,
From a small Boat, that row'd along,
The listning Winds receiv'd this Song.

"This Song" is similar to Old Testament songs, the hymns of the Church, or individual prayers, in being offerings to God for His providence. Just as the Old Testament songs praise God not only for what He has given Israel, but also for Israel's future destiny when it will rule over all nations, so the Church sings of its triumph at the end of time.

What should we do but sing his Praise
That led us through the watry Maze,
Unto an Isle so long unknown,
And yet far kinder than our own?
Where he the huge Sea-Monsters wracks,
That lift the Deep upon their Backs.
He lands us on a grassy Stage;
Safe from the Storms, and Prelat's rage.

The singing of God's glory while being led through the watery maze brings to mind the Israelities crossing the Red Sea during their escape from Egypt: "But God led the people about, *through* the way of the wilderness of the Red sea" (Exodus 13:18). The "Maze" refers to the wanderings of the Israelites. If the voyage to the New World recalls the escape from Egypt, the song of "praise" recalls the song of Miriam (Exodus 15:20). The sister of Moses is a type of the Church. The crossing of the ocean to a land "far kinder than our own" recalls Joshua's crossing of the River Jordan. The island that is "so long unknown" is a new Promised Land. The journey to the Bermudas is to found a Church in the New World. It is where the Temple is to be built, a shadow of the heavenly Jerusalem and a return to Paradise. It is a shadow of the harbour promised to the faithful at the end of time.

"That lift the Deep upon their Backs" refers to the water spout coming out of the back of the whale; but "Deep" brings to mind the seas at the Creation: "And the earth was without form, and void; and darkness *was* upon the face of the deep. And the Spirit of God moved upon the face of the waters" (Genesis 1:2). The separation of the dry land from the sea (Genesis 1:10) is a sign of the escape of the Israelites through the Red Sea. Just as God defeats the Leviathan at the Creation, He defeats Pharaoh by dividing the waters so that his people can pass over:

> For God *is* my King of old, working salvation in the midst of the earth. Thou didst divide the sea by thy strength: thou brakest the heads of the dragons in the waters. Thou brakest the heads of leviathan in pieces, *and* gavest him *to be* meat to the people inhabiting the wilderness. (Psalm 74:12-14).

Within the multiple contexts brought to mind by the poem, "He lands us on a grassy Stage" may recall the greenness of the Creation, the Garden of Paradise, Noah's ark resting on the mountain of Ararat, and the progress of the Church. Noah's ark is a type of the Church and contains the remnant who are saved when the sinful world is destroyed. The landing of the ark is a new creation; it inaugurates a new humanity, a new covenant with God. Noah is a type of Christ, a new Adam. His deliverance prefigures the Exodus. "Stage" also brings to mind the various stations or journeys of the Israelites on their way to the Promised Land.

"Safe from the Storms, and Prelat's rage" literally refers to the dangers of the sea voyage and to Archbishop Laud from whom the Puritans were fleeing; but we should also remember the Israelites escaping from Pharaoh, who stands for the Devil. Pharaoh enraged against the fleeing Israelites says "I will pursue . . . my lust shall be satisfied upon them . . . my hand shall destroy them" (Exodus 15:9).

The storm recalls the strong winds which make the waters roll back so that the Israelites can pass through the sea (Exodus 14:21).

> He gave us this eternal Spring,
> Which here enamells every thing;
> And sends the Fowl's to us in care,
> On daily Visits through the Air.
> He hangs in shades the Orange bright,
> Like golden Lamps in a green Night.

"Gave us", read in association with the various plants on the island, brings to mind the sixth day of Creation when God gives man every herb bearing seed and every fruit tree (Genesis 1:29). The subsequent activities ("He hangs", "He makes", "He cast") recall God's creation of the Garden of Eden: "God planted" (Genesis 2:8), "God formed" (Genesis 2:19). Paradise was often allegorised as the Church, with its trees representing the saints and the tree of life being Christ.[2] "Eternal Spring" refers the mind to eternal life after the Day of Judgment when death will no longer have dominion and there will be eternal May.

While spring seems to refer to the season, a spring is also a brook of running water or a well. It is fitting that there should be a spring on the island since "a river went out of Eden to water the garden" (Genesis 2:10). "Eternal Spring" thus alludes to the waters of grace bringing forth perpetual life for the elect. Israel "shalt be like a watered garden, and like a spring of water, whose waters fail not" (Isaiah 58:11). Jesus says "But whosoever drinketh of the water that I shall give him shall never thirst; but the water that I shall give him shall be in him a well of water springing up into everlasting life" (John 4:14).

The description of the island includes allusions to the Garden of Eden, Canaan, the Tabernacle, the Church and the heavenly Paradise. The fowls bring to mind the fowls of Paradise (Genesis 2:19) and the quails sent by God to the Israelites (Exodus 16:13). They are signs of God's care and promises of salvation. Paradise was a garden offering shade and protection, oranges were sometimes said to be among its various fruits. The oranges "He hangs" in the shady boughs of the tree are "like golden Lamps" and since they shine in a "green Night" are also similar to stars.

The symbolism is complex as might be expected from the implied double metaphor — oranges: lamps: stars — and from the implied comparison of branches and leaves to "a green Night". Christ is the fruit bearing tree of life, the shade He offers is man's hope; and since green is the colour of hope, the shady orange tree whose boughs are "a green Night" is a witty and learned allusion to Christ. He who hangs the oranges in the tree is God "which hath shewed us light".

The oranges as lights in a green night can also recall the creation of the "lights in the firmament of heaven to divide the day from the night; and let them be for signs . . . give light upon the earth" (Genesis 1:14-15). The mind of Marvell's Mower "in the greenness of the Grass / Did see its Hopes as in a Glass". The oranges shining like lamps in a green night bring to mind man's hopes of salvation as promised in the signs of the Creation.

Marvell's description of the island includes signs of God's promises throughout history. The various fruits and wonders of the island are signs of the presence of the Church and recall similar signs of its manifestation in the past:

And does in the Pomegranates close,
Jewels more rich than *Ormus* show's.
He makes the Figs our mouths to meet;
And throws the Melons at our feet.

The pomegranate was often included in descriptions of Paradise. It is among the fruits of the Promised Land,[3] and is a common symbol for the Church. Its seeds are the faithful community of believers. God both makes the figs and makes them "our mouths to meet". "To meet" probably includes a punning allusion to Genesis 1:30 where God gives man every fruit tree "for meat": that is, for food and contemplation. We can contemplate God's goodness through the abundance of pleasant fruits He has given man. The appearance of the fig in the Bible often has eschatological associations, since the Arabic root for fig means time, or the time is come (Matthew 24:32-34).[4] In Canticles 2: 13 "The fig tree putteth forth her green figs" is a sign of the coming of spring, and spiritually a sign of the coming of the day of grace. Putting the figs into the mouths of the voyagers would be symbolic of making them bearers of the Gospel. Figs were also among the fruits of the Promised Land. The melon thrown at the feet of the voyagers is a sign of Christ's presence in His Church. Christ is read into the apple tree of Canticles 2:3; but early biblical commentators, worrying about the possible associations of *malum* (Latin) with malice, preferred to speak of the fruit as a *melum* (Greek).[5] Thus the tree of Canticles 2:3 becomes "some Fruit-tree"; it also becomes the melon which causes the speaker in *The Garden* to stumble. The allusion is to the biblical stumbling stone: "The stone which the builders rejected, the same is become the head of the corner" (Luke 20:17).[6] The melons thrown at the feet of the Pilgrims can be seen to recall Christ the stumbling stone Whom the Jews rejected, but upon Whom the Church is built.

But Apples plants of such a price,
No Tree could ever bear them twice.

In contrast to the abundant oranges, figs, pomegranates and melons, there are costly apples, or is it "Apple's plants"? Does God (He) plant apple trees; or do the trees bear Apple's plants? Presumably the first reading is literally correct, but the ambiguity seems intentional as if Marvell wanted the two lines to be read both ways. The ambiguity is furthered by the problem of whether the apples might be pineapples. The ambiguity is intended to recall that God planted both the tree of knowledge and the tree of life in Paradise (Genesis 2:9). The fruit of the tree of knowledge was often supposed to be the apple, and Adam's eating of it might well be described as costly. According to legend Adam carried a fragment of the tree with him when he was expelled from Paradise; it later grew into the tree from which the wood of the Cross was taken. Christ's Sacrifice recapitulates Adam's Fall; Adam eats the apple, Christ climbs the tree of the Cross:

> Man stole the fruit, but I must climb the tree;
> The tree of life to all, but only me.[7]

The recollection of the price paid by Christ to redeem man is at the heart of the liturgy: "For ye are bought with a price" (I Corinthians 6:20). The "Tree" thus recalls the precious wood of the Holy Cross bearing the ransom of the world. "No Tree could ever bear them twice" reminds us that Christ dies once, unlike Old Testament sacrifices which are performed yearly (Hebrews 9:28).

If we are reminded of the consequences of Adam's disobedience and of Christ's Sacrifice, "Apples", "Tree", "bear" bring to mind Canticles 2:3 "As the apple tree among the trees of the wood, so *is* my beloved among the sons. I sat down under his shadow with great delight, and his fruit *was* sweet to my taste". Matthew Poole interprets the fruit as "the benefits which I received by him [Christ], the clear, and full, and certain knowledge of God's will, and the way of salvation, adoption and remission of sins, faith and repentance, and all manner of grace, and assurance of glory".[8] Since in classical Latin *caritas* could mean either dearness of price or affection, the apples "of such a price" recall the fruits of Christ's love.[9] "The tree of life, which bare twelve *manner of* fruits" (Revelation 22:2) is interpreted as Christ. But is it possible for the "Tree" of Marvell's poem to recall the tree of knowledge, the Cross, and the tree of life? In the passage from Herbert's *Sacrifice* which I quoted above, the three trees and their significance are recalled and the allusions almost fused into a single image.

> With Cedars, chosen by his hand,
> From *Lebanon*, he stores the Land.
> And makes the hollow Seas, that roar,
> Proclaime the Ambergris on shoar.

In Psalm 104, where God's providence is praised, we read: "The trees of the LORD are full *of sap*; the cedars of Lebanon, which he hath planted" (Psalm 104:16). The cedars of Lebanon are not only a sign of God's works to all mankind in the creation of the visible world, but they are also associated with the special favours to His Church. Solomon builds his temple from the cedars of Lebanon (II Chronicles 2:8) and cedars are brought from Lebanon to rebuild the temple (Ezra 3:7). While Solomon commands "that they hew me cedar trees out of Lebanon" (I Kings 5:6), the trees in Bermudas are chosen by God. The island is a temple which God Himself builds. The cedar which God will plant in Ezekiel 17:23 is usually understood as the Gospel.

"Ambergris" has a fragrant odour and was used as a base for perfumes. In Renaissance poetry it often stands for the divine odour of Christ.[10] The divine odour is a pleasing sacrifice (Philippians 4:18), of which Old Testament sacrifices were types. In Revelation 5:8 the prayers of saints are described as odours. Just as incense is a prayer to God, so prayers have a good odour. To proclaim the ambergris would be similar to John the Baptist's proclamation of Christ as the anointed one. The announcement of the oil of holy anointments is made in Exodus 30:31: "And thou shalt speak unto the children of Israel, saying, This shall be an holy anointing oil unto me throughout your generations". Do the "hollow Seas" of Europe proclaim the sacraments on the shores of the New World?

> He cast (of which we rather boast)
> The Gospels Pearl upon our Coast.

The voyagers bring salvation in the form of the Church, its sacraments and the Gospel to the Americas. They and the Church bringing the divine Word to the nations of the world are the chosen people journeying to the Promised Land. Their boasting is of Christ's kingdom: "In God we boast all the day long, and praise thy name for ever" (Psalm 44:8). It is a sign of their confidence in God. Jonah tossed on shore brought God's world to Nineveh. Jonah is a type of Christ, and of preachers. Casting "the Gospels Pearl" alludes to Matthew 7:6: "Give not that which is holy unto the dogs, neither cast ye your pearls before swine", which is one of the common justifications for allegorical interpretation of the Bible. We may see it as an allusion to the method of the poem.

> And in these Rocks for us did frame
> A Temple, where to sound his Name.

Christ, the rock, has created the Church which praises Himself. Just as God was in the Old Testament Tabernacle, so Christ is in the body of His Church. The renewed Temple is a sign of the Messianic era. Whereas the Old Testament Temple was a building, the Church is in the body of believers: "Know ye not that ye are the temple of God, and *that* the Spirit of God dwelleth in you?" (I Corinthians 3:16).[11]

Christ is the rock or foundation upon which the faithful build their Church (I Corinthians 3:11). In Canticles 2:14 the Church is allegorised as taking refuge from its enemies in the clefts of the rock: "O my dove, *that art* in the clefts of the rock, in the secret *places* of the stairs, let me see thy countenance, let me hear thy voice; for sweet *is* thy voice, and thy countenance *is* comely". The voice of the bride is the prayers and praises of the Church.

Oh let our Voice his Praise exalt,
Till it arrive at Heavens Vault.

Bermudas recalls the duty of the faithful and the Church to praise God for His providence. The Church is the new Israel which thanks and praises God for favours of which the favours granted the Israelites were shadows. *Bermudas* echoes the Psalms because the Psalms are songs of praise. The Psalms recall the past and future of Israel. They were supposedly written by David who was the founder of the Temple, and Israel is their speaker. Just as Israel looks forward to its eventual triumph over the nations of the world, so the Church sees in the Psalms prophecies of its future. The song of praise sung by the voyagers is not only directed towards God in Heaven, but also to the world at large:

Which thence (perhaps) rebounding, may
Eccho beyond the *Mexique Bay*.

Just as Israel is to be a kingdom of priests to the other nations (Exodus 19:5-6), so Christ tells the disciples: "Go ye therefore, and teach all nations, baptizing them in the name of the Father, and of the Son, and of the Holy Ghost" (Matthew 28:19). The injunction to preach the Gospel is connected with the future hopes of the Church. The Gospel must first be preached to the whole world before the Second Coming.

Thus sung they, in the *English* boat,
An holy and a chearful Note,
And all the way, to guide their Chime,
With falling Oars they kept the time.

The shift in tense to "Thus sung they" helps shape our response to the nature of the Pilgrims' song. The Pilgrims were singing of a land they had not yet seen while journeying towards the future. Their song is "holy" and "chearful", being religious and happy. They do not fear for the end of their journey. In keeping the time they are participating in the divine scheme, sharing in the work of mankind's restoration: "All things are best fulfilled in thir due time, / And time there is for all things".[12] They are obeying God's will in preaching the Gospel which will someday bring about the return of eternal spring: "Work your work before the time: and he will give you your reward in his time" (Ecclesiasticus 51:38).

CHAPTER FIVE

The Nymph complaining for the death of her Faun

For thou wast slain, and hast redeemed us to God by thy blood. (Revelation 5:9)

It is surprising that some critics have insisted upon reading *The Nymph complaining for the death of her Faun* as a realistic portrait of a young girl lamenting the death of an animal, when the poem is so artificial and unrealistic. The continual shifts forward and backward in time, and the fragmented narrative line, warn us that we are in the presence of allegory. *The Nymph* is in part modelled on Ovid's *Amores*, Book 2, Chapter 6, where Corinna mourns for her dead bird, thinks back on his innocent and peaceful life, and concludes by saying that after his death he will go to Elysium and over his bones a tomb will rise decked with a funeral stone. The Ovidian influence does not mean the poem is secular. Ovid was often moralised and allegorised. In the Middle Ages, "even the *Art of Love* was allegorised for the benefit of nuns".[1] The conclusion of Corinna's lament (upon which stanzas ten and eleven of *The Nymph* are based) is particularly suitable for allegorisation, since the Elysium to which the bird goes is a holy hill, perpetually green, only accessible to good birds, and from which the bad are debarred.

Even if we were not aware of allegorisations of Ovid and the tradition of pastoral allegory, stretching from Mantuan and Boccaccio through Spenser to William Browne and Phineas Fletcher, we would be forced by the pressure of Marvell's language to see a religious significance in *The Nymph*. Individual words suggest a further dimension to the story: "Pray'rs", "Heaven", "Heavens King", "justice", "Stain", "bless", "Gifts", "virgin", "holy", "Image". Phrases point towards analogies: "nor cou'd / Thy death yet do them any good", "to offer for their Sin", "dy'd in such a Purple Grain", "And dye as calmely as a Saint". The artificiality of the diction and syntax causes us to reflect upon certain words and phrases: "There is not such another in / The World, to offer for their Sin".

Using the death of a fawn as its central figure, the beginning and conclusion of Marvell's poem are reminiscent of the Marian lament in which the Virgin stands at the foot of the Cross and sorrows for her dying Son. In literary and artistic representations of the Virgin's sorrows, she often thinks back to the childhood of her Son and their mutual joys.[2] The description of the Nymph's previous life with her Faun, which occupies the centre of the poem, has similarities to the Virgin's reminiscences of Christ's childhood. Marvell's poem might be said to be an allegory based on the birth, life and death of Christ in the tradition of the medieval Marian *planctus* and narrative meditations. Such devotions often used the imagery of Canticles and the speaker often assumed the viewpoint of the Virgin. The Song of Songs, or Canticles, has usually been read allegorically, although there is no agreement as to what exactly it represents. The Church Fathers and later commentators treated it as figurative of the mutual love of God and man's soul, Christ and the Church, Christ and the Virgin Mary.[3] There have been varied and contradictory readings of it as representing the history of the Church in its various stages of development. In most commentaries of Canticles, and in sermons, meditations, hymns and poems based on them, it is common to move back and forth freely between these various interpretations, with the result that a multiplicity of meanings may be suggested by a single verse or phrase. As we will see in *The Nymph*, Marvell makes use of such simultaneity of significance.

The symbolism of Canticles is recalled in the poem's main actors. A fawn is a young deer; the bridegroom in Canticles 2:9 is described as a roe, a young hart. Commentators sometimes compared the bridegroom's actions to those of a fawn. A nymph is a virgin or a young bride, as is the bride in Canticles. While it is usual to allegorise the bride as the soul and the Church, it is necessary to remember that poems, hymns and devotions on the Virgin often employ imagery from Canticles. During the Middle Ages when Canticles was the most important influence on Mary-poetry, the Madonna was usually characterised not as an ascetic Virgin, or a sublime Mother of God, but as a young bride. The traditional association between the Virgin and the bride of Canticles is reflected in the manuscript of Lord Fairfax's poetry, where "The Songs of Mary the Blessed Virgin", "Zachariah's Song" and "Simeon's Songe" (from Luke 1 and 2) are followed by his metric version of "The Songe of Solomon".[4]

We should not assume that Marvell would have regarded devotion to Mary as Papist. Seventeenth century Anglicans did not follow the Puritans in demoting the role of the Virgin; however, Anglicans differed from Catholics in believing that all grace was from Christ and not from the Virgin. Christ was the sole mediator between man and God; the Virgin was not, as Roman Catholics claimed, co-mediator. We need not be troubled, however, by doctrinal differences. It is sufficient for our purposes that Mary was traditionally thought of as the Tabernacle or Church of God in which the Messiah promised the Israelites was actualised.

The Nymph is divided into eleven verse paragraphs or stanzas, because eleven is the traditional symbolic number for mourning.[5] The poem begins by recalling the Crucifixion, moves backward in time to the Incarnation, alludes to the life of Christ and His presence with His mother and the early Church, and ends with His death and Ascension. The shooting of the Faun is the first and main event of the poem because Christ's death is the central event in created time; it is Christ's death which effects the reconciliation between God and man:

> The wanton Troopers riding by
> Have shot my Faun and it will dye.
> Ungentle men! They cannot thrive
> To kill thee.

The abrupt beginning is similar to the meditative practice of creating similitudes or metaphorical representations to fix the mind on a theme. In meditation we would be there, imagining ourselves present at the Crucifixion; but Marvell's method is different. The figures of the Faun and Troopers stand between the meditative mind and the Crucifixion. The "Troopers" are described as "Ungentle men", identifying them with the Jews (ungentile). "They cannot thrive / To kill thee" alludes to sacrificial killing. The killing of the harmless Faun recalls the prophecy of Christ in Isaiah 53:7: "brought as a lamb to the slaughter".

> . . . Thou neer didst alive
> Them any harm: alas, nor cou'd
> Thy death yet do them any good.
> I'me sure I never wisht them ill;
> Nor do I for all this; nor will:
> But, if my simple Pray'rs may yet
> Prevail with Heaven to forget
> Thy murder, I will Joyn my Tears
> Rather then fail. But, O my fears!
> It cannot dye so. Heavens King
> Keeps register of every thing.

"Good" is used in the sense of "blessing". "Yet" suggests that the Faun's death will result in good in the future. The shift from the present to the implied future might be described as an allegorical tripwire or trigger. A sacramental vision can only be reproduced in literature through techniques which suggest the simultaneity of past, present and future. We are reminded of the Virgin sobbing at the foot of the Cross and Christ's tears. Tears are "simple Pray'rs". Christ wept for mankind; the Church joins its tears with those of Christ and prays for its persecutors (Luke 23:34). "Prevail with Heaven" both recalls the atonement and the intercession of the saints. Heaven will not forget the Troopers' murdering of the Faun since the names of unrepentant sinners and the enemies of God are recorded in the Book of Fate in Revelation. Even the death of a sparrow is not "forgotten before God".

Animals are part of God's creation, to be used with prayers, thanksgiving, and as an aid to contemplation. When Adam is given dominion over "every beast of the field", the animals are brought before him so that he can praise the variety and goodness of God's creation. God says "every beast of the forest *is* mine" (Psalm 50:10):

And nothing may we use in vain.
Ev'n Beasts must be with justice slain;
Else Men are made their *Deodands.*

Things of the world are to be used towards an enjoyment of God, while misuse, or abuse, is vain (useless), and results from vanity or self-love. "Else Men are made their *Deodands*" is an example of double syntax, since "their" could refer to men or beasts. A deodand (a theological word) is an animal or moving thing which, having occasioned the death of a man, is forfeited to the crown or lord of the manor. Originally it was a forfeit to God for pacification of wrath. While slain beasts are sin offerings, they are sacrificed to make an atonement (Numbers 6:11 ff). Since it is the reasonable soul which distinguishes man from beast, if man acts unjustly or wantonly, he is worse than a beast. If man is no better than a beast, why not sacrifice men for beasts? It is because men act unjustly that Christ becomes a sacrificial deodand, saving man from divine wrath. "Ev'n Beasts must be with justice slain" brings to mind Christ's trial: "Then Pilate said unto them, Why, what evil hath he done? And they cried out the more exceedingly, Crucify him" (Mark 15:14).

The prophetic relationship of the Old to the New Testament is recalled:

Though they should wash their guilty hands
In this warm life blood, which doth part
From thine, and wound me to the Heart,
Yet could they not be clean: their Stain
Is dy'd in such a Purple Grain.
There is not such another in
The World, to offer for their Sin.

The ritual sacrifice of beasts after Mosaic law prefigured the death of

Christ (Hebrews 10:18-23). Sacrifices were sin and trespass offerings. They were accompanied by the washing of whatever was stained in the sacrificial blood (Leviticus 6:27). In Deuteronomy the rules for purification after the discovery of a murder include the washing of hands over a sacrificial heifer (Deuteronomy 21:6-8). The heifer is usually seen as a type of Christ, and the ceremony as prefiguring Pilate's washing of his hands. The sacramental significance of the cleansing of hands is recalled in "Cleanse *your* hands, *ye* sinners" (James 4:8). "Though they should wash their guilty hands / In this warm life blood" recalls Matthew 27:24-25: "Pilate . . . washed *his* hands before the multitude, saying, I am innocent of the blood of this just person: see ye *to it*. Then answered all the people, and said, His blood *be* on us, and on our children". It is "life blood" because it is blood shed for eternal life: "we have redemption through his blood" (Ephesians 1:7). The Nymph's blood "parts" from the Faun's in the sense of "shares" (partakes) or "divides from" (is a portion of), and recalls Simeon's prophecy of Christ's death. Simeon tells Mary "a sword shall pierce through thy own soul also" (Luke 2:35). This is seen as referring to Mary's future anguish at the Crucifixion. It was common to say that the sword pierced both Christ's side and Mary's heart at once.

In "Yet could they not be clean" Marvell is thinking of the distinctions between ceremonial purification, innocence, and being free from sin through the blood of Christ.[6] "For *it is* not possible that the blood of bulls and of goats should take away sins" (Hebrews 10:4). If the slayers of the Faun cannot be clean, it is because their act is wanton (carnal in the sense of being after the Old Law), and because they are a figure for the guilt of the Jews in Christ's death.

"Their Stain / Is dy'd in such a Purple Grain". Purple is a common symbol for royalty, and recalls the purple robe put on Christ before the Crucifixion. The "dyed garments" of Isaiah 63:1 are seen as a prophecy of Christ's Sacrifice: "he *was* clothed with a vesture dipped in blood" (Revelation 19:13). "Stain" alludes to "His blood *be* on us and on our children" (Matthew 27:25). "Grain" recalls that Christ is the promised seed of Genesis 3:15. In John 12:24 Jesus compares Himself to a corn of wheat. A "Purple Grain" would recall that the promised seed is of the royal line of David: Jesus is King of the Jews. "There is not such another in / The World, to offer for their Sin". Christ's atonement is final: "where remission of these [sins and iniquities] *is, there* is no more offering for sin" (Hebrews 10:18). If you incur guilt through killing a unique sacrificial offering, what can you then use to repay or atone for your guilt?

After the description of the shooting of the Faun, the Nymph thinks back to the time when she was given the animal by Sylvio, her former lover:

Unconstant *Sylvio*, when yet
I had not found him counterfeit,
One morning (I remember well)
Ty'd in this silver Chain and Bell,
Gave it to me: nay and I know
What he said then; I'me sure I do.
Said He, look how your Huntsman here
Hath taught a Faun to hunt his *Dear*.
But Sylvio soon had me beguil'd.
This waxed tame; while he grew wild,
And quite regardless of my Smart,
Left me his Faun, but took his Heart.

Sylvio is a common pastoral name suggestive of innocence, trees, forests and the golden age. The natural world, however, fell and grew "wild" when the serpent "beguil'd" (Genesis 3:13) Eve to eat the fruit of the tree of knowledge. One result of the Fall was the promised coming of Christ, figured here by the Faun. While Marvell through Sylvio is alluding to mankind's remembrance of an Edenic golden age, the false lover is also figurative of the Synagogue which hands on the promise of the Messiah. Sylvio is "counterfeit"; something which is counterfeit is a false copy of the real. Christianity views the Synagogue as a shadow or type of the Church. Old Testament types are physical shadows of New Testament images, which in turn refer to heavenly realities. Sylvio's inconstancy fits with God's complaints in the Old Testament that the Israelites have forgotten or rejected Him.

The Faun is given to the Nymph tied in "this silver Chain and Bell". Aaron's bell is a symbol for preaching. The Faun comes tied in Old Testament law and the prophets, which prefigure the Gospel and preaching. "I know what he said then" brings to mind "Mary kept all those things, and pondered *them* in her heart" (Luke 2:19). Some commentators claimed that Mary read and meditated upon such prophecies as Isaiah 7:14: "Therefore the Lord himself shall give you a sign; Behold, a virgin shall conceive, and bear a son, and shall call his name Immanuel". Sylvio's words should probably be viewed as figurative of prophecies of the coming of Christ.

The puns on "Huntsman", "Faun", "*Dear*", and "Heart" play upon and evoke many associations. Origen in commenting upon Canticles 2:8 says that the harts may be understood as Old Testament saints, such as Abraham, Isaac, Jacob, David and Solomon; "those harts the Lord's voice did indeed make perfect, and their fawn is He who was born as a child of them according to the flesh".[7] Both Origen and Bernard say that Christ is a fawn or young hart because "unto us a child is born, unto us a son is given" (Isaiah 9:6). In losing Sylvio, the Nymph is left with desires which will be fulfilled through her love of the Faun. The fulfilment of Old Testament promises is read in Ezekiel 36:26: "A new heart also will I give you, and a new spirit will I put within you: and I will take away the stony heart out of your flesh, and I will give you an heart of flesh".

That Marvell has in mind the passing of the Covenant from the Israelites to the Christians is shown by "This waxed tame; while he grew wild". The opposition of the tame and wild is a favourite motif of Marvell's and here, as in *The Mower against Gardens*, alludes to Romans 11, where the Israelites are the good or tame trees on which are grafted the wild branches of the Gentiles. Sylvio, figurative of the Synagogue, grows wild, deserting his love and the people; but he hands on the Faun, whose tameness is figurative of Christ's obedience.

> Thenceforth I set myself to play
> My solitary time away,
> With this: and very well content,
> Could so mine idle Life have spent.
> For it was full of sport; and light
> Of foot, and heart; and did invite,
> Me to its game: it seem'd to bless
> Its self in me. How could I less
> Than love it? O I cannot be
> Unkind, t' a Beast that loveth me.

"Thenceforth" is an unusual word for poetry; it seems equivalent to such biblical phrases as "and it came to pass" or "in those days". The departure of Sylvio and the gift of the Faun bring to mind the ceasing of Israel's prophetic function with the coming of Christ. The Nymph's solitude with the Faun suggests Christ's early life. Proverbs 8:30 is seen as prophetic of Christ and the Virgin Mary: "and I was daily *his* delight, rejoicing always before him". We are reminded of non-biblical accounts of the Christ Child's gaiety and "sport"; "The Son adorned and nursed by the Sweet Maid, / A Thousand fold of love for love repaid".[8] Usually when the Magi visit Mary they find her "with her sweet child playing".[9] Jeremy Taylor, speaking of the Nativity and Child in the manger, writes of "the great variety of sweetnesses, and amorous reflexes, and gracious intercourses, which passed between the blessed Virgin and the holy Child". "If we could behold his sacred feet with those affections which the holy Virgin did".[10] The Faun blesses "Its self in me" because the members of the Church share in the blood and flesh of Christ.

The Faun's gaiety ("light of foot, and heart") and its invitation "to its game" recall Canticles 1:4: "Draw me, we will run after thee . . . we will be glad and rejoice in thee" and Canticles 3:11 "Go forth, O ye daughters of Zion . . . in the day of the gladness of his heart". The

Faun's lightness of foot is self-explanatory; it brings light. Isaiah 52:7 is read as a prophecy of the deliverance of the faithful and the Church: "How beautiful upon the mountains are the feet of him that bringeth good tidings, . . . that publisheth salvation; that saith unto Zion, Thy God reigneth!" Since Isaiah is rich with passaged which are interpreted as prophesying Christ and His relationship to the Church, such echoes strengthen the symbolic associations felt in the allusions to Canticles. Isaiah is often used to explain Canticles.

The Faun has not died, yet the Nymph speaks of it as if it had:

Had it liv'd long, I do not know
Whether it too might have done so
As *Sylvio* did: his Gifts might be
Perhaps as false or more than he.
But I am sure, for ought that I
Could in so short a time espie,
Thy Love was far more better then
The love of false and cruel men.

The Faun is Sylvio's gift. Origen discussing Canticles says that the gifts which the Church receives in preparation for its divine marriage are the law and the prophets which promise her the coming of the Son of God.[11] The Faun is contrasted with Sylvio's gifts because Christ is the reality of which Old Testament blessings are shadows. Sylvio as the Synagogue hands on God's promise. Christ proves His claim to have come to fulfil Old Testament prophecies by His death. The shortness of the Faun's life recalls the shortness of Christ's life on earth. "Thy Love was far more better then / The love of false and cruel men" contrasts Christ's love with erotic live, such as Solomon's and perhaps imitates Canticles 1:2 where God's gifts are contrasted to sensual delights: "for thy love *is* better than wine". The Nymph alone with the Faun in her garden is an appropriate figure for the undefiled bride of Canticles. She suggests the Church enjoying the spiritual gifts of Christ's presence and at times is a figure for the soul's contemplative life with God.

With sweetest milk, and sugar, first
I it at mine own fingers nurst.
And as it grew, so every day
It wax'd more white and sweet than they.
It had so sweet a Breath! And oft
I blusht to see its foot more soft,
And white, (Shall I say then my hand?)
NAY any Ladies of the Land.

The description of the Nymph feeding the Faun is figurative of the Virgin nourishing the Christ Child. In the New Testament, milk is used to stand for the first principles as contrasted with a mature knowledge of doctrine.[12] In Marvell's poem *Upon Appleton House*, sugar is a symbol for the holy oil: "The Sugars uncorrupting Oyl". If the Nymph feeds the Faun with the sugar's uncorrupting oil, she is giving him the oil used to anoint priests and kings in the Old Testament.[13] Christ is the anointed, or Messiah (John 1:41). As the Faun grows it becomes purer and sweeter. "Grew" and "wax'd" allude to "And the child grew, and waxed strong in spirit, filled with wisdom" (Luke 2:40). The allusion is important since the last event of Christ's boyhood recounted in the Bible is His going to Jerusalem "when he was twelve years old" (Luke 2:42).

The whiteness of the Faun's body recalls the purity of Christ's life, its sweet breath represents God's Word. According to legend the deer with the breath of its nostrils kills serpents. The bestiaries allegorise this as the Gospel which kills the devil.[14] Christ's feet are a well-known symbol for His humanity, the feet being where the earth and divine meet. Commentators said that His two feet are "mercy" and "judgement". The Faun's foot is contrasted with those of the Nymph and other ladies because it was usual to speak of Christ's hands as pure and white.[15]

> It is a wond'rous thing, how fleet
> 'Twas on those little silver feet.
> With what a pretty skipping grace,
> It oft would challenge me the Race:
> And when 'thad left me far away,
> 'Twould stay, and run again, and stay.
> For it was nimbler much than Hindes;
> And trod, as on the four Winds.

In the meditations and *planctus* there are often descriptions of the Boy leaving His mother and returning to her. In the fourteenth century meditation the Virgin seeking her Child says: "Tell me where you are, sweet Son, and I shall come to you or you to me . . . Alas, my Son, do not delay to come to me . . . Show me therefore, where you are and how I can find you".[16] The coming and going of the Faun in the sixth stanza also reflects the coming and going of the bridegroom in Canticles. God's gifts to the contemplative soul and the Church are in the form of visitations. The divine word may show man the way to salvation, but the union of the bride and bridegroom cannot be permanent until the next life.

The Faun's "skipping grace" alludes to Canticles 2:8: "The voice of my beloved! behold, he cometh leaping upon the mountains, skipping upon the hills". The skipping shows Christ bringing grace. "It oft would challenge me the Race" echoes Canticles 2:10: "My beloved spake, and said unto me, Rise up, my love, my fair one, and come away". In Psalm 19:5 the sun declares God's glory "as a bridegroom coming out of his chamber *and* rejoiceth as a strong man to run a race". This is usually read as an allusion to the Incarnation and Virgin Birth; the race is allegorically His life and death.

"And when 'thad left me far away, / 'Twould stay, and run again, and stay". Origen says "So also is it with the soul . . . as long as she cannot find what she is looking for, the Word of God is surely absent from her. But when the thing she sought comes up to meet her, and appears to her, who doubts but that the Word of God is present, illuminating her mind and offering to her the light of knowledge?" He also says: "The Bridegroom is thus sometimes present and teaching, and sometimes He is said to be absent; and then He is desired. And either of these will suit either the Church or the dutiful soul. For when He allows the Church to suffer persecution and tribulations, He seems to her to be absent; and again, when she goes forward in peace and flourishes in faith and good works, He is understood as being present with her".[17] In "trod, as on the four Winds", "trod" recalls the promise in Genesis that Christ will come to tread the serpent underfoot. The four winds bring to mind the four corners of the earth (Revelation 7:1). The Faun thus brings to mind Christ's conquest of death.

Within the frame of the Nymph's recollections, we now move forward in time. The Faun is older and is no longer nursed by the Nymph. Instead we will find him feeding on roses. The break in narrative, I believe, is analogous to the discontinuity which occurs in the biblical life of Christ between His twelfth and thirtieth years. (Such broken narrative is also common to *planctus* poems when the Virgin recalls the life of her Son. In such poems it is used to suggest her emotions.)

I have a Garden of my own,
But so with Roses over grown,
And Lillies, that you would it guess
To be a little Wilderness.
And all the Spring time of the year
It onely loved to be there.

The Nymph's garden recalls the enclosed garden of the bride in Canticles (4:12), allegorised as the Virgin, Church or soul. Commenting upon Canticles 1:6, "*but* mine own vineyards have I not kept", Origen says that the bride has not kept the habits and customs of the Old Law.[18]

The lilies and roses allude to "I *am* the rose of Sharon, *and* the lily of the valleys" (Canticles 2:1), a verse which commentators assigned to both the bride and bridegroom as the speaker is not certain. Unfortunately there are such varied explications of what the lily and roses of Canticles signify that my own interpretation of what Marvell means by them is necessarily impressionistic, although I will attempt to show how my impressions are within exegetical traditions. The roses of Canticles are associated with the prophecy of Christ's flourishing Church or Kingdom in Isaiah: "Sharon is like a wilderness" (33:9); "The wilderness and the solitary place shall be glad for them; and the desert shall rejoice, and blossom as the rose" (35:1); "he will make her wilderness like Eden, and her desert like the garden of the LORD" (51:3). The roses are thus a sign of man's restoration and of the Church. Traditionally the Virgin's garden is "over grown" with lilies: "he shall grow as the lily" (Hosea 14:5). Origen says that the lily of the valleys grows in strong, uncultivated places, meaning among the Gentiles.[19] Bernard interprets the lilies of Canticles more loosely. Christ is a lily, the events of His life and death are lilies, all virtues are lilies: "there are as many lilies as virtues".[20] While there is a strong emphasis in this part of the poem on the mystical, contemplative interpretation of Canticles, Marvell also has in mind Christ's mission and teaching, as is shown by the presence of the flowers.

The Faun is in the garden during the springtime because it is the season of rebirth, the Annunciation, Easter and Christ's Passion. The coming of spring in Canticles 2:12 is allegorised as the day of grace, or the glad tidings of salvation: "*The flowers appear on the earth*: this and the following clauses are here alleged as evidences of the spring time, which in the mystical and principal sense seems to signify the day of grace, or the glad tidings of salvation proposed to sinners in the time of the law, by types, and shadows, and promises, but much more clearly and fully in the gospel".[21]

> Among the beds of Lillyes, I
> Have sought it oft, where it should lye;
> Yet could not, till it self would rise,
> Find it, although before mine Eyes.
> For, in the flaxen Lillies shade,
> It like a bank of Lillies laid

evokes several motifs from Canticles — the bridegroom resting at noon with his flock (1:7), the bridegroom feeding among lilies (2:16) and the bride seeking her lover (3:15). Christ dwells among the faithful and enjoys their company. The lilies are the daughters of Jerusalem, the bridegroom's flock. Origen says that when He became the lily in the valleys, forthwith His neighbours also become lilies in imitation of Himself, that is every single soul that draws near Him and follows His pattern may become a lily too.[22] Solomon's "bed" (Canticles 3:7), surrounded by the valiant of Israel, is interpreted as the Church enjoying the fellowship of Christ.[23] Commenting upon "My beloved is gone down into his garden, to the beds of spices, to feed in the gardens, and to gather lilies" (Canticles 6:2), Poole says that the lilies are the believers whom Christ gathered to Himself in His Church, or the prayers and praises tendered to Him by His people.[24] Commentators also saw the lilies of Canticles as referring to the Apostles and the converted. "Have sought it oft" alludes to "By night on my bed I sought him whom my soul loveth: I sought him, but I found him not . . . nor awake *my* love till he please" (Canticles 3:1,5). The Church and the faithful seek Christ through prayer and meditation, but Christ comes to the soul when He wishes.

Upon the Roses it would feed,
Until its Lips ev'n seem'd to bleed:
And then to me 'twould boldly trip,
And print those Roses on my Lip.

Throughout this section of the poem Marvell is wittily playing against each other the various meanings and readings given the flowers and colour symbolism of Canticles. The bridegroom of Canticles dwells among lilies; he does not feed on them. He feeds on honey, spices, wine, milk and other delights, for which Marvell substitutes roses. The roses appear to change their meaning each time they are mentioned. I imagine that the roses upon which the Faun feeds are sinners, whom he incorporates into himself. Bernard says the bridegroom "finds nourishment in the virtues of those upon whom He has shed the brightness of sanctity; and also that he receives sinners to penitence in His Body, which is the Church; and that it was to unite them with Himself that He was Himself made sin, who did no sin, that the body of sin might be destroyed in which sinners had once been incorporated, and that they might become righteousness in Him, being justified freely by His grace".[25] The Faun's lips, the result of feeding on roses, recall the blood of Christ paid to redeem man. In a poem known as *Meditations on the Life and Passion of Christ*, prophecies of Christ include a description of "His lips like a red rose-bush".[26]

The printing of the roses on the lips of the Nymph suggests "Let him kiss me with the kisses of his mouth" (Canticles 1:2) and the erotic kissing and love play of Canticles 7:8-9. The kisses are signs of love and grace. Bernard says the pressure of the lip signifies the union of souls.[27] Origen says: "The kisses are Christ's, which He bestowed on His Church when at His coming, being present in the flesh, He in His own person spoke to her the words of faith and love and peace".[28] The bold printing of the roses on the lips is figurative of Christ giving the Gospel to his Church to be preached, and of His promised union with the faithful. It is also probable that the Faun printing "those Roses" on the Nymph's lips is figurative of the faithful being fed in the Eucharist. The Last Supper and Christ's Sacrifice are recalled in the

Eucharistic communion when the body of Christ is placed on the lips of the faithful.

> But all its chief delight was still
> On Roses thus its self to fill:
> And its pure virgin Limbs to fold
> In whitest sheets of Lillies cold.
> Had it liv'd long, it would have been
> Lillies without, Roses within.

While the Faun enjoys kissing the Nymph, his chief delight is eating roses and lying among lilies. In Canticles the bridegroom leaves the bride (5:6) and is later found in the garden feeding among lilies (6:3). "How fair and pleasant art thou, O love, for delights!" (Canticles 7:6) is usually understood as the Church's graces. The lilies are "cold" because, despite the obvious erotic significance of the bridegroom feeding among them, they should be understood spiritually. The sheets are "whitest" because the Church is unspotted and undefiled. It is the virgin bride of the celestial Lamb: "arrayed in fine linen, clean and white: for the fine linen is the righteousness of saints" (Revelation 19:8). In his seventy-first sermon on Canticles, Bernard said that Christ "was nourished with food in the house of Martha and Mary; he reclined, even in the body, among the lilies (I speak of them, for they were lilies)".[29]

"Had it liv'd long, it would have been / Lillies without, Roses within". In Canticles 5:10 the bridegroom is "white and ruddy", which is usually understood as His body and blood, or His life and the Passion. Poole interprets it as His Innocence and Passion. The colour symbolism can be found in emblem-books: "White, for his blessed and divinifyed soule; red, for his precious flesh, embrued with his blood".[30] In poetry we usually find red and white as the colours of the Passion. George Herbert says: "Thy bloody death and undeserved, makes thee / Pure red and white".[31] Christ is "the *granum frumenti* white within and red without, dying to live again".[32] One writer meditating upon the Passion says "love that is so fierce / has made thy body a red rose-bush".[33] Marvell cleverly reverses the traditional colour symbolism while recalling that Christ's life was emblematic of virginal innocence and a martyr's love.[34]

After the section treating of the Nymph's life with the Faun, the poem again focuses upon the dying animal. We are reminded of Christ on the Cross, blood streaming like tears from His wounds, His head calmly bowed as He accepts His destiny.

> O help! O help! I see it faint:
> And dye as calmely as a Saint.
> See how it weeps. The tears do come

Sad, slowly dropping like a Gumme.
So weeps the wounded Balsome: so
The holy Frankincense doth flow.
The brotherless *Heliades*
Melt in such Amber Tears as these.

His calmness recalls the prophecy of Christ's Sacrifice in Isaiah 53:7: "He was oppressed, and he was afflicted, yet he opened not his mouth: he is brought as a lamb to the slaughter, and as a sheep before her shearers is dumb, so he openeth not his mouth". "Saint" brings to mind the Church which is a body or communion of saints: "they have shed the blood of saints and prophets" (Revelation 16:6). In early representations of the Crucifixion the robe of Christ is embroidered with the figures of saints, who as members of His body share in His Passion and His triumph.[35]

The Faun's weeping and tears recall Christ "when he had offered up prayers and supplications with strong crying and tears" (Hebrews 5:7). Donne says: "And those teares, Expositors of all sides referre to his Passion, though some to his Agony in the Garden, some to his Passion on the Crosse; and these in my opinion most fitly; because those words of S. *Paul* belong to the declaration of the Priesthood, and of the Sacrifice of Christ; and for that function of his, the Crosse was the Altar".[36] Christ's tears in the Garden were seen as prophetic of His cries on the Cross: "And being in an agony he prayed more earnestly: and his sweat was as it were great drops of blood falling down to the ground" (Luke 22:44).[37]

"Gumme",[38] "Balsome" and "holy Frankincense" allude to the herbs, spices and resins used in the incense and holy oil at the Old Testament atonement ceremony (Exodus 30:23-35). The atonement is for expiation of sins, and the high priest must offer incense and sacrificial blood as a propitiation. The incense is burnt to make a sweet smoke which rises to Heaven. It is thus a form of prayer and by association is seen as similar to tears, which are also prayers of penitence. In *Eyes and Tears* Marvell wrote, "The Incense was to Heaven dear, / Not as a Perfume, but a Tear". The various aromatic gums flow, or drip, like blood or tears and thus are fitting emblems for Christ's tears and blood. The incense was offered at the altar (place of slaughter) of the Holy of Holies, which is a type of the Cross of Christ's Sacrifice.

Hugh of Saint Victor says: "For Christ is so called from chrism and the Christian is named from Christ. Therefore, ever since all began to share the name all had to receive unction because 'in Christ we all are a chosen generation, a kingly priesthood,' (Cf. I Peter 2,9). Chrism is made of oil and balsam, because through oil the infusion of grace is designated, through balsam the odour of good fame".[39] The "holy

Frankincense" has associations with Christ's intercession, which is compared to a sweet odour (Ephesians 5:2), and to incense (Revelation 8:3-4).

> I in a golden Vial will
> Keep these two crystal Tears; and fill
> It till it do o'reflow with mine;
> Then place it in *Diana's* Shrine.

The Nymph's mention of the "golden Vial" looks forward to Revelation 5:8 "the four beasts and four *and* twenty elders fell down before the Lamb, having every one of them harps, and golden vials full of odours, which are the prayers of saints". In Psalm 56:8 the people of Israel ask God to remember them: "put thou my tears into thy bottle". In *Paradise Lost* the tears of Adam and Eve, "sent from hearts contrite", are "Sighs and Prayers", which "in this Gold'n Censer, mixt / With Incense, [Christ] thy Priest" brings to God.[40] The crystal tears recall Christ's blood and tears in the Garden and during the Crucifixion.

Diana is an emblem of chastity; she is often allegorised as the Virgin. (Ephesus, centre of the cult of Diana, was the first Church to worship Mary. It was during the Council of Ephesus in 431 that the role of Mary in relation to the Trinity became doctrinal.[41]) But why does the Nymph place the golden vial or censer in a shrine? I am reminded of the body and blood of Christ on the altar. Christ is both the sweet odour of sacrifice and the sacrificial body of the Host.[42] The association of tears with the Eucharist is found in Donne's sermon on Psalm 11:3. Donne says that God first admitted "thee to him . . . by Water, the water of *Baptisme*: Goe still the same way to him, by Water, by repentant *Teares*: . . . And the last thing that hee [Christ] bequeathed to thee, was his *Blood*, in the Institution of the Blessed *Sacrament*: Refuse not to goe to him, the same way too, if his glorie require that Sacrifice".[43]

> Now my sweet Faun is vanish'd to
> Whether the Swans and Turtles go:
> In fair *Elizium* to endure,
> With milk-white Lambs, and Ermins pure.
> O do not run too fast: for I
> Will but bespeak thy Grave, and dye.

The description of the dead Faun's translation to Heaven ("*Elizium*") and the Nymph's desire to join it bring to mind Christ's Ascension and the desire of the faithful to be among the saints who serve at "the throne of God and of the Lamb" (Revelation 22:3). Just as the sacrificial animals must be without blemish, so Christ is a pure offering made for atonement. "Go" alludes to the Ascension. The various snow white animals, emblems of purity and innocence, are the chaste virgins and saints of the Church who will enter Heaven. Augustine interprets the turtle dove and pigeon of Genesis 15:7-21 as types of Abraham's spiritual seed and "heirs of the kingdom of eternity" ("In fair *Elizium* to endure"). Bernard says that the voice of the turtle in Canticles 2:12 is the preaching of chastity.[44]

The Nymph's cry "O do not run too fast: for I / Will but bespeak thy Grave, and dye" brings to mind the need to bear witness for Christ. The Church and the soul see in Christ's death and Ascension a promise of redemption. The Nymph's words are a confession of faith: "He which testifieth these things saith, Surely I come quickly" (Revelation 22:20). Revelation 22:17 and 22:20 are often seen as anticipated by Canticles 2:17 ("Until the day break, and the shadows flee away, turn, my beloved, and be thou like a roe or a young hart upon the mountains of Bether") and Canticles 8:14 ("Make haste, my beloved, and be thou like to a roe or to a young hart upon the mountains of spices"). Matthew Poole says that Canticles 2:17 refers both to abiding with Christ throughout the ages, and to the general resurrection when there shall be an immediate enjoyment of the bridegroom. Commenting upon Canticles 8:14 Poole says "Seeing we must part for a time, make haste, O my beloved Bridegroom, and speedily finish the work which thou hast to do in the world, that so thou mayst take me to thyself, that I may live in thine everlasting embraces".[45]

The Faun's grave will be a statue or image of the Nymph and Faun standing for the Church and Christ. In "bespeak thy Grave" Marvell brings to mind the entombment and perhaps recalls one of the main events between Christ's death and Resurrection. When Mary Magdalene goes to the sepulchre she learns that Christ is resurrected. She is told that He will go before her to Galilee. She then carries her news to the Apostles. She is both a witness and a link in the founding of the Church. In the last section of the poem, the Nymph's weeping over the death of her Faun recalls John 20:11: "But Mary stood without at the sepulchre weeping". That the Nymph should also remind us of Mary Magdalene is not surprising. The Church celebrates the Feast of Mary Magdalene with quotations from both Canticles and biblical descriptions of the Crucifixion.

In contemplative literature "die" means the swooning or rapture of the soul into an ecstasy of communion with the divine. It was common to draw a parallel between the soul's mystical death and Christ's Sacrifice. "If God give me *mortem raptus*, a death of rapture, of extasie, of fervent Contemplation of Christ Jesus . . . this is . . . that . . . *death of his Saints*, by which they are dead and buryed, and risen again in Christ Jesus".[46] Before the soul can enjoy its rapture, it must be prepared by further contemplation, penitence, and recovery of the divine image within itself. The poem is thus an allegory related to meditations on the life and death of Christ.

The Nymph says that she will have a statue made of herself weeping with the dead Faun at her feet, but it is not necessary for the artist to engrave tears since the statue will itself weep and engrave tears on its breast.

First my unhappy Statue shall
Be cut in Marble, and withal,
Let it be weeping too: but there
Th' Engraver sure his Art may spare;
For I so truly thee bemoane,
That I shall weep though I be Stone:
Until my Tears, still dropping, wear
My breast, themselves engraving there.
There at my feet shalt thou be laid,
Of purest Alabaster made.

The statue of the weeping Nymph with the dead Faun at her feet brings to mind representations of Mary weeping at her Son's death (the Mother of Sorrows of Christian art). Marvell returns here to the tradition of the Virgin's *planctus*; within this formerly well-known tradition Mary weeps and wishes to die rather than survive her Son.[47] It is not surprising that the weeping Nymph should remind classically trained readers of Niobe, since in Catholic devotion Niobe's tears were often incorporated as types of the tears of the Virgin in her sorrow: "For she could not see her Sonne to be so crucifyed, without groanes, and motherlie laments for her dying Sonne, the joy of her hart, and hart of al her joyes, so pierced with a souldiers speare, that even transfixed withal the mothers breast, a verie *Niobe* of teares, or rather *Noome* of bitter groanes".[48] "Laid" may allude to the entombment: "Now in the place where he was crucified there was a garden; and in the garden a new sepulchre, wherein was never man yet laid" (John 19:41).

The Nymph's statue is also a figure for the remembrance by the Church and the individual soul of Christ's Sacrifice. Notice the Nymph's remark "though I be Stone". "Stone" puns on Peter's name; Peter is the stone on which Christ builds His Church. But Marvell also uses the symbolism of the altar.[49] The Nymph is the uncut stone altar of the Old Testament (Exodus 20:25). Durandus explains that the first sanctuary in Bethel was the type of all altars.[50] If the Nymph is a "Stone" altar and the Faun is laid at her feet, he must be in the "confessio" or grave for relics under the altar table. Sometimes the Sacrament of the Eucharist, or Host, was placed in or under altars in place of relics. In the Jewish ceremony, type of the Christian, the blood of the animal was sacrificed at the foot of the altar.[51] The symbolism of the dead animal at the foot of the weeping statue is appropriate since the Church is founded upon Christ's death. As for alabaster, it is whiter than marble and is sometimes symbolic of heavenly purity. The Faun has as its memorial an image of spiritual purity. While we should see the Nymph's statue as the Church recalling through its prayers and art the life and death of Christ, we could apply the Nymph's words to the soul in meditation remembering the events of the Passion. In the New Testament, the message of salvation is written in the human heart (II Corinthians 3:3).

The last two lines of the poem are an example of Marvell's use of double syntax:

> For I would have thine Image be
> White as I can, though not as Thee.

The "Image", while referring to the Faun, can also include the Nymph ("as I can"). Such transformation is possible since man is created in the divine image, the elect are in Christ's image and the Church is the image of Christ: "But we all, with open face beholding as in a glass the glory of the Lord, are changed into the same image from glory to glory, *even* as by the Spirit of the Lord" (II Corinthians 3:18). Jeremy Taylor says "Holy Jesu, since thy image is imprinted on our nature by creation, let me also express thy image by all the parts of a holy life, conforming my will and affections to thy holy precepts"[52] While man may imitate Christ, he cannot be as white "as Thee". "Shall a man be more pure than his maker?" (Job 4:17). Nor can the earthly Church be without stain since its members are not pure. Such purity will occur at the end of time: "That he might present it to himself a glorious church, not having spot, or wrinkle, or any such thing; but that it should be holy and without blemish" (Ephesians 5:27). If the Synagogue is a shadow revealed in types, the earthly Church is an "Image" of the heavenly bride. The lamenting Nymph and the dead Faun are both images in the sense that they are figures for divine realities. They remind the Christian reader of his duty to contemplate the meaning of Christ's life, and to strive for a similar purity. The Nymph's weeping plays its part in such associations, since it is suggestive of penitence.

I have tried to show that *The Nymph complaining for the death of her Faun* is a figurative allegory recalling the birth, life and death of Christ. It is modelled on the poetic tradition of the sorrows of the Virgin Mary and on medieval meditations on the life of Christ. In Sylvio's giving the Faun to the Nymph we are reminded of Old Testament prophecies of the coming of Christ. The echoes of Canticles throughout the central stanzas of the poem are used to recall Mary's life with her Son. We should see the Nymph as the Church as well as Mary and the Faun's life in her garden as recalling Christ's mission. Throughout the poem there is an intermittent analogy to mystical contemplative interpretations of Canticles in which the love of the bride and bridegroom is that of the soul and God. If we read the poem in this way, the soul is seen as gaining various blessings as it meditates on the life of Christ and at the end of the poem prepares for its eventual mystical union after death.

CHAPTER SIX

To his Coy Mistress

Beware lest any man spoil you through philosophy and vain deceit. (Colossians 2:8)

If it has not been recognised that Marvell's lyrics are essentially religious, it is probably because of *To his Coy Mistress*. How is it possible for someone to be a religious poet when he wrote one of the finest and most passionate love songs of the seventeenth century? It is not necessary to resort to a theory of artistic impersonality, or to assume that Marvell was enjoying a pagan holiday, to find a place for *To his Coy Mistress* within the allegorical imagination. A close reading of the poem reveals that it is another, more daring variation on Marvell's usual themes. Perhaps the best way to grasp what Marvell is doing is to imagine a *Dialogue between the Resolved Soul and Created Pleasure* in which only Created Pleasure speaks, and in which the imagery used by the speaker ironically undermines his argument and reminds us of the Resolved Soul's perspective on the temptations of the flesh.

Since my concern is with *To his Coy Mistress* as allegory, I will assume that most readers are aware of the poem's more obvious qualities, such as its sophisticated, sardonic wit. More important for my purpose is the way in which Marvell makes us conscious of the philosophical basis of the speaker's plea to make the most of time. The poem's highly articulated logic ("Had we . . . But . . . Now therefore . . . Thus"), reinforced by images of time and activity ("pass", "grow", "slow", "hurrying", "instant", "devour"), makes us unusually aware of the assumptions behind *carpe diem* poetry. Time is passing, the present is all there is, a life of intense sensation — especially sexual pleasure — alone has value. The clarity with which the speaker in *To his Coy Mistress* presents his argument for a life of sensation shows that Marvell fully understands the assumptions behind his theme.

But does the plea to devour time really convey Marvell's attitude in the poem? Does not the very intensity and violence of the poem's conclusion undermine the persuasiveness of the speaker's argument ("devour" . . . "tear . . . with rough strife, / Thorough the Iron gates of Life")? Love is not mentioned in the last two stanzas of the poem; the picture of passion and lust is not attractive. The lady is said to have a "willing Soul", and it is suggested that she perspires "At every pore with instant Fires". She is invited to be like a bird of prey. There are also a number of individual words which should make us pause: "crime", "Eternity", "Virginity", "Honour", "Lust".

Allegory is the saying of one thing by way of another. Irony was traditionally recognised as a form of allegory, and among the tropes of which knowledge is necessary for a correct understanding of Scripture.[1] If my reading is correct, *To his Coy Mistress* is an example of ironic allegory which implies the opposite of what it at first appears to argue. The speaker's claim that we should make the most of time is finally shown to debase man into an animal. The sense is unmistakable. If the lady gives in to the speaker's argument, they will become predatory, devouring, tearing sexual pleasures from the jaws of time, like animals fighting over food.

The main irony of Marvell's poem is that the imagery and vocabulary the speaker uses allude to the Christian scheme of history and to Christian doctrine. Such expressions as "before the Flood", "the Conversion of the *Jews*" and "the last Age" might at first seem like ironies thrown off by the speaker; but the cumulative effect of such religious allusions is to invalidate the speaker's claims about the nature of time and existence. Instead of persuading us that life consists of passing sensations and that nothing else has meaning, the poem brings to our mind the purpose of God's creation as revealed throughout the Bible and history. The most momentous Old Testament events are recalled: the Flood, the Israelites in exile, the entry into the Promised Land. Allusions are made to the coming of the end of created time, and also to eternity. This allusive reaching forward and backward in time is accompanied by Marvell's habitual drama of the temptation of the soul, which according to its choice may be saved or damned. Moreover, as I will later show, there are reasons to see *To his Coy Mistress* in relation to the Annunciation and Incarnation.

The themes are suggested in the first two lines of the poem, although we would not notice the significance without the suggestiveness of the poem as a whole:

> Had we but World enough, and Time,
> This coyness Lady were no crime.
> We would sit down and think which way
> To walk, and pass our long Loves Day.

The "World" and "Time" began with the Creation. The lady's coyness or modesty is certainly not a crime. Modesty became necessary as a result of the first crime, Adam's Fall. Sexuality before the Fall was innocent and without lust or cupidity; it involved no shame. It may be witty to speak of modesty ("coyness") as a crime against love, but from a Christian point of view crime accurately describes the speaker's attempt to seduce the lady's soul. Basically a contrast is being implied between tender fondness and the passionate lust which will be urged at the conclusion of the poem.

Thou by the *Indian Ganges* side
Should'st Rubies find: I by the Tide
Of *Humber* would complain. I would
Love you ten years before the Flood.

The two lovers so separated bring to mind the dispersal of the world's population after the Flood ("I would / Love you ten years before the Flood"), and the dispersal of the Jews in exile lamenting ("would complain") by the rivers of Babylon: "By the rivers of Babylon, there we sat down, yea, we wept, when we remembered Zion" (Psalm 137:1). Allusion to biblical history and to God's providential scheme is continued in:

And you should if you please refuse
Till the Conversion of the *Jews*.

The conversion of the Jews to Christianity was supposed to occur before the Second Coming. The empires of the modern world supposedly had their origin in antiquity from the sons of Noah, who helped repopulate the world after the Flood:

My vegetable Love should grow
Vaster then Empires, and more slow.

The progression of the argument in the first stanza offers us a recapitulation of history from the Creation to the Last Age:

An hundred years should go to praise
Thine Eyes, and on thy Forehead Gaze.
Two hundred to adore each Breast:
But thirty thousand to the rest.
An Age at least to every part,
And the last Age should show your Heart.

The speaker's mistaken view of the purpose of time and the world is further suggested by his misuse of such words as "praise". "adore", and "love". The enumeration of the lady's charms reads like a parody of Canticles: "Behold, thou *art* fair, my love" (Canticles 4:1): "thou *hast* dove's eyes" (4:1): "thy temples *are* like a piece of pomegranate" (4:3): "Thy two breasts *are* like two young roes" (4:5). "Show" is suggestive of Revelation. The bridegroom in Canticles is a hart (2:9,

2:17), who will appear again at the end of time: "Make haste, my beloved, and be thou like to a roe or to a young hart upon the mountains of spices" (Canticles 8:14). "State" means dignity but could also mean kingdom, in:

For Lady you deserve this State;
Nor would I love at lower rate.

Marvell's meaning will be clear if we remember *The Garden*: "Such was that happy Garden-state".

In the second stanza the speaker uses the passing of time to argue the absurdity of modesty, virginity and honour. His logic seems directed against social convention, which demands the lady's coyness; but his choice of words also directs our attention to such matters as morality and the rewards and punishments after death ("Eternity", "Worms", "Virginity", "Lust", "Grave"). If the first stanza of the poem recalls Eden and the slow but inevitable accomplishment of God's promises throughout history, the second stanza reminds us that the times are drawing to an end and that the day of judgment is coming nearer:

But at my back I alwaies hear
Times winged Charriot hurrying near:
And yonder all before us lye
Desarts of vast Eternity.

Basically the idea, expressed in a pun, is that the time is approaching for the "Desarts" (rewards and punishments) of eternity. In *Paradise Lost*, Adam, after being told of "New Heav'ns, new Earth, Ages of endless date", says:

How soon hath thy prediction, Seer blest,
Measur'd this transient World, the Race of time,
Till time stand fixt: beyond is all abyss,
Eternitie, whose end no eye can reach.[2]

If time's chariot has eschatological resonances, the deserts of eternity in accordance with the speaker's materialism would be mere nothingness. From a Christian standpoint the deserts of eternity are Paradise and Hell. The contrast between time's chariot and eternity thus not only recalls the distinction between the created world and God, but also alludes to the purpose of created time. Historically it is a stage for the working out of the drama of redemption; morally it is a stage upon which to test those fit for Paradise.

Thy Beauty shall no more be found;
Nor, in thy marble Vault, shall sound
My ecchoing Song: then Worms shall try
That long preserv'd Virginity.

The points made by the speaker are common to medieval sermons on the passing of temporal pleasures, and are associated with eternal rewards and punishments. Fire and worms punish the flesh of the ungodly after death; indeed, worms devouring a woman's sexual organs is a traditional representation of *luxuria* or lust. The wit echoes medieval contempt of the world, and is appropriate to disgust with the flesh.[3] (The worms "try" her virginity both in the sense of "test" and "devour".) The themes are found in the Bible, where they include the hope of salvation: "they are laid in the grave; death shall feed on them . . . their beauty shall consume in the grave . . . But God will redeem my soul from the power of the grave" (Psalm 49:14-15). "For I know *that* my redeemer liveth, and *that* he shall stand at the latter *day* upon the earth: And *though* after my skin *worms* destroy this *body*, yet in my flesh shall I see God" (Job 19: 25-26).

The speaker's "ecchoing Song" may not "long" reverberate in "marble Vaults" after death, but it does spread out in ripples of biblical associations, bringing to mind the fall of Babylon in Revelation 18:22-23: "And the voice of harpers, and musicians . . . shall be heard no more . . . and the voice of the bridegroom and of the bride shall be heard no more at all in thee". "Virginity" reminds us that the theme of the poem is the relationship of chastity to the rewards of "Eternity". Marvell can speak at the same time in double entendre while recalling Christian doctrine:

And your quaint Honour turn to dust;
And into ashes all my Lust.
The Grave's a fine and private place,
But none I think do there embrace.

"Quaint Honour" and "Lust" are used by the speaker as puns on the female and male sexual organs, while "embrace" alludes to sexual intercourse. We are, however, reminded that man was created out of dust and to dust he will return (Genesis 3:19).

The imagery of eternal deserts is taken up in the "instant Fires" of stanza three, recalling the eternal fires of Hell. The poem now specifically focuses upon the soul in its moment of decision ("now . . . now . . . now").[4] It can give in to temptation, and spiritually die; or resist, and enjoy the promises of eternity. The pleasures of the passing moment are pitted against faith in God's providence and love. We are reminded of Augustine's contrast between "now" and "there", our world and Heaven. The choice is the essential drama of Marvell's poetry and is an imitation of Christ's temptation in the wilderness, itself a recapitulation both of Adam's Fall, and of the testing of the faith of the Israelites during their wanderings on the way to the Promised Land.

Now therefore, while the youthful hew
Sits on thy skin like morning dew.

We need not worry about whether Marvell originally wrote "glew" for "hew" or "dew"[5] The speaker's sense is that the youthful appearance of the lady is transitory and will eventually pass. While for the speaker this is a reason for enjoying the pleasures of life, the same observation could be used as a persuasion against placing too much faith in present joys. Youth will pass, like the morning's dew, flesh will die, but the soul is eternal. Man's coat of skin is a result of the Fall (Genesis 3:21), in contrast to the immortal soul:

And while thy willing Soul transpires
At every pore with instant Fires.

If the speaker tries to persuade the lady to see herself as "willing" to the point of perspiring with instant fires, we might instead see an allusion to the soul's choice. Will is necessary for salvation. The soul, although clothed by the skin, is immortal. It aspires to Heaven, and not the eternal fires of Hell.

Now let us sport us while we may;
And now, like am'rous birds of prey,
Rather at once our Time devour,
Than languish in his slow-chapt pow'r.

To sport like amorous birds of prey, and to devour time, conveys an impression of bestial sensuality. Intemperance dims the divine image within the soul and turns man into an animal. In Christian allegory those who are seduced by carnal pleasures are turned into beasts. For this reason the seven deadly sins are often portrayed as animals. The violence of the speaker's sentiment contrasts to the slow but steady fulfilment of the divine scheme alluded to earlier in the poem. One should help redeem the time, not devour it. The devouring jaws of time are death; to devour time would be to die. It is man's duty to be patient and keep the time. Satan and Eve fall from wanting to be gods before their time. Macbeth falls into a course of evil by wanting to anticipate the time. In Ecclesiastes we are told: "To every *thing there is* a season, and a time to every purpose under the heaven" (3:1). The voyagers in Marvell's *Bermudas* "kept the time". The slowness of time, which the speaker in Marvell's poem rejects, is the divine plan for man's redemption, symbolised in the creation of the world and time. Augustine says: "The princes of the former eat in the morning, before their hour, expecting not the true time of felicity, but hurrying unto the world's delights headlong: but they of the city of Christ await their future beatitude with patience"[6]

Let us roll all our Strength, and all
Our sweetness, up into one Ball:
And tear our Pleasures with rough strife,
Thorough the Iron gates of Life.

The speaker is trying to persuade the lady to sexual intercourse. Strength and sweetness presumably refer to masculinity and femininity. Seventeenth century poets liked to imagine lovers as two hemispheres which make up a world; behind the image is that of Plato's spherical lovers who are divided into halves ("sorted by pairs") when they descend into the material world, the ball being the symbol of their original perfect unity. Here the ball is, ironically, the physical posture of the two people joined in sexual intercourse. The "rough strife" refers to the motions of love making, while the "gates of Life" include a passing allusion to the woman's sexual organs. The plea to tear one's pleasures through the gates of Life is thus an invitation to sexual ecstasy, and glances at the commonplace of the sexual climax as a form of "dying".

If, however, we read the poem with an awareness of ironies, we notice that the sexual description includes resonances which undermine the sexual plea. The woman's "gates" are not merely those of an enclosed city or fortress of conventional love poetry; they are the "gates of Life". To the speaker life is sensation; but we have been made conscious of the lady's soul and her spiritual life. The iron gates carry associations both with life and death. Spenser writes of "the seuen fold yron gates of grislie Hell"[7] In Dante's *Inferno* (Canto Eight) the iron gates of the City of Dis are the entrance from sins of incontinence to those of violence and fraud. It was believed that in the time between Christ's death and Resurrection He descended into the underworld to free the souls of the dead; in iconography this is represented as tearing off the iron gates of Hell. David, and all Christians, praise "thou that liftest me up from the gates of death" (Psalm 9:13); and petition "Open to me the gates of righteousness" (Psalm 118:19). In typology Samson, a prisoner in Gaza, bursting the doors off their hinges ("all our Strength . . . and tear . . . with rough strife . . . Iron gates") is a figure for the fall of the gates of Hell before Christ, and shadows Christ's vanquishing of death, symbolised by the broken doors of the sepulchre[8]

If the iron gates of life, through which the lady is enjoined to tear her pleasure, allude to her sexual organs, the resulting sexual ecstasy or "death" would damage her hopes to enjoy eternal life after death, as her mind would be on carnal pleasures instead of Christ and eternity. Christians are enjoined to be virgins, who shun the temptations of the world, and to imitate the purity of Christ and the Virgin Mary. In Christian symbolism the Virgin Mary, as mother of the Redeemer, is the gate of life, the gate through which Heaven is entered[9] That Marvell was aware of such symbolism is shown by Stanza XIII of *Upon Appleton House*, where similar imagery of gates and bars is used; gates and bars protect the nun's cloister, which in

Stanza XIV is associated with the enclosed garden of Canticles 4:12.

Thus, though we cannot make our Sun
Stand still, yet we will make him run.

Joshua made the sun stand still (Joshua 10:12-13) during his conquest of the Holy Land. Joshua is the successor of Moses who finally leads the Israelites to the Promised Land. He is therefore a type of the Messiah, who fulfills the promises made to the Israelites. The conquest of the Promised Land corresponds to Christ's victory over death and Hell. Crossing the Jordan is linked in typology and iconography with Christ's freeing the damned imprisoned behind the gates of Hell. One should cross the Jordan and hasten towards a new life in Christ, overthrowing Jericho, one's former way of life.

If the speaker cannot make the sun stand still, he claims he can "make him run". Psalm 19, which praises God for His creation, providence and Holy Scripture, begins: "The heavens declare the glory of God; and the firmament sheweth his handywork"; and continues "Their line is gone out through all the earth, and their words to the end of the world. In them hath he set a tabernacle for the sun, Which *is* as a bridegroom coming out of his chamber, *and* rejoiceth as a strong man to run a race" (Psalm 19:4-5). The creation is a sign of Christ and His prophets and an example to the soul. In *The Nymph complaining for the death of her Faun*, the Faun with "grace", "oft would challenge me the Race". Paul says "let us run with patience the race that is set before us, Looking unto Jesus the author and finisher of *our* faith" (Hebrews 12:1-2). Canticles 8:14 is allegorised as referring to the Second Coming: "Make haste, my beloved".

It is not accidental that *To his Coy Mistress* is printed in the first edition of Marvell's poems shortly after *The Nymph complaining for the death of her Faun*, a poem recalling the life and death of Christ, and before *The Unfortunate Lover*, a poem treating of the Incarnation and Crucifixion. *To his Coy Mistress* ironically treats of erotic love in a manner which also recalls, for purposes of contrast, the Virgin Mary and the Incarnation. In Christian tradition Mary is a modest "Lady", to whom are often applied the Canticle-like praises of the beginning of the poem. Such phrases as "That long preserv'd Virginity" and "the youthful hew / Sits on thy Skin like morning dew" are applicable to her. (The latter phrase might be based on Canticles 6:10, where the Virgin and early Church are supposedly allegorised as the dawn or "morning". [10]) At the Annunciation she is a modest but willing soul. Commentators said that she was naturally modest when spoken to by the Angel Gabriel, but commentators also said that like the bride in Canticles she burned with the desire to be united with Divine Love. She is a closed portal or gate. Throughout the last stanza of the poem the Incarnation is brought to mind. Gabriel, the angel of the Annunciation, supposedly, according to some philologists, meant "strength of God".[11] The Virgin is all sweetness. Thus strength combines with sweetness to produce a son!

Is there a son? Some critics have had the impression that "our Sun" refers to a child which will result from the proposed union. Their impressionistic reading is, I feel, confirmed by the fact that Psalm 19 is a well-known prophecy of the Incarnation. The difference between Marvell's poem and the Annunciation is, of course, that an amorous bird of prey has replaced the dove as a dominant symbol. (Is there a pun on "pray"?) The conception of the child has been by "rough strife", whereas Christ came "into the world so, without doing violence to the virginal and pure body of his mother; that he did also leave her virginity entire, to be as a seal, that none might open the gate of that sanctuary".[12] Jeremy Taylor's "Considerations upon the Birth of our Blessed Saviour Jesus" include comments on time which seem appropriate to quote here:

> yet he did not prevent the period of nature, nor break the laws of the womb, and antedate his own sanctions, which he had established for ever. He stayed nine months, and then brake forth "as a giant joyful to run his course." For premature and hasty actions, and such counsels, as know not how to expect the times appointed in God's decree, are like hasty fruit, or a young person snatched away in his florid age, sad and untimely. He that hastens to enjoy his wish before the time, raises his own expectation and yet makes it unpleasant by impatience, and loseth the pleasure of the fruition when it comes, because he hath made his desires bigger than the thing can satisfy. He that must eat an hour before his time, gives probation of his intemperance or his weakness; and if we dare not trust God with the circumstance of the event, and stay his leisure, either we disrepute the infinity of his wisdom, or give clear demonstration of our own vanity.[13]

As with many of Marvell's poems, *To his Coy Mistress* combines allegory with contemplation. To speak of the poem as related to contemplation may at first seem surprising, but reflexion on the matter will reveal a double pattern of contemplation. The speaker begins by meditating on the mutable world, progresses to thoughts of death, and concludes by pleading for a life of sexual union and ecstasy. The progress of his feeling is a parody of, and thus recalls, true contemplation upon the world, time, death, eternity, and communion with God. We might see the "one Ball" as an ironic parallel to the contracting of the mind within itself, in contemplation, to find the divine image: "in its pure and circling thoughts, express /

The greater Heaven in an Heaven less".[14] My view that the speaker's invitation to sexual ecstasy is an inversion of contemplative mystical communion can perhaps be best illustrated by a quotation from Francis de Sales, where we find bestiality and spirituality treated as contrary states of ecstasy resulting from the choice made by the "willing Soul":

> The philosophers of old knew two kinds of ecstasy: one lifting us above ourselves, the other dragging us below ourselves. They seemed to imply, those writers, that man is some sort of middle being — through his intellectual ability sharing the nature of angels, through his senses the nature of animals. Yet, by his way of life, by taking constant care, he can emancipate himself from that middle state. He can ascend to the spiritual world of the intellect, and become like the angels; or he can descend to the world of the senses, and become like the beasts. Whichever way he takes, he experiences an ecstasy — a going out of himself.[15]

It is an appropriate irony that *To his Coy Mistress* should end with an allusion affirming divine providence, when the speaker has tried to deny any meaning beyond present sensations. The temptation offered by the speaker is not only sexual, but also a denial of divine purpose. The lady addressed in the poem is being tested like Eve by the serpent, Christ by Satan, or any human soul by the temptations of the world. The fine articulate logic of the speaker is Satanic, having as its aim corruption of innocence which it tries to degrade to bestiality. Throughout the poem, however, Christian symbols and biblical allusions provide a proper perspective on the temptation that is offered.

To his Coy Mistress, rather than being unusual among Marvell's poems, is in fact typical in its essential vision. It is also typical of Marvell's wit and sophistication that he should write one of the greatest love lyrics in English poetry and that the poem should allude to the strongest possible Christian arguments against sexual indulgence. It is typical of Marvell that he should create the *persona* of the speaker in *To his Coy Mistress* as a means of introducing a double consciousness into his poem. The speaker is the most intelligent and articulate of Cavalier poets, and all the while we are conscious of the spiritual significance of the temptations that he offers. Only a great writer could top centuries of *carpe diem* poetry in poise and persuasiveness while undermining the entire structure of the poem with irony. Such a complexity of literary effect is the fruition of the allegorical imagination, with its ability to see analogies, to perceive meanings which run contrary to literal statements, to recognise biblical allusions and what they traditionally signify, to understand symbols in all their aspects and therefore to focus upon single words as being meaningful in themselves. The allegorical imagination provides Marvell with the essential materials which his poems express.

CHAPTER SEVEN

The Unfortunate Lover

> *He hath no form nor comeliness . . . He is despised and rejected of men; a man of sorrows, and acquainted with grief . . . he hath borne our griefs, and carried our sorrows . . . he was wounded for our transgressions, he was bruised for our iniquities . . . with his stripes we are healed . . . he is brought as a lamb to the slaughter . . . he was cut off out of the land of the living . . . he bare the sin of many, and made intercession for the transgressors.* (Isaiah 53)

While *The Unfortunate Lover* has the reputation of being obscure, its subject and themes should be obvious to readers familiar with seventeenth century devotional verse. Christ is the Unfortunate Lover and the poem's symbolism alludes to His Incarnation, sufferings and Sacrifice. Some readers however, confuse the description of erotic love in the first stanza with "my poor Lover" in stanza two. In the second stanza the imagery of the Lover's birth is similar to Neo-Platonic descriptions of the soul's entry into the world of time and space and might cause the reader to think that the subject is the soul rather than Christ, especially as words are sometimes made to carry two distinct significances. Another difficulty is the violently paradoxical statements made about the Lover; here the problem is primarily of local interpretation — exactly what is being said at a particular moment. The paradoxes, however, are appropriate to the kind of mysteries being recalled: the God Who takes on Himself the sufferings of humanity, the God Who dies so that man may be reborn, the God Whose blood and flesh are shared in the Eucharist. The style of the poem is meant to focus the reader's mind on the meaning of symbols rather than particulars, on the significance of the Incarnation and Sacrifice rather than the details of Christ's birth and death. Even time and space are treated abstractly and emblematically, as Marvell is thinking upon their spiritual significance.

In the first stanza secular love is mocked as being unable to make an "impression upon Time":

Alas, how pleasant are their dayes
With whom the Infant Love yet playes!
Sorted by pairs, they still are seen
By Fountains cool, and Shadows green.
But soon these Flames do lose their light,
Like Meteors of a Summers night:
Nor can they to that Region climb,
To make impression upon Time.

The irony begins with "Alas, how pleasant" and continues in such puns as "soon these Flames do lose their light". "Infant Love" is Cupid. The lovers are sorted by pairs because, according to Plato, in the ideal world the lover and love object enjoy perfect union. The fountains are a Neo-Platonic symbol of generation and represent the river of life. The soul descends from the garden into the material world. At the beginning of the poem the lovers' days are still pleasant because their souls have not yet encountered the world of time and space. When the lovers descend into the material world division occurs and their love is soon extinguished. "Flames" is, of course, a pun on lovers, but it ironically alludes to divine light. The lovers lose their remembrance of the divine world after their descent into the world of material forms. They stop burning with desire for the good, the beautiful or the true. They are like meteors, they burn themselves out. They have become part of the sublunary world where all is mutable and impermanent. The images of flames burning themselves out and meteors falling suggest passing intensity and passing sensation. It is perhaps not accidental that *The Unfortunate Lover* follows *To his Coy Mistress* in the first edition of Marvell's poems. Just as the lovers in *To his Coy Mistress* cannot make their sun stand still, so these lovers cannot "to that Region climb, / To make impression upon Time". Erotic love does not last, cannot be rekindled, and does not save man from the effects of time. The irony is directed against the claims of Renaissance Neo-Platonists that man could through erotic love remember divine beauty, rise above his senses and ascend to union with the divine.

If the first stanza of *The Unfortunate Lover* rejects erotic and Neo-Platonic love as unable to redeem man from this world, the next seven stanzas treat of a Lover Who takes on Himself the sufferings of the flesh and blood and all the pains that the world of time and space can offer. We are told that He is the only true Lover that love has created. The Unfortunate Lover is Christ, and the poem is primarily about His love as expressed through the Incarnation and Sacrifice. The poem also alludes to the Church and its sacraments, since they are expressions of His love.

The second stanza of *The Unfortunate Lover* contrasts the birth of "my poor Lover" into the world of time and space with "these Flames" of stanza one:

'Twas in a Shipwrack, when the Seas
Rul'd, and the Winds did what they please,
That my poor Lover floting lay,
And e're brought forth, was cast away:
Till at the last the master-Wave
Upon the Rock his Mother drave;
And there she split against the Stone,
In a *Cesarian Section.*

Basically the stanza refers to the Incarnation: the Suffering Servant Who has long been promised is finally born into the temptations and tribulations of this world. The ship is the ark of salvation — the eternal Church of early Christian thought — which, like Christ, has existed since before the Creation. It has been shipwrecked in the world of historical time since Adam's Fall; from it will emerge the Saviour upon which the visible Church will be founded. The seas and the winds bring to mind the fallen state of man and the world into which the Lover must be born, in contrast to the Paradise, recalled in stanza one, which man lost. In *Paradise Lost* man's Fall untunes the world and unharnesses the winds and seas. These are among the tribulations suffered by man as a result of the Fall, and are an aspect of divine punishment.[1]

The Lover floating on the seas of time is on the verge of being born into the material world. He has a pre-existence in the sense that He is eternal and His birth has long been promised. He is not yet manifest in the flesh. The eternally pre-existing Church or ship of salvation has been wrecked in the world of time and space, but from its wreckage the Lover will be born to undo the damage caused by the wreck and found a new Church. The Synagogue is a type of the eternal Church, but, as the Old Testament prophets agree, it is in a deplorable condition ("Shipwrack") and has rejected its destiny. It is argued in the New Testament that the failure of the Synagogue is shown by the fact that Israel is in bondage. God's covenant has passed to the Christians. Our Lover should be viewed as floating on the sea of time within the womb of Israel, and the eternal pre-existent Church, before being brought forth by Mary.

While the seas stand for time and God's judgment, they also bring to mind the Virgin, because of the pun Mary / Mare. The mystery of the Incarnation is spoken of as an "unbounded sea".[2] The second stanza is the most difficult part of the poem, as words and images are often used to convey a multiplicity of associations, which may be compared to the varied meanings which biblical commentators derived from a single text. The scene is emblematic and symbolic with more than one meaning intended. The winds that "did what they please" allude to "The wind bloweth where it listeth, and thou hearest the sound thereof, but canst not tell whence it cometh, and whither it goeth: so is every one that is born of the Spirit" (John 3:8). The wind and seas thus allude to the role of the Holy Ghost and the Virgin Mary in the Incarnation. The seas rule because Mary from free-will could refuse her role. The Annunciation to Mary is like the Spirit which moved over the water at the original Creation of the world. The birth of Christ is a new creation after Adam wrecked the first Creation. "Before I formed thee in the belly I knew thee; and before thou camest forth out of the womb I sanctified thee, *and* I ordained thee a prophet unto the nations" (Jeremiah 1:5). The relationship of the Unfortunate Lover's birth to prophecies of the coming of Christ is recalled by "brought forth": "And behold, thou shalt conceive in thy womb, and bring forth a son" (Luke 1:31).

The Lover ere brought forth "cast away" in a shipwreck recalls mankind's rejection of divine love: Adam's disobedience, the rejection of Old Testament prophets, and Israel's apostasy. The birth of the Lover fulfils God's promise or covenant with mankind as revealed in various previous manifestations. Before Israel is brought forth out of Egypt it is also cast away in bondage. "Every son that is born ye shall cast into the river" (Exodus 1:22). Moses is put in an "ark", which lay "in the flags by the river's brink" (Exodus 2:3). Moses as leader of the Jews is a type of Christ. In the Book of Jonah: "The LORD sent out a great wind into the sea, and there was a mighty tempest in the sea" (1:4); "For thou hadst cast me into the deep, in the midst of the seas; and the floods compassed me about: all thy billows and thy waves passed over me. Then I said, I am cast out of thy sight; yet I will look again toward thy holy temple" (2:3-4). The birth of the castaway Lover upon the rock recalls the whale tossing Jonah upon dry land. Jonah is a type of the Suffering Servant, someone whose destiny is to undergo the pains of the world in order to reveal the Gospel.[3]

The "master-Wave" refers to God the Father Whose providence foresaw the willingness of the Son to be born and suffer in His humanity:

> The Father's wisdom willed it so,
> The Son's obedience knew no No,
>   Both wills were in one stature;
> And as that wisdom had decreed,
> The Word was now made Flesh indeed,
>   And took on Him our nature.[4]

The eternal or pre-existent Church is the mother driven on the rocks of matter, or the material world, where she becomes manifest as the incarnate Church. The wrecked ship of salvation (in the form of the Synagogue) is newly created as the Church with the coming of Christ: "thou are Peter, and upon this rock I will build my church" (Matthew 16:18). The eternal Church brings forth the Christ Child Who will establish it and become its Head. We might also recall that the hill of Calvary is symbolised by a rock. The Unfortunate Lover will die upon a rock and the sacraments of the Church will flow from His wounds.[5]

The mother splitting against the stone gives birth to the Unfortunate Lover. If we see the mother as the Church, the stone might recall the Old Testament laws brought on tables of stone from Mount Sinai. Even before Moses brings the laws from Mount Sinai the Israelites are led by Aaron to worship false gods with the result that Moses breaks the two tables of stone: "he cast the tables out of his hands" (Exodus 32:19). He then has two more made (Exodus 34:28). This is interpreted as a sign that the covenant will pass from the Jews to Christians.[6] The Mother then is the Synagogue splitting into Christians and Jews, believers and non-believers, according to whether they accept the leadership of Christ: "The stone *which* the builders refused is become the head *stone* of the corner" (Psalm 118:22). "Be it known unto you all, and to all the people of Israel . . . This is the stone which was set at nought of you builders, which is become the head of the corner" (Acts 4:10-11). "In a *Cesarian Section*" alludes to the Virgin Birth. "Before she travailed, she brought forth; before her pain came, she was delivered of a man child" (Isaiah 66:7) is interpreted as a prophecy of the coming of the Messiah. We should recall that Christ was born during the reign of, and in a region under the dominion of, Augustus Caesar. It was believed that Christ was born in the Roman Empire so that His Gospel would be disseminated throughout the world.[7]

If one had to concentrate the themes of the second stanza to a single focus, it would be the coming of the Messiah, Who has long been expected and Who will in subsequent stanzas undergo the pains of humanity. He is born in a tempest as the result of mankind's Fall, and although the ark of salvation seems shipwrecked, His death will be the foundation of the sacraments of the new Church.

The Sea him lent these bitter Tears,
Which at his Eyes he alwaies bears.
And from the winds the Sighs he bore,
Which through his surging Breast do roar.
No Day he saw but that which breaks,
Through frighted Clouds in forked streaks.
While round the ratling Thunder hurl'd,
As at the Fun'ral of the World.

The tears and sighs are those of Christ for mankind. The Unfortunate Lover is born bearing tears and sighs as part of His inheritance in taking on the sins and suffering of the flesh. "Who in the days of his flesh, when he had offered up prayers and supplications with strong crying and tears unto him that was able to save him from death, and was heard in that he feared; Though he were a Son, yet learned he obedience by the things which he suffered" (Hebrews 5:7-8). The sea lends bitter tears because Mary is a bitter sea (Mare / amare). Marvell is thinking of the Mother of Sorrows. The wind recalls the Holy Ghost. The images of "surging Breast" and roaring sighs are a sign of the Lover's divine message.[8] Those inspired by prophecy traditionally have been portrayed with swelling chests as inspiration wells up within them before they proclaim their message. Christ is born into a world of clouds and thunder suggestive of the spiritual darkness and divine wrath under which man lived before the coming of the Messiah. The thunder is the Law hurtling down through the clouds of Mount Sinai.[9]

We are reminded both of the situation of mankind before the birth of Christ, and of the Crucifixion and its role in the future history of mankind. The tears and sighs look forward in the poem to Christ's Passion. The paradox that the scene of the birth of the Lover is similar to the funeral of the world can be explained as follows: 1) It is like a funeral of the world because all are under a sentence of death before the coming of the Redeemer; 2) it is the end of the old order, the world governed by law; and 3) it looks forward to the passing away of this world and the creation of a new heaven and a new earth.

Throughout *The Unfortunate Lover* varied events are felt to be simultaneously present. The Crucifixion especially seems present in each stanza. We should not be surprised when a description recalling one event also seems to allude to another situation; Rosemond Tuve has pointed out that iconographic and typological conventions often telescope several different happenings into one symbolic situation.[10] A further double focus occurs in stanza four:

While Nature to his Birth presents
This masque of quarrelling Elements;
A num'rous fleet of Corm'rants black,
That sail'd insulting o're the Wrack,
Receiv'd into their cruel Care,
Th' unfortunate and abject Heir:
Guardians most fit to entertain
The Orphan of the *Hurricane.*

The "masque of quarrelling Elements" represents the instability of the material world as a result of Adam's Fall. Christ came to redeem mankind from its bondage to the elements:

> Even so we, when we were children, were in bondage under the elements of the world: But when the fulness of the time was come, God sent forth his Son, made of a woman, made under the law, To redeem them that were under the law, that we might receive the adoption of sons. (Galatians 4:3-5)

The elements mean carnality. The Lover is an "Heir" because Christ is the new Adam and heir to the creation as well as being the Son of God.[11] He is an unfortunate heir because it is His destiny to suffer. Marvell may have in mind Mark 12:6-8:

> Having yet therefore one son, his wellbeloved, he sent him also last unto them, saying, They will reverence my son. But those husbandmen said among themselves, This is the heir; come, let us kill him, and the inheritance shall be ours. And they took him, and killed *him*, and cast *him* out of the vineyard.

The cormorants are a symbol for the Devil or Satan.[12] Their happiness over the shipwreck is similar to Satan's joy over Adam's Fall. Whereas prelapsarian Adam could entertain the guardian angels, the devils are now "most fit" to entertain the new heir to the creation. By taking on humanity the Son of God has become subject to emotions, passions and temptations. To redeem man's heritage He must reverse Adam's Fall by resisting the temptations of Satan and set an example for mankind. The cormorants mocking the shipwreck, entertaining the heir marooned on his rock, bring to mind the temptations of Christ in the wilderness. In *Paradise Regained* one of the temptations Christ must face is the terror of a storm.[13] The mocking cormorants insulting the abject heir may also recall the Jews, soldiers, priests and thieves who insulted Christ on the Cross while He suffered in His humanity.

Christ in becoming flesh acquires the same physical needs and functions as mankind:

> They fed him up with Hopes and Air,
> Which soon digested to Despair.
> And as one Corm'rant fed him, still
> Another on his Heart did bill.
> Thus while they famish him, and feast,
> He both consumed, and increast:
> And languished with doubtful Breath,
> Th' *Amphibium* of Life and Death.

Hope and despair are among the four basic emotions, joy and sorrow being the other two. Christ suffered in His human nature, "namely, hunger and thirst in the absence of food, sadness and fear in the presence of harm".[14] We might recall the temptations Christ had to face in the wilderness; He fasted and felt despair, which paradoxically increased His strength:

But now I feel I hunger . . .
And from the sting of Famin fear no harm,
Nor mind it, fed with better thoughts that feed
Mee hungring more to do my Fathers will.[15]

It is through His weakness that He will overcome Satan:

To conquer Sin and Death the two grand foes,
By Humiliation and strong Sufferance:
His weakness shall orecome Satanic Strength.[16]

We are also reminded of Christ on the Cross, desolate, given vinegar or gall, hanging between life and death: "languished with doubtful Breath". Christ's experience of the fear of death was a commonplace of medieval Christian literature.

The food images in stanza five, anticipating similar images at the end of stanza seven, bring to mind the relation of the Sacrifice to the Last Supper. The images are symbols of the Eucharist recalling both Christ and the Church. The images of famine and feast recall the Passover, a time of both fasting and feasting. But "they famish him, and feast" (upon him) would seem to allude to the body of Christ represented by the bread: "And he took bread, and gave thanks, and brake *it*, and gave unto them, saying, This is my body which is given for you: this do in remembrance of me" (Luke 22:19). He is "consumed" in the Mass and "increast" through communion with the bodies of the faithful.[17] "Increast" may also allude to Christ's growing up. "And Jesus increased in wisdom and stature, and in favour with God and man" (Luke 2:52). It seems likely that we should read stanza five as referring both to Christ's life and to the sacrament of the Eucharist. The Lover is both fed with human emotions and also becomes the substance of a feast. A once common religious emblem was that of Christ the Pelican Who feeds its young from the blood streaming out of its breast. The Lover is the "*Amphibium* of Life and Death" because of the inert state of Christ on the Cross, passing from life to death, but also because of the paradox that His death shall bring eternal life. The word "*Amphibium*" brings to mind His dual nature, God and man.

Christ's Sacrifice is an act of atonement which redeems man from God's wrath:

And now, when angry Heaven wou'd
Behold a spectacle of Blood,
Fortune and He are call'd to play
At sharp before it all the day:
And Tyrant Love his brest does ply
With all his wing'd Artillery.
Whilst he, betwixt the Flames and Waves,
Like *Ajax*, the mad Tempest braves.

"And now" pinpoints the event at a moment in time. It recalls the theme of now-ness which runs throughout the New Testament, signifying a turning point in history. The spectacle of blood is Christ on the Cross; the duration of the Crucifixion is alluded to in "all the day".[18] The Lover is like a swordsman engaged in serious sword-play with Fate. He will be wounded and His death will overcome His adversary. His wounds are those of love. He is an intermediary between the flaming lightning of God's wrath and the sinful world; "Upon the wicked he shall rain snares, fire and brimstone, and an horrible tempest" (Psalm 11:6). Ajax in his anger is an example in classical literature of the Herculean hero; Hercules is often allegorised as a type of Christ. Christ's power wrestles with sin, death and God's wrath and overcomes them like a hero ("braves").[19]

The themes of Christ the victorious mediator, Christ suffering on the Cross and Christ the Lover Who offers His blood and flesh in the Eucharist are developed in stanza seven through symbolic imagery and outrageous puns. Both the images and the puns are traditional to their themes and can be found in other seventeenth century poets. Marvell's originality lies rather in their violent compression than in their invention. Christ the superior hero, victorious over both divine wrath and man's stubborn heart, is suggested by:

> See how he nak'd and fierce does stand,
> Cuffing the Thunder with one hand;
> While with the other he does lock,
> And grapple, with the stubborn Rock.[20]

The thunder is God's wrath; Christ's claim to divinity is proved by His ability to grasp the thunder and redeem man from the Old Law. The stubborn rock with which the Lover "does lock, / And grapple" is the heart of man hardened against Christ's love.[21] The Lover is fierce because He is heroic. He is naked because the Son of God in being born lays aside His robes of glory, and because of Christ's nakedness on the Cross. The Lover not only grapples with the rock but is present upon it, recalling the symbolism of the Church as a rock. The Church's sacrament of baptism is traditionally prefigured in the water which Moses brought out of the rock: "thou shalt smite the rock, and there shall come water out of it, that the people may drink" (Exodus 17:6).

In devotional poetry Christ's nakedness on the Cross is often contrasted to His being "drest" in blood:

> From which he with each Wave rebounds,
> Torn into Flames, and ragg'd with Wounds.
> And all he saies, a Lover drest
> In his own Blood does relish best.

A flame can be a lover or a ribbon worn by a lover, similar to a pennant. The body of Christ is torn into flames or symbols of love; we recall the breaking of the bread or wafer in the Eucharist, symbolic of Christ's body. Since the Eucharist is a love feast the image of flames is appropriate. "Torn into Flames, and ragg'd with Wounds" also brings to mind the flagellation and the parting of Christ's garments (Mark 15:24) at the Crucifixion. Marvell's seemingly audacious pun on "drest" — preparation of food / clothed — alludes to the paschal lamb, Christ's humanity, the flagellation, and the Sacrifice.[22] "Relish" undoubtedly includes a pun on savour / Saviour: "Whoso eateth my flesh, and drinketh my blood, hath eternal life; and I will raise him up at the last day" (John 6:54).[23] To understand why Christ's Passion and Sacrifice is connected with imagery based on the Last Supper, we need to remember that Christ's death is voluntary and that it was anticipated in the offering of the Last Supper which instituted the sacrament of the Eucharist: "And he said unto them, This is my blood of the new testament, which is shed for many" (Mark 14:24). It is the Unfortunate Lover, "drest / In his own Blood" Who makes an "impression upon Time", by cuffing the thunder of God's wrath and by being present in the Eucharist.

If we recall Christ's body "torn into Flames" at the flagellation and in the Eucharist, and if we also remember that flames can stand for a lover's ribbon or the pennant of a chivalric lover, the "*Banneret*" of stanza eight will offer no problem of interpretation:

This is the only *Banneret*
That ever Love created yet:
Who though, by the Malignant Starrs,
Forced to live in Storms and Warrs;
Yet dying leaves a Perfume here,
And Musick within every Ear:
And he in Story only rules,
In a Field *Sable* a Lover *Gules*.

A banneret is a grade of knighthood instituted by Charles I, conferred on the battle field. In *Dialogue — Lucasta — Alexis*, Lovelace writes:

Love nee're his Standard when his Hoste he sets,
Creates alone fresh-bleeding Bannerets.

Marvell was a friend of Lovelace and is here parodying the chivalric love tradition still found in Lovelace's poetry. Marvell is specific; the Unfortunate Lover is "the only *Banneret* / That ever Love created yet". Christ is the only real symbol of love because He is present in His symbol. His is the only banner to be followed. He is the only knight of love. "He brought me to the banqueting house, and his banner over me *was* love" (Canticles 2:4).

The Lover has been forced by the malignant stars to "live in Storms and Warrs". The storms and wars are the created world, the tempest and turmoils of life after man's Fall. The stars were supposed to govern the events in the temporal world; malignant stars would be those responsible for storms and wars. Such stars were sometimes thought of as the fallen angels. "Yet dying leaves a Perfume here" alludes to the perfume of grace made possible by Christ's Sacrifice. The perfume is the incense of a pleasing sacrifice. The "Musick within every Ear" refers to the Gospels.[24] The significance of the perfume and music is that although Christ has died, He leaves His Church behind to help others "to that Region climb".

"And he in Story only rules, / In a Field *Sable* a Lover *Gules*" alludes to medieval and Renaissance stories and chronicles which depict or allegorise Christ as a knight carrying a shield and as a chivalric lover adorned with various ribbons and devices. In romances and in sermons influenced by them, the shield represents the Cross. The red stands for Christ's blood in the Passion and the black stands for His death. Marvell's ironic "only" means that all chivalric representations of divine love trivialise what He suffered. He is the Unfortunate Lover Who had to be born into the world, wage a war against sin and die to redeem mankind.

The Unfortunate Lover consciously avoids the trivialisation of the sacred which often occurs when divine mysteries are depicted in poetry. Its violence, extravagance and obscurity force the mind to focus upon the mystery of the Incarnation and Sacrifice. While outwardly expressionist in imagery and style, it is an intellectual *tour de force*. It is easy to dislike the poem. It offers no easy satisfactions to the mind or eye; it does not offer sensuous pleasures; it has no tenderness. *The Unfortunate Lover* shows Marvell's imagination recapturing qualities of the earliest Christian philosophers, when divine truths were explored on analogy to Neo-Platonic mysteries and when the nature of Christian revelation could only be explained through paradox:

> Very Flesh, yet Spirit too;
>   Uncreated, and yet born;
> God-and-Man in One agreed,
> Very-Life-in-Death indeed,
> Fruit of God and Mary's seed;
>   At once impassible and torn
> By pain and suffering here below:
> Jesus Christ, whom as our Lord we know.[25]

Marvell has presented such divine paradoxes as a series of emblems, each of which recalls some stage in the life and death of Christ. Once we have learned to adjust to the kind of poem *The Unfortunate Lover* is, we can see that it is a major and daring work of art. Marvell has taken a standard Renaissance poetic subject, the shipwrecked lover cast on a strange island, and turned it into a powerful emblem of Christian mysteries. It may not be immediately likeable; but it has an undeniable magnificence and intellectual vigour of a kind found only in the greatest art.

CHAPTER EIGHT

The Definition of Love

For love is of God; and every one that loveth is born of God, and knoweth God, He that loveth not knoweth not God; for God is love. In this was manifested the love of God toward us, because that God sent his only begotten Son into the world, that we might live through him. Herein is love, not that we loved God, but that he loved us, and sent his Son to be the propitiation for our sins. (I John 4:7-10)

It is best to think of *The Definition of Love* as a humorous poem on a serious topic. It appears to imitate the Socratic method of tracing some particular quality through various classes of being to its universal essence. Love in the poem includes the lover, the object of his love and the bonds of love between the two. All three categories are subsumed under the general class of love and are aspects of it. But as an exercise in philosophy *The Definition of Love* is more than a little absurd. Although it appears to define its subject, it is really a riddle, similar to Old English riddles, and part of the pleasure that it gives results from our puzzlement at the clues that are offered. The various parts to the puzzle are tantalisingly scattered about. For example, it is not revealed until the final stanza that Fate which separates the two lovers is also an aspect of love. Nor is the reader's immediate comprehension helped by such oxymorons as "Magnanimous Despair" and "feeble Hope". The poem puzzles the reader and forces him to recall the spirit of the doctrine behind the letter. By causing the reader to think about the relationship of fate to love, and of hope to despair, the Christian doctrine of love is more fully brought to mind.

The conceptual frame of the poem is the traditional Christian doctrine of love. Rather than quote from the Bible, Augustine, Bernard, Bonaventura and others I will attempt to summarise it.[1] God created the world out of an act of love and His love is present in all of creation. Love stretches forth from the Creator throughout the creation, infusing it with life and motion. The world is kept in its order and course through bonds of love. All things are in love with their Creator and seek union with Him. But not being themselves divine, they cannot merge with their Creator and are fated by their nature to remain distinct and separate. The distance between the created world and God is filled with various hierarchies of angels, some of whom act as intelligences governing the motions of the various spheres. These angelic intelligences operating through the influence of the stars determine the fate of the mutable world. The centre of creation is man, whose soul was created in the divine image. As a result of Adam's Fall, man forgot the divine nature of his soul, became distracted by carnal temptations, and no longer inclined to love God. Man's love of God can only be restored through an act of grace; but to accept God's love it is necessary to have an inclination of the will towards God.

To love something we must desire it and to desire it we must have some knowledge of it. Having lost the knowledge of God's goodness and having suffered under the burden of Old Testament law, man fell into despair, and despite the prophecies of the Bible no longer hoped for God's love. The Incarnation and Sacrifice of Christ, themselves acts of love, made possible faith and hope in God's love. The love of God now became possible. The main commandment of Christianity is to love God. Having through Christ found faith, charity and hope, man seeks to draw closer to God. Such union is not possible in this world. The immortal soul seeks to fly to Heaven but is weighed down by the mortal body. In contemplation, however, the mind and soul may be said to achieve communion of wills with the divine, although the body is still anchored to this world. Such an experience looks forward to the love which is to be experienced by the soul in Heaven and to the joys of the resurrected at the end of time.

The first stanza of *The Definition of Love* is particularly difficult as Marvell does not give us sufficient information:

> My Love is of a birth as rare
> As 'tis for object strange and high:
> It was begotten by despair
> Upon Impossibility.

It was a commonplace of Renaissance theories of love that kinds of love are distinguished by their objects. Here the object is "strange and high". While "high" might lead us to think of a noble lady, "strange" is unlikely to refer to a woman. Something strange is unusual or foreign. A love object is something we desire or have an inclination towards. The most likely, although perhaps not the only, love object which would supply an answer to the proposed riddle is God. God is the highest good; He dwells "in the high and holy *place*" (Isaiah 57:15), and would fit various meanings of "strange", such as unique or from a distant place. The Promised Land, which is a type of the heavenly Paradise, is a "strange country" (Hebrews 11:9). Christ speaks of Himself as a stranger (Matthew 25:43). The main theme of the poem is the desire to transcend this world and fly directly to God.

How can "My Love" have as its parents Despair and Impossibility? An answer is supplied if we think of the condition of mankind before the coming of Christ; man was in despair at the impossibility of saving himself. Since there was no mediator to redeem man, he despaired of his salvation. He had no hope or expectation of being reconciled with God. In the tenth book of *The Confessions*, Augustine asks whom he could find to reconcile himself to God and says that it is impossible without Christ. Thinking of the Pauline doctrine of hope he continues: "Rightly do I place in him my firm hope that you will cure all my ills through him who *sits at your right hand and pleads for us:* otherwise I should despair . . . We might have thought that your Word was far distant from union with man, and so we might have despaired of ourselves, if he had not been *made flesh and come to dwell among us*".[2]

That Marvell wants us to recall the Pauline doctrine of hope is suggested by the prominence given such words as "love" (charity) and "Hope", and by the distinctions made between the speaker's condition before and after the birth of his love. The nature of divine love was revealed to man through the Incarnation and Sacrifice of Christ, which saved man from despair and gave him hope. It only became possible to love God, that is to incline our will to accept His love, after Christ's Sacrifice had redeemed man from the effects of Adam's sin, freeing him from the bondage of the flesh so that he could rise above carnal love and have faith and hope and charity: "Now faith is the substance of things hoped for, the evidence of things not seen" (Hebrews 11:1). Bernard says: "But if you have not the knowledge of God, could there be a hope of salvation for you without that knowledge? No, not even a hope. For you cannot love One whom you do not know, nor have eternal happiness in the possession of One whom you do not love".[3]

While there is no explicit mention in *The Definition of Love* of Christ's birth and His role as mediator, we are reminded of His role in the drama of mankind's redemption by the associations brought to mind through such words as "begotten", "birth", "high", "Despair", "divine", "Hope", "Heaven" and "fall". Several times Christ is asked who can be saved and He replies that what is impossible with man is possible with God.[4] This recalls other biblical passages where God makes seemingly impossible promises. When God promises

Abraham that Sarah will bear a son named Isaac and He will "establish my covenant with him for an everlasting covenant" (Genesis 17:19), Sarah objects that she is too old to bear children. God says "Is any thing too hard for the LORD?" (18:14).[5] The promise to Abraham is recapitulated in the Annunciation. The angel says "thou shalt conceive in thy womb, and bring forth a son, and shalt call his name JESUS. He shall be great, and shall be called the Son of the Highest: and the Lord God shall give unto him the throne of his father David" (Luke 1:31-32). Mary asks, "How shall this be, seeing I know not a man?" (1:34); "And the angel answered and said unto her, The Holy Ghost shall come upon thee, and the power of the Highest shall overshadow thee: therefore also that holy thing which shall be born of thee shall be called the Son of God . . . For with God nothing shall be impossible" (1:35-37).

In the second stanza hope and despair are ingeniously paired off against each other in a manner which is opposite to their usual mode of operation:

Magnanimous Despair alone
Could show me so divine a thing,
Where feeble Hope could ne'r have flown
But vainly flapt its Tinsel Wing.

Hope is one of the three theological virtues necessary for salvation, whereas despair is normally used in theology to describe a fear of God without hope, and is a sin that can result in damnation. How then can hope be feeble and vain while despair is magnanimous and reveals the divine? Marvell is wittily and sensitively playing upon nuances of meaning. "Magnanimous" means great-souled or great-spirited. The greatness of the soul is that it is immortal and created in the divine image.[6] Bernard says "the soul is great because it is capable of things eternal".[7]

A knowledge of the Augustinian tradition of meditation helps to fill in the conceptual frame of the poem. Despair comes from the ignorance of God. The mind, ignorant of the love of God, despairing of salvation, finds within itself the immortal soul in which the divine image of God is implanted. The mind asking how it could have such knowledge within itself traces the source of the soul back to its Creator, and in asking how it can be saved from its condition gains a fuller knowledge of how divine love is expressed through Christ. The mind having rediscovered the divine image within its soul no longer despairs at the seemingly insurmountable distance between man and God and now having hope for its immortal soul inclines to love God. Bernard says that while a sinful man might perhaps return to the right frame of mind, condemning himself for all the evil action which he has done and propose to reform, he will think his sins too many and feel unable to make satisfactions for offences so numerous, if he "is ignorant how good and merciful God is, how gentle and favourable to the penitent".[8]

"So divine a thing" is the love object and perhaps the soul itself. Such a double interpretation is possible if we remember that the soul contains the divine image within itself, expressing the "greater Heaven in an Heaven less".[9] The greatness of the soul shows its Creator. However, "so divine a thing" is also an implicit allusion to Christ. Mary is told "that holy thing which shall be born of thee shall be called the Son of God" (Luke 1:35). While "that holy thing" shows that the Son will not be a mere man, a "holy thing" is also a sacrificial offering. Christ is "whom God hath set forth *to be* a propitiation through faith in his blood" (Romans 3:25). Christ is the holy propitiating thing.

"Where feeble Hope could ne'r have flown / But vainly flapt its Tinsel Wing" alludes to the condition of the mind before divine love was revealed to it by the soul.[10] Not having any notion of the object of its love, it could never have flown so high. Not having any knowledge of the extent of divine love, it could not hope. Hope is an expectation of some future good. Before the coming of Christ mankind had no hope of a heavenly life:

> That at that time ye were without Christ, being aliens from the commonwealth of Israel, and strangers from the covenants of promise, having no hope, and without God in the world: But now in Christ Jesus ye who sometimes were far off are made nigh by the blood of Christ. (Ephesians 2:12-13).

Despair is the condition of man under the Old Law without the aid of the Gospel. Without Christ it would be vain to expect God's love. It would be vain in the sense of fruitless; it would also be vain in the sense of proud or presumptuous. Vanity or self-love cannot have a knowledge of so high or "so divine a thing" as God. Bernard says; "I rise not, I am not lifted up nor brought out of the dust, I do not breathe the free air of hope, unless the Prophet Himself shall come down".[11]

In stanza three despair has passed and we have moved into the present, a period of hope. The soul is stretched forth to God;[12] but the speaker complains that Fate prevents him from achieving such union:

> And yet I quickly might arrive
> Where my extended Soul is fixt,
> But Fate does Iron wedges drive,
> And alwaies crouds it self betwixt.

Bernard says, "the growth and extension of the soul is charity"; "although the soul, being of a spiritual nature, does not admit of material extension, nevertheless grace confers upon it what is denied by nature".[13] The mind has achieved a knowledge of the object of its love from its immortal soul, but is prevented from actual union with it by the created world. This seeming paradox is really a distinction and part of the definition. The mind can ascend to God in the sense of having knowledge of Him, but being wedded to the body it cannot achieve actual union. The speaker's soul may partake of spiritual knowledge, but the speaker cannot have a direct apprehension of "so divine a thing". The distinction between body and soul is central to the poem. The poem treats of abstractions and abstractly defines love because it is an expression of the mind's way of thinking. The immortal soul, created in God's image, is capable of sharing in the divine life; the body cannot share the same experience as the soul, being prevented from doing so by Fate.

Fate is an aspect of divine love. The creation and God's concern for His creation bring about Fate. In older Christian literature the heavens are moved by angels whose special function is to perform the work of divine providence in upholding and continuing creation. Fate is the condition brought about by the angelic intelligences, to whom God has given the job of keeping the created world in motion. Fate is that which results through the disposition of the created world. Boethius says: "Fate, on the other hand, is the planned order inherent in things subject to change through the medium of which Providence binds everything in its own allotted place . . . Fate controls the motions of different individual things in different places and in different times".[14] The mind by its very nature is fated not to merge with God, since it is imprisoned in the body.

If Fate is a disposition inherent within created things, Fate also can mean an influence which determines conduct. The stars were usually regarded as a source of such influence. And since the stars were governed by angelic intelligences, there is nothing improper in a Christian writer saying that Fate is determined by the stars, providing one makes a basic distinction between influences on the body and on the soul. Only material things are subject to Fate. The immortal soul has free will and is not subject to Fate.

The comedy of personifying Fate as consciously interposing herself between the mind and the object of its love derives from imputing conscious motives to an abstract term. The distinction between the corporal and the divine derives from the Creation of the world, when the corporal was given existence. The iron wedges that separate the creation from its Creator are a way of expressing the various stages of the chain of being. Marvell pretends that Fate is responsible for the boundaries between the two substances and will not let them join for fear that she will lose her kingdom. While it is true that if the divine and the corporal were to merge there would be no world of time and mutability over which Fate could reign, the argument is absurd. Fate is only a byproduct of the Creation. As in Marvell's Mower sequence, where a personification of time laments the end of his reign with the coming of the last days of the world, Fate's point of view is another of those absurd perspectives in which Marvell delights.

The comic description of Fate as a jealous lover crowding herself between the lover and love object is a parody of the Platonic notion of triads. According to Plato two dissimilar things can only be joined by a third which acts as a mediator. The chasm between the mortal and the divine, for example, can only be bridged by the spirit. Plato describes love as such a mediator:

> 'He is a great spirit, and like all spirits he is intermediate between the divine and the mortal.' 'And what,' I said, 'is his power?' 'He interprets,' she replied, 'between gods and men, conveying and taking across to the gods the prayers and sacrifices of men, and to men the commands and replies of the gods; he is the mediator who spans the chasm which divides them, and therefore in him all is bound together, and through him the arts of the prophet and the priest, their sacrifices and mysteries and charms, and all prophecy and incantation, find their way. For God mingles not with man; but through Love all the intercourse and converse of God with man, whether awake or asleep, is carried on.'[15]

In Christianity the only mediator between God and man is Christ: "For *there is* one God, and one mediator between God and men, the man Christ Jesus" (I Timothy 2:5). But if Christ the mediator is a bond of love, Fate, resulting from God's care for His creation, can also playfully be described as a mediator.

The two perfect loves in stanza four[16] are the love of God for man and the love of the soul for God:

> For Fate with jealous Eye does see
> Two perfect Loves; nor lets them close:
> Their union would her ruine be,
> And her Tyrannick pow'r depose.

"Close" means coming together, and during the seventeenth century often referred to lovers embracing. "Their union" points towards the theme of the poem, man's desire for union with the divine. Fate is personified both as a jealous woman and as a queen ruling over a kingdom, the corporal world. She has despotic power and in the next stanza issues decrees. The union of the earthly and heavenly kingdoms would depose or take away Fate's power. Why is Fate's power described as "Tyrannick"? Again Marvell is using a word in two senses. It is tyrannic in the sense that it is absolute ("Decrees of Steel") but a tyrant is also a usurper ("And alwaies crouds it self betwixt").

And therefore her Decrees of Steel
Us as the distant Poles have plac'd
(Though Loves whole World on us doth wheel)
Not by themselves to be embrac'd.

Fate has decreed the separation of the lovers at two distant poles and has in the process usurped the space between them. Our Platonic mediator has become a tyrant who separates while acting as an intermediary. As an intermediary she even manages to share the embraces meant for others. "Embrace" is of course a pun. The two perfect lovers are not comprehensive of love; they need "the Love which us doth bind". We should also remember that in mystical contemplation one seeks God's embraces.

The two distant poles of a globe or a sphere are held together by an axis which acts as an intermediary. The poles here are those of the celestial sphere. The human and divine are at opposite ends of the universe. The lovers are not physically at opposite ends of the axis, they are metaphorically "as" at opposite ends of the axis. In between are the angelic orders. The earth and heavens also are separated by the stars and the planets, governed by angels. God's love of man is the central feature around which the creation turns. The word "wheel" both means "move" and suggests a moving circumference. The *primum mobile* is moved by its love of God and communicates motion to the rest of the universe:

> This great Bowle of the *Heavens*, roules and turnes about an Axeltree, fixt in a certain place, and flyes with the winged swiftnes it hath; the Angel gives it the whirle about, and makes it turne round according to the Divine providence, crowning the world with its vaulted Arch enameled al with starres.[17]

In stanza eight the stars are seen both as a plane between the human and the divine, and presumably as a sphere around the earth, since they are capable of moving into opposition.

Unless the giddy Heaven fall,
And Earth some new Convulsion tear;
And, us to joyn, the World should all
Be cramp'd into a *Planisphere*.

The planisphere is a flat circular map which attempts to depict a curvature such as the earth or the heavenly spheres.[18] "Giddy" is used in the sense of circling and alludes to the wheeling spheres of stanza five and to the movement of the stars in stanza eight. The giddiness of the heavens is also a witty way of saying that they are possessed by the divine.[19] The first convulsion of the earth was the result of man's Fall which led to the present imperfection of the physical world. It was widely believed that the earth was a perfect sphere and the heavens moved in perfect circular motion at the creation of the world, but as a result of Adam's Fall the creation became deformed.[20] The word "fall" may recall either the Fall of Adam and Eve or of Satan — the latter of whom carried a third of the angels with him. Satan was traditionally supposed to have felt giddy emotions at the start of his rebellion.[21] Marvell is not merely up to his usual trick of transposing associations from one thing to another (Fall of earth to Heaven); he is using the transposition to recall related themes and their associations.

But what is the "new Convulsion" which would tear the earth? An earthquake supposedly occurred at the Resurrection of Christ (Matthew 27:54). When might Heaven fall? An earthquake and the fall of stars are foreseen in Revelation 6:12-13. It is also prophesied that at the Second Coming the first Heaven and the first earth will pass away and the heavenly Jerusalem will come down from God out of Heaven to man and there shall be no more death (Revelation 21:1-4) Isaiah 24:20 is usually regarded as a prophecy of the Apocalypse: "The earth shall reel to and fro like a drunkard".

In stanza seven two kinds of loves are described and are compared with oblique and parallel lines. The contrast is between carnal and spiritual love;

> As Lines so Loves *oblique* may well
> Themselves in every Angle greet:
> But ours so truly *Paralel,*
> Though infinite can never meet.

Oblique lovers come together; the parallel love of man for God and God for man can never directly join. Any educated Renaissance reader would know that whereas the rational soul is a circle, being the image of perfection, the vegetative soul is a triangle and the sensible soul is a quadrangle. Aspects of the vegetative soul are begetting, nourishing, and growing, and the sensible soul is a quadrangle because it adds feelings to the other three aspects. Angular love belongs to this world; it is a form of self-love or cupidity ("Lines . . . themselves . . . greet").[22] Bonaventura speaks of the will being *obliquus* if it love something more than God.[23] "Angle" as used here includes a pun on "angel". According to Renaissance Neo-Platonists, between the soul and God there is the angel, the equivalent to the intermediary of the Platonic triad, and corresponding to the angelic orders in Christianity which inhabit the heavens between the human and the divine. Ficino explaining the movements of the soul says that it seems to move straight when it descends to the body and sense, obliquely when it is reflected in itself or in the angel, in a circle when it turns to God.[24] An oblique love then reflects itself; it is a form of self-love.

The two perfect loves, although parallel, can never meet. What kind of lines cannot meet in infinity? The circle is an infinite line having neither beginning, middle, nor end. Two parallel circles would always remain equidistant from each other. The two concentric circles are symbols for God and the rational soul, the circle being an image of their perfection. Kenelm Digby says "But mans soul is a Circle, whose circumference is limited by the true centre of it, which is onely God".[25] Donne says "God is a circle himselfe, and he will make thee one".[26] The two loves are not only infinite in the sense of endless, but also in remaining distinct from each other. The allusion is to the difference between the soul's immortality and God's eternity:

> But although God is a Spirit and the human soul is a spirit, yet God is a Spirit uncreated and the Creator, and the soul is a created spirit; from this it follows that there is an infinite distance between the spirit which is the human soul and the Spirit which is God.[27]

Therefore the Love which us doth bind,
But Fate so enviously debarrs,
Is the Conjunction of the Mind,
And Opposition of the Stars.

In "Conjunction of the Mind" Marvell is punning upon the seventeenth century meaning of conjunction as sexual intercourse. This significance is cleverly set against the astronomical meaning of conjunction and opposition. "Conjunction" means apparent proximity or union. "Opposition" is diametrically the opposite position to conjunction. Love binds the mind to God; presumably the stars intervene between the mind and the object of its love. This is literally true in the sense that both the starry spheres and the angels are between the human and the divine. They are links between the two orders; but as intermediaries they separate them. The love which created the world leads man's mind to its Creator, but the same love has also created the angels and the stars which stand between man and God.

"Opposition" also alludes to the supposed influence of the Zodiac upon lovers. To say that the stars were in opposition to your love would mean you were star crossed, unlucky, that Fate was against you. The word "Fate" when associated with stars suggests the angels which act as the guardians or intelligence over the stars, and through them influence the material world. They are here described as envious, and the stars are in opposition. Previously Fate was described as "jealous". It would, as stanza six suggests, result in the destruction of the present order of the world if Heaven and earth were to join, and Fate would no longer influence the mutable world. Might there not also be an allusion to the fallen angels, whose rebellion, according to tradition, began as jealousy over the proposed creation of man, and who in seducing man from his Maker brought about the present rule of death and Fate? Satan is usually described as the adversary or the opponent. The levelling of Heaven and earth at the end of time will result in the end of Satan's dominion over the material world. "Fate so enviously debarrs" thus seems to include an allusion to Satan whose envy is a cause of the Creation, man's Fall, and the rule of Fate. Both Heaven and Hell are traditionally guarded by barred gates. The fallen angels presiding over stars were sometimes said to be the cause of bad luck in this world. In Marvell's *The Unfortunate Lover* it is the "Malignant Starrs" which force the Lover to live in a world of storms and wars.

"Conjunction" is not only an astronomical term. It has a technical meaning in contemplative literature.[28] It is necessary to be in conjunction before you can leave behind meditation and enter contemplation itself. This moment corresponds to annihilation when the mind no longer fixes the imagination or senses on objects, and the soul delights in being alone, enjoying its own peace. In contemplation it is common to feel that one has passed the stars and moved beyond images of this world to those of eternity. But in fact the mystic does not achieve direct union with God. The mind achieves conjunction, but a union of substances is impossible. Bernard says: "But to be borne upon the clouds, to penetrate into the fulness of Light, to burst into the abysses of Glory, to dwell in the Light which none can approach unto, for this the present is not the time, nor is your mortal body capable of sustaining it. That felicity is reserved for you at the last".[29] The word "Conjunction" recalls our hopes, since the conjunction of the stars was believed to be a sign of great events:

> when the Sun and the Canicular *Starre* are in conjunction, and match togeather, the world burnes with outrageous heats.[30]

> As *stars* (not powerful else) when they *conjoin*,
> Change, as they please, the Worlds estate;
> So thy *Heart* in *Conjunction* with mine,
> Shall our own fortunes regulate;
> And to our *Stars themselves* prescribe a *Fate.*[31]

To regard the opposition of the stars as a reason for despair would be a mistake, since they are also part of "the Love which us doth bind". If the stars in Marvell's poem are now in opposition, presumably at some future time they will be in conjunction. All creation is a sign of divine providence. Even the reign of Fate looks forward to the end of time, when man will have a more direct "Conjunction" with the divine. When the giddy heavens fall and there is a new heaven and earth, there will no longer be an insurmountable distance between God and man. "Conjunction" in the future need not only take place in the mind.

The Definition of Love might be described as a comedy of philosophy trying to define spiritual matters. It is witty to attempt to explain divine matters on analogy to astronomy, geometry and statecraft; but such analogies result in further obscurities. We would not be aware of the Christian doctrine of love in the poem if we did not already know it. Nor would we even know what Marvell was writing about in the various stanzas unless we were familiar with the symbols, concepts and definitions that he uses. For the educated Christian reader, *The Definition of Love* is a riddle requiring elementary doctrinal answers. God is Love, just as Christ is divine. God is the object of our love. Christ makes such love possible. It is difficult not to feel that the poem shows Marvell's amusement with poetry which attempts such impossible tasks as defining love. But it is also important to realise that the comedy results from using inappropriate kinds of logic to explain the simple basic distinction between the earth-bound soul and the object of its love during spiritual contemplation. Indeed the poem is as much about the limitations of mystical contemplation as about divine love.

CHAPTER NINE

The Picture of little T.C. in a Prospect of Flowers

The Picture of little T.C. in a Prospect of Flowers has similarities to Renaissance paintings in which several seemingly unrelated events are depicted; the connection between the events and other details of the scene is to be found in an underlying allegory. In the foreground of Marvell's picture is T.C., a young girl lying on the grass playing with some flowers. Next we see T.C. as she will be in the future, conquering men with her chaste charms. As in mannerist paintings where the artist, or some figure, points towards a symbolic scene, Marvell brings himself into the poem and points towards its allegory: "let me in time compound . . . Where I may see thy Glories". In the fourth stanza we focus on the significance of the flowers in the scene. The poem concludes by warning about the right and wrong use of nature.

As with many Renaissance paintings, close attention to the details of the picture reveals a profound and elaborate allegory. T.C. is imagined as a new Adam having dominion over the created world and meditating upon its significance. She is thus a figure for the soul faced by the choice between falling into sensual temptation or remaining chaste in preparation for her eternal life. Throughout the poem we are reminded of God's promises to man, as revealed through biblical prophecy and events. T.C. is first shown in the morning of her life; the mention of her laws and commands recalls the Mosaic era; while "chaster Laws" suggests a contrast between Old Testament law and New Testament commandments. In the second and third stanzas, for example, T.C. is imagined as a conquering army and as a chariot destined for some glorious triumph. This brings to mind the journey of the Israelites to the Promised Land, and the Church's progress towards its eventual triumph and marriage with the heavenly Lamb.

See with what simplicity
This Nimph begins her golden daies!
In the green Grass she loves to lie,

And there with her fair Aspect tames
The Wilder flow'rs, and gives them names:
But only with the Roses playes;
And them does tell
What Colour best becomes them, and what Smell.

Certain words stand out and demand attention: "simplicity", "Nimph", "golden", "Grass", "Roses", "tames". Simplicity, with its meanings of innocence, humility and soberness of mind, is a spiritual state. "But I fear, lest by any means, as the serpent beguiled Eve through his subtilty, so your minds should be corrupted from the simplicity that is in Christ" (II Corinthians 11:3). Lying on the grass naming flowers T.C. is engaged in a simple meditation on God's creation. Her simplicity recalls Adam before the creation of Eve and the Fall.[1] Eden is further suggested by "begins" and by "golden daies". "Begins" implies "In the beginning", while "golden daies" recalls the age of gold, the equivalent of the age of innocence, or man's first Paradise. "Begins" is also similar to the "now" of "Courage my Soul, now learn to wield", or "Welcome" of "Welcome the Creations Guest",[2] in pointing to a moment of moral decision. Since "nymph" can mean a virgin or soul, as well as a young girl or bride, the scene is related to Marvell's other poems on the theme of the Resolved Soul and Created Pleasure.

If Marvell were a Neo-Platonist we would say that the poem allegorises the moment of the soul's descent into the world of matter, where it faces the dangers of sensual corruption. Marvell is not a Neo-Platonist; there is no mention of the soul's pre-existence. The implied parallel to Genesis sets the poem within a Christian frame of reference. T.C., like all humans, recapitulates the choices of Adam and Eve. The flowers tamed by T.C. are similar to the animals of Genesis who were supposed to recognise God's image in Adam's beauty. The taming of the wild flowers, and the giving them names, shows a purposeful, rational use of creatures. According to some authorities, the naming of the animals stimulated man to contemplation and praise of God.[3] Adam's taming of the wilder animals was a sign of his control over sensuality. The question raised by the poem is the use T.C. will make of her life. God created the grass, greenery and flowers both for man's delight and for contemplation. Since all flesh is grass and will fade as the flowers of the field (Isaiah 40:6), a nymph (soul) lying on the grass (flesh) should be aware that the proper object of her love is God, not the material world.

"What Colour best becomes them" brings to mind the difference between the red rose of this world and the white rose of Paradise. "And what smell": the fragrance of the rose is a reminder of the splendours of Paradise. In Canticles 6:10 the bride, and figuratively the progress of the Church, is described as "she *that* looketh forth as the morning, fair as the moon, clear as the sun, *and* terrible as *an army* with banners". "Morning" is interpreted as the Church before written law; "fair as the moon" shows her under Mosaic law; the sun signifies the Gospel, and the army is allegorised as the Church Militant. We need not worry over whether the parabolic implications of T.C. as a figure for the Church raise doctrinal matters. It is sufficient for our purposes that T.C. as an individual can represent the Church Militant as one of the faithful.

A link between Adam naming the animals and T.C. as a figure of the Virgin is in Luke 1:30-31, where Mary is told that she has found favour with God and that she shall call her Son Jesus, i.e. Joshua or Saviour. Commentators saw this as evidence that Mary had a clear notion of what kind of person her Son was, and that as Adam gave names according to natures, so Mary would name her Son according to His office.[4] In stanza two T.C. is "This Darling of the Gods". Another link between the Virgin and the naming of the creatures is in Genesis 2:20: "And Adam gave names to all cattle, and to the fowl of the air, and to every beast of the field; but for Adam there was not found an help meet for him". Just as Adam had understanding of the creatures, he had knowledge of the correct use of "an help meet". The first help meet precipitated Adam's Fall; Mary, the second Eve, helps redeem man through her purity.

Who can foretel for what high cause
This Darling of the Gods was born!
Yet this is She whose chaster Laws
The wanton Love shall one day fear,
And, under her command severe,
See his Bow broke and Ensigns torn.
Happy, who can
Appease this virtuous Enemy of Man!

"Who can foretel for what high cause / This Darling of the Gods was born!" warns us to read *T.C.* allegorically, and to see the poem as looking forward to the future history of mankind. "Where I may see", "ere", "in time compound" and similar words and phrases contribute to the prophetic dimension of the poem. T.C.'s high cause is that of mankind. It is the eventual triumph of the Church over death. When we read "Yet this is She whose chaster Laws / The wanton Love shall one day fear" we are reminded of Diana, goddess of chastity, who was often treated as a type of the Virgin Mary. While "Laws" and "command" recall Moses receiving the law on Mt Sinai, "chaster Laws" would be those of the Gospel. Christ's commandments are chaster, being spiritual; Old Testament law is after the flesh: "For the law made nothing perfect, but the bringing in of a better hope *did*; by the which we draw nigh unto God" (Hebrews 7:19). The description of love as "wanton" identifies him as vulgar Eros or Cupid, in contrast to divine love.

T.C.'s chaste laws associate her with the conquest of sensuality (carnality introduced through the Fall). Chastity does not mean sexual virginity, although that is a common sign of chastity. It means purity of mind, an unwillingness to be tempted by sensual or created pleasures. Wanton love is erotic love which results from the Fall and is a misdirection of love from God. His defeat by "chaster Laws" looks forward to Christ's conquest over the serpent. The bows and ensigns are the usual accoutrements of Cupid — the ensigns being the pennants, banners and ribbons of chivalric love. Cupid "fears" T.C. because her "chaster Laws" bring an end to his influence on mankind; sensuality and cupidity will no longer govern man.

Marvell's imagery reflects a long tradition of Christian literature in which Satan is portrayed as an archer whose bow is broken by Christ. In Saint Bernard one reads of "the angels of Satan, who transform themselves into the Angels of light (2 Cor. xi:14), who prepare their arrows within the quiver (that is, in concealment) that they may privily shoot at the upright in heart (Ps. xi:2)".[5] A common *exemplum* in medieval sermons was of Death the bowman shooting Adam.[6] In the *Ancrene Riwle* Christ's love is depicted as breaking the Devil's bows: "His place is in peace. There hath He broken the powers of bows: the shield, the sword, and the battle". "He breaks his bows, which are secret temptations that he shoots from afar".[7] T.C. is a "virtuous Enemy of Man" because her virtue keeps her chaste despite the men who attempt to gain her affection. She is unlike the mistress of Petrarchan poetry, often called an "enemy".

Only a major poet is capable of successfully balancing the playfulness and profundities of stanza three. T.C. is not the usual cruel mistress of love poetry. Each young man who falls in love with her will be despised, not because she is cruel, but rather because he has given in to Cupid and therefore to his wanton or sensual nature:

O then let me in time compound,
And parly with those conquering Eyes;
Ere they have try'd their force to wound,
Ere, with their glancing wheels, they drive
In Triumph over Hearts that strive,
And them that yield but more despise.
Let me be laid,
Where I may see thy Glories from some Shade.

To "compound and parly" would be to make peace; to "in time compound, / And parly . . . Ere" would be to make peace before she conquers. The allegorically minded reader will see "in time" as meaning in this world. Literally the speaker will surrender to T.C. before her time of conquests; more imaginatively, he is thinking of her future spiritual glories.

The eyes are next imagined as a triumphal chariot driving over those who resist and also over those who yield to her charms. Her "glancing wheels" driving in triumph (at the exact centre of the poem) recall the symbolism of Christ's victory chariot and the chariot of the Church Triumphant.[8] Her triumph is that of the faithful, implicit in the blessing to subdue the earth in Genesis 1:28, foretelling the subduing of the world for God. We may recall the Israelites' conquest of the Promised Land, itself a type of the Church's eventual triumph. The ark of the covenant was portrayed in the Middle Ages as borne on four wheels, resembling a chariot and foretelling the Church Triumphant.[9] "Drive" is often used in the Bible in association with Israel's conquests on its way to the Promised Land: "Thou shalt drive them out" (Exodus 23:31); "I drive out before thee the Amorite, and the Canaanite" (Exodus 34:11). When Joshua commands that the ark of the covenant be carried across the Jordan before the people, he says "ye shall know that the living God *is* among you, and *that* he will without fail drive out from before you the Canaanites, and the Hittites" (Joshua 3:10).

The speaker, having prophesied T.C.'s conquests, wishes to see into the future and enjoy a vision of the glories that await her. The glories are divine or religious; they allude to the marriage of the heavenly bride and bridegroom: "That he might present it to himself a glorious church, not having spot, or wrinkle, or any such thing; but that it should be holy and without blemish" (Ephesians 5:27). Why does the speaker need shade? One always needs covering when in the presence of divinity. When God talks to Moses and renews the tables He covers him while His "glory passeth by" (Exodus 33:22). The tree which provides the speaker with "some Shade"[10] is probably the apple tree of Canticles 2:3; Christ is the shadow which saves man from God's wrath.[11] "Shade" in the Bible often means death; the dead are shades.[12] To see glories from the shade would be to be among those resurrected at the last age: "They that dwell under his shadow shall return; they shall revive" (Hosea 14:7).

Mean time, whilst every verdant thing
It self does at thy Beauty charm,
Reform the errours of the Spring;
Make that the Tulips may have share

Of sweetness, seeing they are fair;
And Roses of their thorns disarm;
But most procure
That Violets may a longer Age endure.

"Mean time" points towards the simultaneous vision implicit within the poem; the present moment is between various times. Through mankind's Fall the natural world fell into carnality and corruption, and it will be redeemed when man is restored (Romans 8:19-22).[13] Just as Adam's Fall disrupted the harmony of the world, so each person is responsible for setting things right by the course of his life. Donne says "our businesse is, to rectifie Nature, to what she was".[14] T.C. in reforming "the errours of the Spring" gives the flowers qualities which they lack since the Fall. As the destiny of man and nature has been linked by the Fall, reforming nature implies participating in the salvation of mankind. Eternal spring was lost with Adam's Fall, which also led to the disruption of the natural world.

In Renaissance emblem-books flowers are often associated with various virtues and vices. For each of the cardinal vices there was often assumed to be a matching virtue, and a poet could utilise either aspect of the meaning of the appropriate image. In *T.C.* Marvell makes use of the contrast between the fallen aspect of the flower and its virtuous aspect. What the flowers are like *now* shows us their fallen aspect; but when T.C. reforms the "errours of the Spring" they take on a virtuous aspect. The rose can stand for worldliness or for the Virgin and the Church. The unthorned rose was in Paradise; the thorns are a result of the Fall. To disarm the rose of thorns would be to restore it to its paradisial state. Violets, symbols of modesty and virtue, are shortlived; to make them "longer" endure is to make modesty and innocence endure. To endure is to persevere or to be patient in adversity. Those who endure are saved (Matthew 10:22). Enduring until a longer age would involve being patient for the coming of the last age. The tulip was often treated as representative of innocence because of its whiteness. After the introduction of vari-coloured tulips in Holland during the sixteenth century the flower took on the symbolic meaning of false sanctity. The tulips in *T.C.* appear to be innocent, since they are white or "fair". Primitive tulips, however, lack any notable attractive smell (unlike the flowers of Paradise). T.C. in giving them a "share of sweetness" is presumably bringing virtue or the odour of sanctity to their beauty. She is improving on their fallen nature. T.C. surrounded by the tulip, rose and violet brings to mind the Virgin in her garden surrounded by the rose, lily and violet. Why is there a tulip instead of a lily in T.C.'s garden? A well-known gardening book, which Marvell knew, seems to clear the matter up. In Gerard's *Herball* we read that the lilies of the

Bible are in fact tulips.[15]

But O young beauty of the Woods,
Whom Nature courts with fruits and flow'rs,
Gather the Flow'rs, but spare the Buds;
Lest *Flora* angry at thy crime,
To kill her Infants in their prime,
Do quickly make th' Example Yours;
And, ere we see,
Nip in the blossome all our hopes and Thee.

The imagery once again reminds us of mankind's dominion over the creatures, and the homage paid by the natural world to man who is created in God's image. Nature, however, has a dual aspect; it can both be used and misused. The proper use of nature is contemplation of God's works. The improper use of nature is for satisfying sensual appetites. In the first stanza of the poem T.C. makes proper use of nature. She is engaged in an elementary form of meditation upon God's creation. In doing so she recalls Adam in Eden; but she is also like any soul faced by the temptations of the world. She can misuse her dominion. "Gather the Flow'rs" may mean study nature, but "spare the Buds" is a warning against falling into sensual temptations.

The injunction against picking the buds and the subsequent warning that death might result have to do with the misuse of both nature and time. Just as in time the buds will form flowers, so T.C. may one day fulfil a high destiny, and so one day wanton love and sin will find its power over man destroyed. All things happen in time, but they happen gradually in accordance with God's plan. To anticipate the future is a sin. Whereas *carpe diem* poetry usually says "seize the day because time is passing", T.C. is told not to anticipate pleasures ("Buds"), but to let them ripen in the fullness of time. In *Clorinda and Damon*, Clorinda says "Seize the short Joys then, ere they vade", only to be told "These once had been enticing things" before Pan (Christ) told Damon "Words that transcend".

"Buds" are slang for female genitalia and thus there is a warning about sexual indulgence. Since the buds are described as "Infants", there is an implied parallel between them and T.C. The gathering of the buds before their time is destructive not only of the flowers but also of T.C. "Example" has the sense of *exemplum*, a moral illustration: "Let no man despise thy youth; but be thou an example of the believers, in word, in conversation, in charity, in spirit, in faith, in purity" (I Timothy 4:12). Flora, the goddess of flowers and springtime, awaits the blossoming of her realm. Since, according to Paul, redemption of nature awaits the redemption of man, Flora would be right to make an example of T.C. for misusing her life. If T.C.

anticipates the future and indulges her senses, she may die and end our hopes.

Marvell may be referring literally to death of the body, but, as the word "hopes" suggests, his main concern is the life of the spirit. The warning at the end of the poem is against the dangers of sensuality and the corruption of spirit: "For to be carnally minded *is* death" (Romans 8:6). If chastity leads to eternal life, to succumb to temptation leads to the death of the soul. As one of Marvell's contemporaries puts it:

> *Adams* innocency is the time of child-hood; and there is a time in the entering in of the understanding age, wherein every branch of mankinde is put to his choice, whether he wil follow the Law of Righteousnesse, according to the Creation, to honour the Spirit.
>
> Or whether he wil delight self, in glorying in the objects of the earth unrighteously. Now if he chuse to satisfie his lusts and his self-wil, and forsake Reasons Law, he shal fal downwards into bondage, and lie under the powers of darknesse, and live no higher then within the circle of dark flesh, that hath no peace within it self, but what he fetches from creatures without him.[16]

Marvell does not need to explain such ideas in *The Picture of little T.C.* As can be seen from Milton's *Maske* they would be known by educated readers during the seventeenth century. Marvell with his usual lightness of touch assumes the reader's knowledge of the moral choice involved in the fifth stanza. T.C. serves as an example to all men. The "hopes" of the final line of the poem allude not only to the future of the girl and the wishes of her family, but also to the spiritual life of mankind and its hopes of eventual restoration.

I pointed earlier to the similarities between the situation of T.C. and that of the soul in the *Dialogue between the Resolved Soul and Created Pleasure.* Many of Marvell's poems have at their core the drama of an innocent soul facing the temptations of the created world. There are also similarities between *The Picture of little T.C.* and the myth of Persephone, who having strayed from her mother Demeter to pick flowers was abducted and carried to Hades by Pluto. T.C. gathering flowers, warned against being nipped in the bud, brings to mind Milton's description of "Proserpin", who, "Her self a fairer Floure . . . Was gatherd".[17] Since Persephone's abduction is often allegorised as the Fall,[18] it is not surprising that T.C. is warned to spare the buds. Marvell's poem belongs to the same intellectual milieu as Milton's *Maske*:

> So dear to Heav'n is Saintly chastity,
> That when a soul is found sincerely so,
> A thousand liveried Angels lacky her,
> Driving far off each thing of sin and guilt,

And in cleer dream, and solemn vision
Tell her of things that no gross ear can hear,
Till oft convers with heav'nly habitants
Begin to cast a beam on th'outward shape,
The unpolluted temple of the mind,
And turns it by degrees to the souls essence,
Till all be made immortal: but when lust
By unchaste looks, loose gestures, and foul talk,
But most by leud and lavish act of sin,
Lets in defilement to the inward parts,
The soul grows clotted by contagion,
Imbodies, and imbrutes, till she quite loose
The divine property of her first being.[19]

The Picture of little T.C. has many of Marvell's best qualities. Its civilised urbanity of manner blends compassion, scepticism, courtly grace and wit. Its tone ranges easily from the lyrical and complimentary to the earnest and profound. The sensibility revealed is extraordinary in its harmonious juxtaposition of the social, moral and divine. The vision is large, rich and comprehensive, while realised with a light and allusive touch. There is security and poise in treating an unusual complexity of effects and themes. This is poetry of the highest order.

CHAPTER TEN

The Mower Sequence, I

The Mower against Gardens

When lust hath conceived, it bringeth forth sin: and sin, when it is finished, bringeth forth death. (James 1:15)

In the first edition of Marvell's poems, *The Mower against Gardens*, *Damon the Mower*, *The Mower to the Glo-Worms* and *The Mower's Song* are printed consecutively. The four poems are a sequence both narratively and allegorically. We first see the Mower at home in the uncultivated fields, inveighing against the ways of civilisation as represented by the cultivated plants and trees of the enclosed garden. Then Juliana comes and the Mower falls in love with her. Although she ignores him, her presence has the effect of alienating him from the world of nature which is his home. Incurably in love, yet rejected by Juliana, he sees death as the only means of ending his sorrow. Allegorically the four poems span the history of the world. The main allegorical themes are the Fall of man and the consequent rise of civilisation (in *The Mower against Gardens*), the coming of divine love and the approaching day of judgment (in *Damon the Mower*), the appearance of signs of the final harvest of the earth (in *The Mower to the Glo-Worms*), and the destruction of death (in *The Mower's Song*). If we remember that the Bible is a history of the world from the Creation to the end of time, the Mower poems form a selective analogy to biblical history with the main emphasis on events in Genesis and Revelation.

In three poems the Mower cutting grass with his scythe clearly has associations with death, time, and the consequences of sin in the fallen world. In *The Mower against Gardens*, however, there is no reason to make such an identification; basically, the Mower would seem to be the voice of natural innocence crying out against the sophistication of the fallen world. Throughout the poem it is implied that gardens and horticulture are in some way sinful. Images suggesting sexuality and lust abound: "Luxurious", "Vice", "seduce", "allure", "taint", "dealt between", "Forbidden mixtures", "adult'-rate", "Eunuchs", "Sex". Contrasted to the implied sinfulness of cultivated gardens are the sweet fields of nature which retain their original innocence and with which the Mower is associated.

The Mower's complaint against enclosed gardens may be said to represent the view of pagan pastoral poetry, with its nostalgia for a golden age of primitive innocence in contrast to the subsequent corruptions introduced by civilisation. It would, however, be wrong to accept the Mower's point of view. For a Christian the golden age was the Garden of Eden, and the loss of innocence resulted from Adam's Fall. The innocence the Mower claims for the natural world no longer exists; the natural world fell with man, and with man awaits its redemption. Nature requires grace to be restored:

> For the earnest expectation of the creature waiteth for the manifestation of the sons of God. For the creature was made subject to vanity, not willingly, but by reason of him who hath subjected *the same* in hope, Because the creature itself also shall be delivered from the bondage of corruption into the glorious liberty of the children of God. For we know that the whole creation groaneth and travaileth in pain together until now. (Romans 8:19-22).[1]

The enclosures, the arts, the civilisation against which the Mower inveighs are not necessarily evil. Arts and sciences can be misused; but they can also be used properly for the glory of God. Indeed all the arts have their origin in the divine mind, and are signs of divine goodness and harmony. All the human skills mentioned in *The Mower against Gardens* may be instances of man misusing God's creation, but they may also be seen as part of God's goodness in providing man with talents, enabling him to improve upon the primitive condition of the fallen world.

While the Mower claims that civilisation only produces vice, he inadvertently implies grounds for the contrary. We may read his description of the garden as an allegory of the Fall and of its consequences; but a close reading of *The Mower against Gardens* reminds us of the reasons for the arts of civilisation. The early history of man, as recorded in Genesis, is recalled, and has the effect of bringing to mind the divine scheme, for the fulfilment of which man, nature and all history work. As in *To his Coy Mistress*, Marvell's imagery works ironically against the assumptions of the speaker. The Mower is not, then, a reliable guide. His identification with the uncultivated fields prejudices him against the encroachments of civilisation. His associations with time and death in the other Mower poems would be reason enough for his resentment at mankind fulfilling its destiny and thus contributing towards the passing away of the present order. The Mower only sees in civilisation the works of the progeny of Cain; but inadvertently he reminds us of the increase and multiplication of those who are of the promised seed.

The kinds of complexities found in *The Mower against Gardens* can be seen from the first two lines:

Luxurious Man, to bring his Vice in use,
Did after him the World seduce.

An analogy is suggested between the history of man and the natural world. The world fell with man from its original perfection; the remainder of the poem may be said to be a clever illustration of the corruption mankind forces upon nature[2] The plant kingdom falls from innocence into various kinds of sins, and simultaneously progresses in cultivation or civilisation.

If the seduction of the world reminds us of the effects of Adam's Fall the sequence "Man . . . Did after him . . . seduce" recalls the seduction of Adam by Eve. Eve first eats the apple; but the world falls with Adam who is seduced by Eve. "Man" in line one does not prevent such an interpretation; Eve is "man" in Genesis 1:27, where "man" is read as the human race rather than Adam. "Luxurious" had the sense of *luxuria*, the sin of Adam and Eve. It is excessive appetite, especially carnal appetite, and includes all sins. Man is given dominion over the world for use. "Vice" is a misuse of the world for purposes of self-love rather than love of God. "Seduce" has the sense of "deceive" or "draw away". Man draws the flowers and plants from the fields into his gardens; through Adam's Fall he draws them away from their original, divinely created innocence:

And from the fields the Flow'rs and Plants allure,
Where Nature was most plain and pure.

The wild flowers and plants of the field are the descendants of the plants and herbs which God created in Genesis. They were given to man for use as food, pleasure, and for contemplation. They were plain and pure at the Creation and in the Garden of Eden. Like man, they have become tainted by carnality; they do not have their original smell, colour, or shape. They fade, perish, and are a common biblical metaphor for the transitory nature of the carnal world. Man may have originally caused them to fall from innocence along with his own Fall, but their restoration is in his hands.

Since the sense of the poem is so obviously the corruption of nature by man, are we entitled to see in it a contrary significance, that of the regaining of Paradise? The enclosed garden of the next two lines is our first justification for this; the image may pertain to both good and evil:

He first enclos'd within the Gardens square
A dead and standing pool of Air.

Square gardens allude to a seventeenth century fashion for enclosed gardens laid out in geometric patterns. They are also the gardens of the world — the square being a common symbol for the world, just as a circle is a symbol for the soul or eternity. But the enclosed garden may also bring to mind the enclosed garden of Paradise, the enclosed garden of Canticles, the Church as the enclosed garden, and the enclosed garden of Revelation. It is interesting to note that Sir Thomas Browne says that the word "Paradise" meant in Hebrew an enclosed field, and the word "garden" derives from the same root. Browne also says that the form of the first city, Babylon, was square, and the last city, the holy city of Revelation, will also be square.[3] The flowers and trees of the poem recall the luxuriant varied plants associated with the Garden of Eden. Traditionally Paradise, the Church and the soul of the believer are enclosed gardens separated from the world, watered by the streams of grace (Isaiah 58:11), perfumed by the flowers of virtues.

The enclosed garden of the poem, although a place of corruption to the Mower, is a figure calling to mind spiritual realities. It encloses such flowers as the rose, the tulip, the pink, and the Marvel of Peru, besides various fruits. The rose is commonly associated with the Virgin, and the tulip was sometimes seen as the lily of Canticles 2:2: "As the lily among thorns, so *is* my love among the daughters".[4] The pinks usually have the emblematic significance of being bashful or modest. The Marvel of Peru is similar to the five o'clock or other flowers which open during a certain hour of the day. It would be appropriate for the floral sundial in Marvell's *Garden*, a flower with which to keep holy hours and meditate upon the harmony of God's creation. Since some writers claimed to have located Eden in Peru, the flower has paradisial associations. The fruit trees of Paradise, however, would be ungrafted, just as the flowers of Paradise would be less sophisticated in their development than those in the poem; the garden of the poem is not Paradise, it is a figure which both recalls and contrasts with what it recalls. The luxuriance of the garden both brings to mind the luxuriance of Paradise, and is a parody of such natural abundance, since it is luxury forced from nature.

If the world fell with man, and will be liberated from corruption with man, the natural world provides an analogy to the history and development of the human race. The fruits and plants must also increase and multiply to the greater glory of God. Their progress parallels the development of human arts and sciences. They "grow", are "taught to paint", seek complexity ("complexion") and even "learn'd to interline" (on analogy to the making of interlinear Bibles):

And a more luscious Earth for them did knead,
Which stupifi'd them while it fed.
The Pink grew then as double as his Mind;
The nutriment did change the kind.
With strange perfumes he did the Roses taint.
And Flow'rs themselves were taught to paint.
The Tulip, white, did for complexion seek;
And learn'd to interline its cheek.

The paradigm upon which the analogy is based can be found in the readings of Genesis and the first five books of the Old Testament as the early history of civilisation.[5] The first builders of cities, tent makers, musicians and iron workers were of the line of Cain (Genesis 4:17-22); Nimrod was the first tyrant; Noah the first coloniser, and so on. The early history of man as found in the Old Testament was read as prophetic: the promises God made to the Israelites, the various sacrificial laws, the bringing of the Ten Commandments, the vision of the Promised Land, were seen as types of events in the life of Christ and the future of the Church. The progress of civilisation after man's Fall is thus a drama of restoration.

It would be misleading to ask whether each botanical image in the poem is to be read in the good or bad sense. They recall biblical events and have Christian associations. Several responses may be simultaneously implied by the same pattern of imagery. (As is shown by George Herbert's *Prayer,* the common mode of most seventeenth century religious symbolism is open-ended in the many associations brought to mind.) The enclosure of plants within the garden recalls both the beginning of private property and the separation of the tame from the wild, the elect from the unregenerate.[6] The "more luscious Earth" recalls the lushness of Paradise, the curse of the earth as a result of Adam's Fall, and the command "to till the ground" (Genesis 3:23). The description of what happens to the seduced world in Marvell's poem recalls the various emotions supposedly felt by Adam and Eve at the time of eating the forbidden fruit ("more luscious", "stupifi'd", "double as his Mind", "strange perfumes", "Palate in dispute"). One of the first effects of the Fall was the heightening of sensation, followed by an increase of carnal appetite and lust. In *Paradise Lost*, after eating the apple Adam begins to lust for Eve and compliments her on the elegance of her taste in enjoying the forbidden fruit.[7]

It was traditional to see all sins as proceeding from man's disobedience. The seduction from obedience to God led to carnality, a turning of the mind away from God, with the result that appetites usurped the governance of reason. Lust gives birth to sin. Gluttony for the forbidden fruit leads to the Fall. The corruption of the senses and the proliferation of vices thus result from lust as represented by gluttony. Sir Thomas More says that gluttony was the sin of our first parents, but gluttony is not so pernicious as the sins which were its result.[8] The world having been seduced and allured by man participates in various sins. It gluttonously feeds on the luscious earth, becomes slothful or "stupifi'd", avaricious ("grew then as double"), lecherous ("tainted"), proud ("were taught to paint"), and envious ("for complexion seek"). The flowers do not become wrathful; but later in the poem there occur the words "Tyrant" and "enforc'd". A similar pattern of associations can be found in Quarles's *Emblems*, where after addressing "Uxorious Adam" and asking "What hast thou done", the poet describes the fallen world as bringing forth the seven sins:

See how the world (whose chaste and pregnant womb
  Of late conceiv'd, and brought forth nothing ill)
Is now degenerated, and become
  A base adult'ress, whose false births do fill
The earth with monsters, monsters that do roam
  And rage about, and make a trade to kill:
    Now glutt'ny paunches; Lust begins to spawn;
    Wrath takes revenge, and avarice a pawn;
Pale envy pines, pride swells, and sloth begins to yawn.[9]

Quarles introduces this emblem by quoting James 1:15.

The Mower against Gardens is obviously about something more than the old debate over nature versus nurture, innocence versus art. In the fallen world such questions are misleading or irrelevant. Nature having fallen with man can be both plain and impure; pinks can grow fulfilling God's command to increase and multiply while being emblematic of man's double mind: "For to be carnally minded *is* death; but to be spiritually minded *is* life and peace" (Romans 8:6).[10] The rise of civilisation, as instituted by the lineage of Cain, is part of the same history as the rise of the Israelites, prophetic of the redemption of man. If "the nutriment did change the kind", we are reminded of the various places in the Old Testament where a change of names is indicative of God's plan; Jacob is told "thy name shall not be called any more Jacob, but Israel" (Genesis 35:10). The change in name signifies that the covenant has passed to Jacob, and is followed by a passage seen as prophesying the coming of Christ: "and kings shall come out of thy loins" (Genesis 35:11). The Fall has its dual aspect. Feeding on the forbidden fruit makes man mortal, but it also results in the divine scheme of redemption. Throughout the poem we are reminded that history is a story both of fall and of redemption.

Its Onion root they then so high did hold,
That one was for a Meadow sold.
Another World was search'd, through Oceans new,
To find the *Marvel of Peru.*
And yet these Rarities might be allow'd,
To Man, that sov'raign thing and proud.

The high value placed on tulip bulbs ("Onion root") refers to the tulip mania in Holland; the discovery of the Marvel of Peru reminds us of the exploration of the New World. Neither might seem to have any religious significance. But if we remember the Israelites lusting for "the leeks, and the onion, and the garlick" (Numbers 11:4-5) of Egypt;[11] and regretting their journey to the Promised Land ("for a Meadow sold"), and if we see the search for another world and crossing of new oceans to find the Marvel of Peru as an analogy to the search for the Promised Land, then the history of horticulture becomes filled with often unrecognised signs of the divine scheme operating through unlikely vehicles.

Man is that "sov'raign thing" having been given dominion over the earth and its creatures; he is told to "subdue it" (Genesis 1:28), which is prophetic of Israel's subduing its enemies, and of the Church's triumph. He is proud, which is the cause of the Fall. His vice is the desire to be "Luxurious". In misusing the world he seduces it, and taints it. But his skills include teaching, seeking, learning "to interline" and searching: arts of restoration. Man's dignity is that of a rational creature created in the image of God. His rationality may be misused for vice; or it may be used to the glory of God. A garden can have either use. The enclosed garden of the Church or soul is not the plain fields of fallen nature.

The second half of the poem begins by offering us a horticultural court of perverted love. Lust and sexual degeneracy are rife. There are pimping ("dealt between"), incest ("Forbidden mixtures"), illegitimacy ("No plant now knew the Stock from which it came"), exoticism ("upon the Wild the Tame"), adultery ("adult'rate fruit"), concubinage ("*Seraglio*"), "Eunuchs" and unnatural birth:

Had he not dealt between the Bark and Tree,
Forbidden mixtures there to see.
No Plant now knew the Stock from which it came;
He grafts upon the Wild the Tame:
That the uncertain and adult'rate fruit
Might put the Palate in dispute.
His green *Seraglio* has its Eunuchs too;
Lest any Tyrant him out-doe.
And in the Cherry he does Nature vex,
To procreate without a Sex.

The Mower describes the various grafts as examples of man's tyranny over nature. He sees them as parallel to the degeneration of family lines and the growth of despotism.

There are a number of biblical allusions which may at first seem solely to be examples of the speaker's wit, but which on further reflexion bring to mind the divine scheme operating throughout history. The forbidden mixtures and mixing of the stock recall the prohibition against mixed plantations in Leviticus 19:19 and Deuteronomy 22:9; the latter continues into a prohibition of adultery (Deuteronomy 22:22). The mixing of the wild and tame by grafting is a key image in the poem. The mixture recalls the grafting of Gentiles on to the Jewish tree of salvation — the root of David (Revelation 22:16), Jesse (Isaiah 11:1, 10) — from which the Messiah is born. The true believers are ingrafted into Christ, the tree of life which bears "twelve *manner* of fruits" (Revelation 22:2). Marvell is using well-known biblical imagery with its varied but related associations. Romans 11 offers many of the same images for the grafting of the wild upon the tame: "And if some of the branches be broken off, and thou, being a wild olive tree, wert graffed in among them, and with them partakest of the root and fatness of the olive tree" (Romans 11:17). The Israelites are the good tree, the Gentiles the wild tree (Romans 11:23-24). The Israelites are the stock[12] and the plants the saved. The word is "engrafted": "receive with meekness the engrafted word, which is able to save your souls" (James 1:21). Common allegorisations of such images include the grafting of Christ's grace upon the soul, and the grafting of the soul to Christ in spiritual marriage.[13]

The "uncertain and adult'rate fruit" which puts "the Palate in dispute" contrasts to the ungrafted trees of Paradise, in which various plants were still distinct from each other. "Uncertain" and "adult'rate" are words belonging to the fallen world, reminding us of the nature of human society in which believers and the unregenerate are mixed. By their fruits "Ye shall know them" (Matthew 7:16), but we are also told "Judge not, that ye be not judged" (Matthew 7:1). With the wild and tame so completely mixed, it is not surprising that the palate is in dispute. Are the enclosed gardens places of vice and unnatural tastes, or a means of working towards man's redemption? God knows; but the Mower does not. The fruit is "uncertain". "Adult'rate" probably includes a pun on "adult", the mature or fulfilled fruit in contrast to the green or primitive fruit.

The next lines suggest that man's dominion over nature has become a tyranny which is paralleled in the plant kingdom:

His green *Seraglio* has its Eunuchs too;
  Lest any Tyrant him out-doe.
And in the Cherry he does Nature vex,

To procreate without a Sex.
'Tis all enforc'd; the Fountain and the Grot.

In terms of the implied analogy between the garden and Old Testament history this would seem to recall Nimrod, the first tyrant, the various concubines of the Patriarchs, and the founding of the kingdoms. A link between "Tyrant" and "enforc'd" is that Nimrod was supposed to have been violent, he was also supposed to be the founder of monarchy (Genesis 10:10). Nimrod, "the mighty hunter before the LORD" (Genesis 10:9), read in the bad sense alludes to the Devil; read in the good sense he recalls Christ hunting men's souls. "Eunuchs" recalls Matthew 19:12: "and there be eunuchs, which have made themselves eunuchs for the kingdom of heaven's sake".[14] The patterning of Marvell's imagery suggests that he has in mind Christ's remarks on marriage, adultery and virginity, in Matthew 19:2-12. The growth and multiplication of Christianity through virgin martyrs would be an analogy to procreation without sex.

Perhaps here, as in many of Marvell's lyrics, there is an allusion to the Annunciation and Incarnation. From the Mower's perspective, the Christ Child might seem an "uncertain and adult'rate fruit", procreated tyrant-like, without normal sexual intercourse. The coming of Christ "grafts upon the Wild the Tame".

The Mower claims that the primitive innocence of nature has been forgotten by man:

While the sweet Fields do lye forgot:
Where willing Nature does to all dispence
A wild and fragrant Innocence.

We should read the Mower's remarks as having a theological import, the sweet fields with their abundance and fragrances being the innocence of Eden. Compared with Eden, the enclosed garden of the poem is indeed a parody or travesty. Its plants are forced, grafted and sophisticated. But if society has "forgot" (probably in the Augustinian sense of having clouded over the image in the memory) the innocence of Paradise, the Mower has forgotten that Eden was an enclosed garden and that after the Fall man was commanded to labour and "till the ground" (Genesis 3:23). The contrast between the labour imposed upon man and the kind of moral value the Mower finds in the fields is ironically made explicit by:

And *Fauns* and *Faryes* do the Meadows till,
More by their presence then their skill.

The Mower is thinking of a pagan golden age of fauns, fairies and gods, not the biblical Paradise recalled earlier in the poem:

Their Statues polish'd by some ancient hand,
May to adorn the Gardens stand:
But howso'ere the Figures do excel,

The *Gods* themselves with us do dwell.

The Mower's fields are obviously not tilled by the descendants of Adam. If they are seemingly uncursed or unfallen, they also lie outside the Christian scheme of salvation. They certainly cannot offer a dispensation of innocence. They are the fields of pagan pastoral poetry, not the heavenly meadows of the Christian imagination. Eden, the Church, the contemplative life are enclosed gardens. Christ, God and Adam are gardeners. Eden may sometimes be spoken of as a wilderness, but that is because it is isolated from the world. The Mower's claim to dwell among pristine innocence ignores the need for grace. The Mower may claim that the gardens have art ("Statues") while the fields have the reality of which art is a figure ("Figures"), but the art of the garden and the poem recalls a different paradisial innocence, and divinity, from the Mower's realm. The arts of the garden correctly may be said "to adorn". The Mower's mistaken claim to innocence might be seen as analogous to the Jews as described by Bernard: "The Synagogue still feasts without, and with demons for friends". "In her scorn of the righteousness of God and desire to establish her own righteousness, she declares that she has no sin, . . . because she supposes herself to be pure and righteous by the works of the Law".[15]

The trouble with the Mower's claim is that it is theologically incorrect. By rejecting civilisation man does not become pure or innocent. Since man was corrupted by the Fall, he needs grace if he is to rise above himself. Adam's Fall makes possible the grand scheme of redemption through time; it is a fortunate Fall in that God brings greater good out of evil. The Bible is a record and prophecy of the divine scheme. Civilisation has its place in the scheme; man must work towards redemption, reforming "the errours of the Spring".[16] The Mower is a romantic or a sentimental primitivist. If the enclosed garden is often allegorised as the Church containing the faithful, the benefits of the sacraments are only within its walls. The Mower's position is close to that of certain forms of radical Protestantism which assume that instant innocence, purity and salvation are possible by rejecting the corruptions of established society and the established Church. Indeed, Marvell's benign amusement at the expense of the Mower can be more fully appreciated if we see the Mower as a seventeenth century Leveller arguing against civilisation and property rights, and arguing in favour of political and religious reform.

The Mower's radicalism can be seen in one of the basic metaphors he uses. He uses "luxury" in the senses both of "sensual" and "luxury-seeking". The desire for refined sensations harms the world, and nature itself becomes corrupted with luxury. The changes which take place in the plant world suggest the equivalent to refined clothing and the use of perfumes and cosmetics. An important image is "enclos'd". The Mower claims that sin brought enclosures. This was a common argument used by the Levellers and Diggers against property rights. The world was originally given to all men for communal use. Sin brought lust which gave rise to the accumulation of property and the desire for luxuries. The buying and selling of the tulip bulb, the searching of the world for strange flowers, show the further consequences of acquisitive desires that resulted from the Fall. Pride, lust, tyranny and monarchy result from the corruption of a world which was once freely enjoyed. In contrast, the meadows of the poem are like the public grounds which the Diggers hoped to farm, a place where nature still does "to all dispence", and therefore a place of innocence, free from the lusts which make man acquisitive. The meadows are a return to the original Eden of communal lands and pure, unsophisticated tastes, sought by the Diggers.[17]

The parody of Digger polemics in *The Mower against Gardens* is typical of the subtle wit that pervades Marvell's lyrics, requiring us to adjust our response in relation to the character of the narrator. While it might not matter whether we identify the Mower with the Levellers, we are required to see the development of gardening through the Mower's eyes as an allegory of the Fall, and also see beyond his vision to signs or promises of redemption. Marvell's poetry is similar to medieval art in being a mirror through which to study God's traces in the world; but as mirrors offer reverse images, we should not be surprised that Marvell's poems sometimes suggest the opposite of what is being said.

CHAPTER ELEVEN

The Mower Sequence, II

Damon the Mower

For when we were in the flesh, the motions of sins, which were by the law, did work in our members to bring forth fruit unto death. (Romans 7:5)

Damon the Mower is within the tradition of the pastoral allegory which, under the guise of depicting homely personages, insinuates greater matters. The Mower is not a mask for Marvell; Marvell quotes the Mower's song. By the use of a narrative frame Marvell implies that the Mower may have a different perspective on the events from his own. The literary convention of the poem is the pastoral lover's "complaint", in which the "scene" sympathises with or responds to the participants. Throughout the poem there is also the common Petrarchan theme of a lover rejected by a cold mistress who outshines the sun. The lover feels pains and sorrows and says that he will kill himself if his love is not returned. The use of the Petrarchan like the pastoral convention is an example of Marvell's sophisticated wit building his allegory upon seemingly inappropriate materials.

The Mower, who in *The Mower against Gardens* seems associated with the innocence of the natural world, takes on further, sometimes sinister, aspects in the other poems of the sequence. He is identified with time, death, Old Testament Law, the mutability of the created world, and even Satan. This is not surprising. There is no true innocence after man's Fall; the natural world is in "bondage" to time, change and death. The Mower's dominion is over mutable and transitory things. The Mower even identifies himself with death: "For Death thou art a Mower too". The emblematic significances of the Mower are traditional; time carrying a scythe, mowing a field, can be found in a number of poems.[1] There are passages, however, where

Marvell treats the Mower as a figure for God's avenging justice on sinners, on Israel, and at the day of wrath.

While the Mower is a common emblem for time and death, the name Juliana does not have any well-known significance. In *Damon the Mower* she is associated with July, the month when the sun is in Leo. The Lion is a common symbol for Christ, and in medieval iconography the zodiacal sign of Leo is taken as representing the harrowing of Hell when Christ freed man's soul from bondage. But Marvell's allegory is too fluid to allow us to draw such a simple parallel, since in *The Mower's Song* Juliana is associated with spring harvests, May games, and implicitly with the Annunciation and Pentecost. Spring is also traditionally the season when the created world will end and be replaced by a new order.[2] Juliana is a figure for divine love in its many aspects. She causes the mind to be affected by an overwhelming love which alienates it from the things of this world. The main paradox of the Mower poems is that whereas divine love brings hope of redemption to the world, the coming of Juliana blights the Mower's hopes. Divine love destroys death.

Heark how the Mower *Damon* Sung,
With love of *Juliana* stung!
While ev'ry thing did seem to paint
The Scene more fit for his complaint.
Like her fair Eyes the day was fair;
But scorching like his am'rous Care.
Sharp like his Sythe his Sorrow was,
And wither'd like his Hopes the Grass.

There is no reason to suspect the first stanza of being allegorical until we reach the last line: "And wither'd like his Hopes the Grass". In the Bible we are told that man's days are like grass or all flesh is grass, and that like grass man will wither and die. Sometimes the metaphor includes warnings against the scorching sun or day of harvest, standing for the day of God's judgment. Hope is an expectation of a future good, in particular the belief that there is redemption or salvation according to the promise of God. The Mower, whose hopes are withered like grass on a fair but scorching day, provides an ironic figure for the kind of hopes which the grass, sun and seasons should recall. The promise of eternal life is seen in the greenness of the Creation, the creation of the grass and the seed (Genesis 1:11). The created world contains signs of God's providence, which Marvell uses as emblems for man's hope to be redeemed from the world of time and death. But from the standpoint of time and death the same signs (July, the hot sun, the withered grass) foretell the harvest at the end of the world which brings an end to their own reign.

Oh what unusual Heats are here,
Which thus our Sun-burn'd Meadows sear!
The Grass-hopper its pipe gives ore;
And hamstring'd Frogs can dance no more.
But in the brook the green Frog wades;
And Grass-hoppers seek out the shades.
Only the Snake, that kept within,
Now glitters in its second skin.

The "unusual Heats" bring to mind the sun of justice as prophesied in Malachi 4:1-2: "For, behold, the day cometh, that shall burn as an oven; and all the proud, yea, and all that do wickedly, shall be stubble: and the day that cometh shall burn them up, saith the LORD of hosts, that it shall leave them neither root nor branch. But unto you that fear my name shall the Sun of righteousness arise with healing in his wings; and ye shall go forth, and grow up as calves of the stall".[3] Since Malachi is the last book of the Old Testament, it is common to see a parallel between its imagery and the Day of Judgment in Revelation. (In reading *Damon the Mower* we will find patterns which suggest Marvell's familiarity with traditional Christian commentaries on the later prophets.) While the sun of justice is usually interpreted as an image of Christ, it is sometimes associated with the "woman clothed with the sun" of Revelation 12:1, representing the Church clothed in the body of Christ.[4] If we think of the meadows as the fallen world, no wonder they are seared by the coming of such unusual heats: "I am come to send fire on the earth" (Luke 12:49).

The grasshopper and frog are emblematic of those who live for transitory pleasures. The season of destruction and judgment, however, is also a time of rebirth and conversion. The green frog presumably wades in the baptismal water of regeneration. The grasshopper, by seeking shade, brings to mind the protection given by Christ from God's wrath. The imagery of seeking shade from the sun of justice is common in seventeenth century poetry and is based on the shade-giving apple tree (Christ) of Canticles 2:3. The new skin of the snake signifies putting off the old man (Adam) and putting on the new (Christ). The scene is of chastisement and rebirth, bringing to mind the refining fires of divine love and judgment.

This heat the Sun could never raise,
Nor Dog-star so inflame's the dayes.
It from an higher Beauty grow'th,
Which burns the Fields and Mower both:
Which made the Dog, and makes the Sun

Hotter then his own *Phaeton.*
Not *July* causeth these Extremes,
But *Juliana's* scorching beams.

Juliana's beams are supernatural as they are figurative of divine love. Juliana brings both destruction and love. Juliana's flames "from an higher Beauty grow'th", recalling the imagery of Luke 1: "the Son of the Highest" (1:32); "the dayspring from on high" (1:78). The effect of Juliana on the sun and dog star is accounted for by the prophecy of "the heavens being on fire" (II Peter 3:12) at the day of the Lord. The Dog-star, or Sirius, was supposed to reign in July, bringing hot days and diseases. The days of the dog star inaugurate the final period before the Last Judgment. In the Folio the text reads "made the Dog". In the Bodleian manuscript this is corrected to "mads the Dog". Extreme heat supposedly makes dogs mad. But the dog is also a biblical symbol for the wicked, the devil and death. "Deliver my soul from the sword; my darling from the power of the dog" (Psalm 22:20). The Hebrew root for the word mad is almost a synonym of prophecy and denotes either prophetic ecstasy or the raving of a madman. A prophetic dog star is an appropriate sign of the coming day of judgment.[5] Since Phaeton almost destroyed the world by taking his father's chariot, if the sun is hotter than Phaeton, it would certainly be a sign of the day of God's wrath.

Tell me where I may pass the Fires
Of the hot day, or hot desires.
To what cool Cave shall I descend,
Or to what gelid Fountain bend?
Alas! I look for Ease in vain,
When Remedies themselves complain.
No moisture but my Tears do rest,
Nor Cold but in her Icy Breast.

The imagery is common to seventeenth century devotional literature on the theme of the sun of justice. Quarles's *Emblems* offer a relevant parallel for the associations Marvell assumes:

Where shall I turn? To whom shall I apply me?
  Are there no streams where a faint soul may wade?
Thy Godhead, Jesus, are the flames that fry me;
  Hath thy all-glorious Deity ne'er a shade,
Where I may sit and vengeance never eye me;
Where I might sit refresh'd or unafraid?
  Is there no comfort? Is there no refection;
  Is there no cover that will give protection
T' a fainting soul, the subject of thy wrath's reflection?[6]

If the fountains and caves are useless to the Mower, it is probably because the rivers are dried up and the mountains overthrown on the day of wrath. Natural "Remedies themselves complain" as nature cannot help. While tears are natural prayers, associated with penitence and grace, the Mower as a figure of time and death cannot benefit from them.

How long wilt Thou, fair Shepheardess,
Esteem me, and my Presents less?
To Thee the harmless Snake I bring,
Disarmed of its teeth and sting.
To Thee *Chameleons* changing-hue,
And Oak leaves tipt with hony due.
Yet Thou ungrateful hast not sought
Nor what they are, nor who them brought.

"How long" echoes the many biblical passages where Israel prays God for deliverance. Christ is a shepherd of souls; a shepherdess could bring to mind both Christ and His Church. Prophecies of Christ often include promises of the bringing of presents. The Mower's presents to Juliana recall the gifts brought to the Christ Child. But the Mower's presents are rejected, unesteemed. Juliana does not love or respect the Mower or his offerings. The three gifts the Mower brings to Juliana are animals and leaves: appropriate gifts for pastoral poetry, but carnal presents with pagan associations. The rejected presents recall Cain's unacceptable offering: "But unto Cain and to his offering he had not respect" (Genesis 4:5). Cain is the founder of the fleshly city in contrast to those of the city of God. Cain's offerings are seen as a type of blood sacrifices and other carnal gifts to God offered by Israel. The rejection of such offerings by the later Hebraic prophets is seen as foretelling the coming of Christ: "Wherewith shall I come before the LORD, *and* bow myself before the high God? shall I come before him with burnt offerings, with calves of a year old?" (Micah 6:6). The Mower complains that Juliana has not sought them or himself. Divine love has no esteem for death or carnal worship. In the next three stanzas the Mower gives us a fuller picture of what he represents.

I am the Mower *Damon*, known
Through all the Meadows I have mown.
On me the Morn her dew distills
Before her darling Daffadils.
And, if at Noon my toil me heat,
The Sun himself licks off my Sweat.
While, going home, the Ev'ning sweet
In cowslip-water bathes my feet.

Damon belongs to the idealised world of pastoral poetry. It is, however, also a place of mutability and death, as is shown by the presence of the Mower. (Since Abel can mean meadows, perhaps the Mower mows all types of Abel?[7]) Since the fallen world is the Mower's dominion, he foolishly assumes its goodness was instituted to aid his labours. *Clorinda and Damon* warns us however, that such pastoral nostalgia has a different meaning since the coming of Christ, and its motifs must be read with the new significance.

> What, though the piping Shepherd stock
> The plains with an unnum'red Flock,
> This Sithe of mine discovers wide
> More ground then all his Sheep do hide.
> With this the golden fleece I shear
> Of all these Closes ev'ry Year.
> And though in Wooll more poor then they,
> Yet am I richer far in Hay.

The contrast between the shepherd and Mower brings to mind Abel and Cain: "Abel was a keeper of sheep, but Cain was a tiller of the ground" (Genesis 4:2). The shepherd is a figure for Christ. Christ is "that great shepherd of the sheep" (Hebrews 13:20) Who pipes the Gospel (John 10:16) while tending His flock (Luke 12:32). His flock are the heirs of God's covenant with Abraham (Acts 13:26), "a great multitude, which no man could number, of all nations, and kindreds" (Revelation 7:9). Contrasted with the shepherd is the Mower with his scythe. The shepherd covers the earth with the faithful who increase and multiply. But death continues his dominion over the earth. Despite the shepherd's flock, the curse of death still prevails.

The "golden fleece" is the wheat or the harvest, and is metaphorically contrasted to the shearing of sheep. The Mower reaps the fields, he harvests at the end of the year, and allegorically he shears the skin of clothes (Genesis 3:21). Why does Marvell metaphorically describe wheat as "fleece"? "Fleece" are among the offerings given to Levites or priests. In the seventeenth century it became a sarcasm for tithing. But behind the word is the older symbolic meaning of harvesting the soul. Thus the shepherd gathers souls or wool, the Mower gathers the withered grass, flesh, hay. Christ saves, the Old Law kills.[8] Behind the stanza lies the parable of the Sower of Matthew 13:37-40:

> He answered and said unto them, He that soweth the good seed is the Son of man; The field is the world; the good seed are the children of the kingdom; but the tares are the children of the wicked *one*; The enemy that sowed them is the devil; the harvest is the end of the world; and the reapers are the angels. As therefore the tares are gathered and burned in the fire; so shall it be in the end of this world.

Nor am I so deform'd to sight,
If in my Sithe I looked right;
In which I see my Picture done,
As in a crescent Moon the Sun.
The deathless Fairyes take me oft
To lead them in their Danses soft:
And, when I tune my self to sing,
About me they contract their Ring.

The Mower claims that he is not "deform'd to sight"; but might what he represents be unattractive to the mind? "We walk by faith, not by sight" (II Corinthians 5:7). Marvell is punning upon various meanings of "formed". In Isaiah 53:2 the Messiah has "no form nor comeliness". Professor Legouis has pointed out that "Nor am I so deform'd to sight" is an echo of the wooing of Alexis by Corydon in Virgil's second Eclogue (line 25): "nec sum adeo informis".[9] Virgil's poem, however, was treated allegorically in the Middle Ages, with the shepherd standing for Christ and Alexis representing man's soul: "By this Coridon is understonde Criste and by this Alexis mannis soule".[10] It is one of Marvell's ironies that the Mower inadvertently refers our mind to the Messiah.

This echo of Virgil can be seen as an allegorisation of Christ wooing man's soul. What is going on? The next lines explain: "I see my Picture done, / As in a crescent Moon the Sun". The light of the sun is reflected on the moon. The moon is thus a mirror of its opposite. Both the Mower and his "Sithe" are mirrors which shine with, and reflect, other lights (—the Son). Thus the Mower can both be an emblem of death, and bring to mind God's reaping angels; he can be a figure for time's dominion over the world, and intermittently bring to mind the Messiah. Even the scythe can be a mirror for "beholding as in a glass the glory of the Lord" (II Corinthians 3:18). The moon which reveals its opposite, the sun, suggests how the poem should be read. We are reminded of hopes which the Mower does not understand. The scythe is in the shape of a crescent. The waning moon is a sign of death; but it also leads to rebirth. Like the dying and rising sun it is a sign of the Resurrection and coming victory of Christ. The phases of the moon are also a testament of the light which it borrows from the sun, since we see the moon by the light of the sun. The Mower looking at his scythe should see death reflected, but he implicitly compares himself to the sun. He is unknowingly correct. A traditional symbol for the Virgin Mary at the Incarnation is a crescent moon. Thus the Mower sees himself in his "Sithe" as the Son can be seen in the Virgin. Just as the withered grass is a sign of the coming harvest, the harvest is a reminder of the eventual fulfulment of man's hopes.

The "deathless" fairies are not part of the Christian scheme of salvation. The fairies were supposed to dance in the forest away from human eyes. Damon, as an earth daimon, would be at home in their company. He is a pagan Pan, not the allegorised figure of Pan as Christ found in Marvell's *Clorinda and Damon*.[11] As leader of their dances he would be married to their queen ("contract their Ring"). The usual explanation of fauns, sylvans and other incubi during the Middle Ages was Isaiah 13:21: "and satyrs shall dance there."[12] The satyrs dance over fallen Babylon, which has now become a desolate place; their appearance is a sign of the coming of God's wrath (Isaiah 13:21-22), the end of the world.

How happy might I still have mow'd,
Had not Love here his Thistles sow'd!
But now I all the day complain,
Joyning my Labour to my Pain;
And with my Sythe cut down the Grass,
Yet still my Grief is where it was:
But, when the Iron blunter grows,
Sighing I whet my Sythe and Woes.

When the Mower's happiness is destroyed by love, we are reminded of Adam, who, through love of Eve, falls from happiness. The ground is cursed, he is sentenced to hard labour to earn his food; thorns and thistles grow to make his work more difficult. But the story of the Fall is also a prophecy of man's redemption. The effects of Juliana on the Mower recall the eventual conquest of divine love over death. The thistles which love sows among the grass, and which make the Mower's labour more difficult, are signs of the appearance of the divine word. "Sow'd" alludes to the parable of the Sower: "The sower soweth the word" (Mark 4:14). In the parable the Sower is Christ, the good seed is the saved, and the tares are the children of the devil. To apply literally the parable to the poem, the meaning is that the wicked remain despite the effects of the curse, death and judgment. However, Marvell sees hope in this as the thistles also have good associations: "Love here his Thistles sow'd".

The Mower's labour pains result from the thorny thistles. As both painful labour and birth pains are consequences of Adam's sin, the pun links the Fall to the doctrine of restoration. In Romans 8:22 Paul speaks of the whole creation labouring in pain for deliverance from bondage. The Mower, however, complains since the coming of divine love makes Satan's harvest of souls less easy.[13] He can cut the grass, but the thistles (grief) remain. Abel was glossed as meaning grief, which was in turn applied to all sons of God. In Isaiah the Messiah is "a man of sorrows, and acquainted with grief" (Isaiah 53:3); "he hath borne our griefs" (53:4).[14] One of the thistles or thorns often mentioned in the Bible is the Palma Christi.[15]

The Mower then is correct to see love as an enemy which makes his work more difficult. Death's blade is dulled by the endurance of the faithful; their appearance is a sign that the days of death are coming to an end. The image of the blunted blade is traditional. In George Herbert's *Time*, the scythe also becomes dull after the coming of Christ. The Mower can prepare his scythe for the harvest at the end of time, but the coming of Juliana has transformed his once hopeful labours into his woes. His lament is a swan's song, a sign of his approaching death. The days of mankind's bondage to sin and the Law are to be over:

While thus he threw his Elbow round,
Depopulating all the Ground,
And, with his whistling Sythe, does cut
Each stroke between the Earth and Root,
The edged Stele by careless chance
Did into his own Ankle glance;
And there among the Grass fell down,
By his own Sythe, the Mower mown.

The return of the narrator ("While thus he") reminds us of the distance between Marvell and the Mower. The Mower's complaint is humorous. The humour is not intended by the Mower; it comes, rather, from outside, from the way the Mower is made to speak and act. There is a discrepancy between the Mower's emotions and our response, which contributes towards our reading the Mower poems as figurative and allegorical. The ironies which result from the interplay between figure and allegory are those of an extremely civilised sensibility. Marvell is capable of creating parodies of Christian doctrine and symbol which have the effect of affirming what is being humorously imitated. In the Mower poems there is no doubt that Godot came and will come again. The humour is playful rather than tragic.

The comic apocalypse of "Depopulating all the Ground" plays with "All flesh *is* grass" (Isaiah 40:6). If you cut all grass, you depopulate the earth of all flesh. The analogy is to "and the earth was reaped" (Revelation 14:16), and also recalls previous biblical acts and prophecies of God's judgment. The Mower's elbow might be seen as an ironic contrast to God's rainbow, "token of a covenant" that God will no more destroy "all flesh that *is* upon the earth" (Genesis 9:13-17). El is one of the Old Testament names for God. "Ground" occurs in the parable of the Sower and biblical interpretations of it. Indeed it has been suggested that the parable should be called the Seeds and the Ground.[16] The Mower has become a figure for the destroying angel of the Apocalypse: "the sword shall devour round about thee" (Jeremiah 46:14).

The Mower's scythe cuts "between the Earth and Root". In Malachi 4:1 "the day that cometh . . . shall leave them neither root nor branch". "Now also the axe is laid unto the root of the trees" (Matthew 3:10). Cutting is a reminder of God's judgment as in "thou also shalt be cut off" (Romans 11:22). If we are reminded of God's judgment, the Mower has other aims in cutting between the earth and root. The Messiah is "a root of Jesse, which shall stand for an ensign of the people" (Isaiah 11:10). Jesus is "the root and the offspring of David" (Revelation 22:16). In Isaiah 53:8 the Messiah will be "cut off out of the land." Death is presumably attempting to separate all flesh from Christ: "Who shall separate us from the love of Christ? *shall* tribulation . . . or sword? . . . For thy sake we are killed all the day long" (Romans 8:35-36).

In the Old Testament, God often threatens to punish the Israelites before restoring them. Such punishment is usually described in images of general destruction. The New Testament parallels such prophecies with the day of judgment. It is in the nature of Marvell's allegory that the Mower can be a figure for death, and through the words he uses indirectly bring to mind the Messiah. The complexities Marvell creates reflect the complexities of what is being recalled; Israel is God's own people bearing the promise of redemption; Israel is also the dead who reject the Messiah and remain wedded to carnal worship. The Mower is a figure of Death the Leveller, and since the Levellers were filled with Messianistic hopes, he is a comic Anti-Christ who brings to mind the true Saviour.

> Alas! said He, these hurts are slight
> To those that dye by Loves despight.
> With Shepherds-purse, and Clowns-all-heal,
> The Blood I stanch, and Wound I seal.
> Only for him no Cure is found,
> Whom *Julianas* Eyes do wound.
> 'Tis death alone that this must do:
> For Death thou art a Mower too.

While the final line of the poem links the Mower to Death, our response is complicated by imagery recalling Christ's Passion. The Mower dies of love, is a kind of physician, and applies the "seal". He is a parody of "him whom man despiseth" (Isaiah 49:7). The imagery of "Blood", "wound" and "seal" recalls Christ, the divine physician who is wounded so His patient might recover: "With his stripes we are healed" (Isaiah 53:5).[17] Christ is an all-heal or saviour.[18] The word "seal" is another of Marvell's etymological puns. *Sphragis* was originally a word for a seal used to impress a mark on wax. *Sphragis* consists of the sign of the Cross marked on the forehead at baptism.[19] Those so marked are to be spared by the destroying angel (Revelation 7:3):

> The redemption accomplished by Christ becomes a saving sign (*semeion*) for those who share in it. And seeing this sign, God saves those who have been anointed by faith. For there is no other way to escape the destroying angel than by the blood of God, Who by love has poured out His blood for us. And by this blood, we receive the Holy Spirit. Indeed the Spirit and the blood are related in such a way that by the blood which is connatural to us, we receive the Spirit which is not connatural, and the gate to death is closed to our souls. Such is the *sphragis* of the blood.[20]

The Mower dies from the wound given by Juliana's eyes. He has healed his body but not his soul.

Why do Juliana's eyes wound? The eyes of a mistress often wound in love poetry, but imagery of eyes wounding is also common in the Bible as a metaphor for divine power. The contrast between the Mower healing himself and the wound given by Juliana's eyes recalls Old Testament passages where wounds are cured by false prophets (Jeremiah 6:14), while God's judgment on Israel is an incurable wound. In Jeremiah, the imagery of wounds and cures forms an extended metaphor of God's relation to Israel: "Hast thou utterly rejected Judah? . . . *there is* no healing for us" (Jeremiah 14:19); "Why is my pain perpetual, and my wound incurable" (Jeremiah 15:18). "Thy bruise *is* incurable, *and* thy wound *is* grevious . . . thou hast no healing medicines" (Jeremiah 30:12). Matthew Poole says that the wounds literally refer to the period of Babylonian captivity, but should be understood as the sinful state of Israel "with reference to God's purpose"[21] The incurable wound is also associated with the day of judgment. "For this *is* the day of the Lord GOD of hosts, a day of vengeance, that he may avenge him of his adversaries . . . in vain shalt thou use many medicines; *for* thou shalt not be cured" (Jeremiah 46:10-11). It is not surprising that the coming of Juliana gives an incurable wound to the Mower. Marvell seems to imagine the meadows or grass as the Israelites under the bondage of the Mower as a figure for Time, Death and Old Testament Law. But to make allegory so explicit is to destroy its very imaginative nature and reduce it to a running analogy without taking into account its purposeful ambiguities and shifting significances.

If the only cure for the Mower's wound is death, and if death is also a Mower, then the last lines of the poem allude to the death of death. The Mower's destruction of his dominion in *The Mower's Song* in order to make a tomb for himself confirms this interpretation of his death as a figure for the end of created time.

Readers of Marvell are aware that many of the lyrics have a humorous resonance. It might be thought that an attitude of amused detachment argues that Marvell was not really involved in the significance of his allegorical lyrics, or that there was a conflict in his personality between what he wrote and what he felt. A better explanation is that the allegorical tradition itself gives sanction to a special kind of wit. Christian writers have often accepted the Socratic view that mysteries should be couched in irony. The injunction not to cast pearls before swine is explanation enough for the kind of humorous relationship between narrative and meaning which one sometimes finds in allegorical literature. In the case of Marvell, there is something added to the allegorist's delight in incongruity, obscurity and misdirection. Marvell enjoyed the fluid relationships found in allegorical symbolism as an educated and sophisticated game. He delighted in making seemingly insubstantial vehicles contain profound significances; he delighted in bringing to mind both the "good" and "bad" meaning of a symbol; he delighted in the varied and often absurd conventions which were part of allegorical interpretation. The seeing of divine truths in multilingual puns and complex typologies was not necessarily absurd to Marvell, since such matters had their appeal to educated minds for centuries. But Marvell also was conscious of the erudition in his poetry as a form of display. While allegorical tradition may direct one to speak ironically and obscurely when alluding to spiritual matters, self-consciousness in performing is characteristic of seventeenth century poetry. In Marvell's lyrics an awareness of the paradoxes and ingenuities inherent in allegorisation is subtly heightened and becomes a form of wit, related to the self-conscious displays of cleverness in the poetry of Donne, Carew, Cowley and Dryden.

CHAPTER TWELVE

The Mower Sequence, III

The Mower to the Glo-Worms

And the light shineth in darkness; and the darkness comprehended it not. (John 1:5)

The Mower to the Glo-Worms is a comedy of reversals. The Mower is extremely articulate and sophisticated for a rustic labourer;[1] his diction is educated ("meditate", "portend", "officious", "courteous") and his speech is a witty exercise in courtly compliment modulated into the pastoral mode. But the main comedy is the incongruity between what the Mower says and the symbolic or figurative significance of the glo-worms and Juliana. The Mower assumes an intimate relationship with nature, but in fact he does not comprehend its emblematic and spiritual significance. Although he uses such words as "meditate", "studying", "portend" and "presage", he does not realise that the glo-worms are in themselves signs of what the coming of Juliana represents. Their lights are indeed wasted on him, but not in the sense he means; they are wasted in that he has no understanding.

The poem consists of a single sentence[2] in which the glo-worms are praised, and then told that their lights have been useless since the coming of Juliana, who has "displac'd" the Mower's "Mind". The clauses in the first three stanzas are used to suggest the emblematic function of glo-worms, and are a means of shaping our response. The glo-worms are natural lights by which to meditate, to foresee ("presage") and to see "the way". If their light is now wasted, it is because a stronger light has come in the person of Juliana. Just as Juliana in *Damon the Mower* outshines the light of the sun, so here she is superior to another natural light. If we were to meditate, ask what she presages and what her flames show, we should see her as a figure for the consummation of the natural order. But the joke is that the glo-worms all along were signs that the Mower's reign was coming to an end, and that he would some day lose his home in the fallen world. The glo-worms are signs of this, since they were supposed to appear immediately before the time of harvesting. Pliny's *Historie of the World* says that glo-worms never appear before the hay is ready for harvesting and never after it is cut. Pliny, in Holland's translation, says that we can see the "incredible goodness of Nature, in teaching vs by that silly creature".[3] Marvell uses this natural sign allegorically, and imagines the glo-worms as symbols for the harvesting of mankind at the Day of Judgment.

When we turn to the text of the poem, we notice that it is surprisingly packed with religious resonances. When the Mower addresses the glo-worms or refers to the natural world, his vocabulary and phrases ironically bring to mind spiritual associations. These in turn imply a further dimension of significance in the scene, although the Mower is not aware of it.

> Ye living Lamps, by whose dear light
> The Nightingale does sit so late,
> And studying all the Summer-night,
> Her matchless Songs does meditate.

The nightingale is a well-known emblem for philosophers who stay up late at night studying the mysteries of life, and for the contemplative soul meditating and singing God's praises.[4]

The glo-worm as a testimony or sign is, despite the Mower's claim to the contrary, at least as significant as comets in what it portends:

> Ye Country Comets, that portend
> No War, nor Prince's funeral,
> Shining unto no higher end
> Then to presage the Grasses fall.

The appearance of comets was usually regarded as a warning of some calamity including the Apocalypse. The Mower says that the Country Comets, or glo-worms, shine "unto no higher end" than to signify the time of harvesting hay (grass). But the Mower misreads the signs. The fall of the grasses recalls the destruction of the carnal world; the harvest recalls the Day of Judgment: "*As for* man, his days *are* as grass" (Psalm 103:15); "And another angel came out of the temple, crying with a loud voice to him that sat on the cloud, Thrust in thy sickle, and reap; for the time is come for thee to reap; for the harvest of the earth is ripe" (Revelation 14:15). Marvell's metaphor is also found in Christ's parable of the tares: "The field is the world . . . the harvest is the end of the world" (Matthew 13: 38-39).

Ye Glo-worms, whose officious Flame
To wandring Mowers shows the way,
That in the Night have lost their aim,
And after foolish Fires do stray.

The glo-worms showing the Mowers their way bring to mind the pillar of fire leading the Israelites on their wanderings to the Promised Land; "And the LORD went before them by day in a pillar of a cloud, to lead them the way; and by night in a pillar of fire, to give them light; to go by day and night" (Exodus 13:21). The Promised Land is a shadow of the heavenly kingdom promised to the faithful of the Church, the new Israelites: Christ is "A light to lighten the Gentiles" (Luke 2:32). In discussing the star of Christ's nativity Jeremy Taylor compares it to "the angel, that went before the sons of Israel in a pillar of fire by night" and says "it was no prodigy nor comet, foretelling diseases, plagues, war and death, but only the happy birth of a most excellent prince".[5]

The glo-worms are signs of man's salvation written in the Book of Creatures, just as the biblical Exodus story is written in the Book of God's revelations. Just as God's flame leads the Israelites out of their bondage, so the natural lights of the glo-worms are signs to those who have lost sight of God's promises and strayed after foolish doctrines or carnal lusts ("Fires"). The glo-worms are similar to John the Baptist in being fore-runners; they prepare for the coming of the real Light. Those who wandered in the night by the dim light of reason are now to be given the light of revelation: "The people that walked in darkness have seen a great light: they that dwell in the land of the shadow of death, upon them hath the light shined" (Isaiah 9:2). Just as the pillar of flame in Exodus is prophetic of the Redeemer, prophecies are recalled through the figure of Juliana: "Then spake Jesus again unto them, saying, I am the light of the world: he that followeth me shall not walk in darkness, but shall have the light of life" (John 8:12):

Your courteous Lights in vain you wast,
Since *Juliana* here is come,
For She my mind hath so displac'd
That I shall never find my home.

If courtesy is vain it is because such aids are no longer necessary since Juliana has come — the joke being that Juliana herself is a figure of what is to come.[6] "When *Juliana* came" and "For *Juliana* comes" in *The Mower's Song* have associations with traditional prophecies of the coming of the Messiah. "Until Shiloh come" in Genesis 49:10 was a well-known prophecy of the Messiah, often linked with "Blessed *is* he that cometh in the name of the Lord" (Matthew 21:9); "Art thou he that should come" (Luke 7:20); and "behold, I come quickly" (Revelation 22:12).

In the last two lines of the poem the Mower complains that he will never find his home again. The secular meaning of "home", as used by the Mower, is being played against the religious significance. Within the figurative analogies of the Mower sequence the coming of Juliana is a sign of the coming destruction of the Mower's world: "all / Will in one common Ruine fall"[7] The Mower, as a figure of death, is at home in this world, not the next. His existence is predicted upon the changeable world, the growth and fall of grass, life and death. He has no other home, no other hopes. Man's home is the mansion of God;[8] but what the Mower represents cannot enter the heavenly kingdom. The Mower has mistaken the significance of "Grasses fall"; it prophesied the destruction of his home. The Mower has lost his harmony with the natural world; a superior object of love has come: "For She my Mind hath so displac'd".

"Mind" is similar to "meditate" and "presage" in helping us to read the poem. Marvell is wittily alluding to the mind as memory — as explained by Augustine and as held by most medieval and Renaissance writers on contemplation[9] The mind has all ideas within it: memory including a knowledge of man's original happiness in Eden. But the Mower as reaper, a figure of time and death, has other memories and hopes than mankind, and they are ended with the coming of Juliana, just as Death's hopes are ended with the coming of Christ. The Mower's home is the created world, which will pass away (Revelation 21:1). As with the courtly lovers of romantic poetry, the object of his love is also his enemy and destroyer.

The displacing of the Mower's mind from the things of the world to Juliana is analogous to the transformation of pagan pastoral poetry to Christian allegory. Pastoral poetry shows man's remembrance of his first Paradise by depicting a golden age when man was in harmony with nature. But now the light of revelation has come, bringing promises of an end to created time. The dim remembrance of Paradise found in classical pastoral poetry has been superseded by the beauty of divine love, which transforms the created world into symbols of man's restoration. In Marvell's *Clorinda and Damon* such a distinction is explicit:

D. These once had been enticing things,
Clorinda, Pastures, Caves, and Springs.
C. And what late change? *D.* The other day
Pan met me. *C.* What did great *Pan* say?
D. Words that transcend poor Shepherds skill,
But He ere since my Songs does fill:
And his Name swells my Slender Oate![10]

If I correctly understand *The Mower to the Glo-Worms*, the social comedy is parabolic. What appears to be a witty pastoral lover's lament is figurative of the approaching end of the dominion of time and death over the created world. The coming of the glo-worms and of Juliana presages the apocalyptic drama figured in *The Mower's Song*. Let me make clear that the Mower and Juliana are not symbols for death's reign and Christ. Marvell's method is playful suggestiveness, bordering on parody, rather than the making of metaphoric equations. The playful humour of Marvell's poem brings to mind doctrinal truths. The wit is in what can be implied, suggested, or brought to mind by the Mower's uncomprehending lament for a superior lady. The religious resonances the Mower uses are simultaneously comic in the situation and recall prophecies of which the speaker is unaware.

CHAPTER THIRTEEN

The Mower Sequence, IV

The Mower's Song

I will ransom them from the power of the grave; I will redeem them from death: O death, I will be thy plagues; O grave, I will be thy destruction: repentance shall be hid from mine eyes. (Hosea 13:14).

With *The Mower's Song*, the eschatological drama shadowed in Marvell's four Mower poems comes to its conclusion. The events correspond to the last moments of created time, as foreseen in Revelation. The appearance of Juliana heralds the renewal of nature, the destruction of the world and the death of the Mower. To understand the paradox of nature both being renewed and destroyed, we need to recall that the world is linked to man's destiny. Nature fell with man and will be restored with man. But redemption from the bondage of corruption results in the destruction of death and the passing away of the present world.

It would be a mistake, however, to read the poem as a single metaphor, in which the events recall those in the Book of Revelation. The associations range in time from the greenness of the Creation, through the coming of Christ, to the end of the world. The range of events recalled is suggested through the sequence of tenses, from "was once" to "grew more", "shall now", to "shall adorn". Similarly the shift from "when *Juliana* came" to "for *Juliana* comes" contributes to the multiple perspective; Christ came and His Sacrifice fulfils the promise in Genesis 3:15 that the head of the serpent will be bruised. From the standpoint of eternity, death dies with Christ on the Cross; but the actual destruction of death in the temporal order occurs at the Second Coming, with the passing away of the heavens and the earth.

Since the natural world is a sign both of the Creation and of its eventual destruction, our imagination moves backward and forward in time during our reading of the poem. For example, one of the key phrases in the sequence of Mower poems occurs in stanza four: "in one common Ruine fall". While the ruin brings to mind the passing away of the created world, it also recalls the Fall of Adam and Eve, which resulted in the corruption of nature from its original innocence.

My Mind was once the true survey
Of all these Medows fresh and gay;
And in the greenness of the Grass
Did see its Hopes as in a Glass;
When *Juliana* came, and She
What I do to the Grass, does to my Thoughts and Me.

The Mower saw in the abundance of green grass the expectation of much hay. As a reaper, he is a figure for death. The mutable world is his dominion, which he harvests, and which, by its redemption, disappoints his hopes. Paradoxically, the Mower's relation to the meadows and grass, before the coming of Juliana, was in a way similar to that of Adam before his Fall. The world consisted of green signs which he contemplated: "My Mind was once the true survey". The freshness of the meadows and the greenness of the grass recall the Creation, each event of which was a sign. The Creation is a mirror of the divine, but the Mower looking at the grass sees only himself reflected. As a figure for death, he is right to see his hopes in grass, since the Bible often says that flesh is like grass, and will soon wither and die. It is one of Marvell's ironies that the greenness of the grass should be a source of hope to the Mower. Green is a common emblematic colour for hope. Hope is the expectation of a future good. The Mower's hopes are for a good harvest; death hopes for continued dominion over the created world.

But to see things through the Mower's eyes would be to read the poem in the "bad" sense, i.e. as pertaining to the Fall and the results of sin. Our reading is directed towards the "good" sense, seeing in the natural world signs of Christian hope. We are reminded of the goodness of God's creation, of Adam's happiness in contemplation, his garden Paradise, and the fact that the natural world contains signs of God's love and man's redemption. The natural world is still to be used as a glass through which to contemplate God's work.

The first phrase of the refrain ("When *Juliana* came") recalls the many "come" and "came" phrases in the Bible which refer to the Messiah. As I have indicated in the last chapter, "Until Shiloh come" in Genesis 49:10 was a well-known prophecy of the Messiah, often linked with "Blessed *is* he that cometh in the name of the Lord"

(Matthew 21:9). "What I do to the Grass, does to my Thoughts and Me" may bring to mind the prophecy of the fall of Babylon in Jeremiah 50:15: "as she hath done, do unto her". God's vengeance on Babylon is a prophecy of the destruction of the earthly city in Revelation. The long sweeping movement of the refrain is not only appropriate to the swing of the Mower's scythe, but also to the effect of Juliana upon him. The motion consists of two strokes. The Mower reaps the grass; Juliana reaps the Mower. Death is destroyed along with his hopes.

> But these, while I with Sorrow pine,
> Grew more luxuriant still and fine;
> That not one Blade of Grass you spy'd,
> But had a Flower on either side;
> When *Juliana* came, and She
> What I do to the Grass, does to my Thoughts and Me.

The appearance of the flowers is a reminder of Christ's life and a sign of the Apocalypse. The symbolism derives from Canticles 2:12: "The flowers appear on the earth". Bernard says:

> Those, too, who first believed from among the people, the firstfruits of the saints, they were flowers. Their flowers were miracles which, like flowers, produced the fruits of faith.[1]

> The Lord gave His blessing, and our earth yielded her flowers, so that in one day three thousand of the people believed, and in another there were five thousand (Acts ii. 41, and iv. 4); in so short a time did the number of flowers, that is, the multitude of believers, increase. Nor was the cold and frost able to prevail against the flowers which appeared, nor could it cause to perish, as is frequently the case, the fruit of life of which they gave promise.[2]

The flowers are the good seed, or the fruitful, which have multiplied in the world since the coming of Christ's Gospel. The Word must be spread throughout the world before the end of time. The increase of the faithful is a sign that the Mower has lost his dominion and his reaping will soon be brought to an end. The luxuriant meadows contrast to "Luxurious Man" in *The Mower against Gardens*: "Luxurious" in the fallen world includes all sin; but the unfallen creation and the heavenly Paradise are "luxuriant".[3]

Unthankful Medows, could you so
A fellowship so true forego,
And in your gawdy May-games meet,
While I lay trodden under feet?
When *Juliana* came, and She
What I do to the Grass, does to my Thoughts and Me.

The Mower sorrowing and rejected by the meadows ironically brings to mind the prophecy of Christ in Isaiah 53:3: "He is despised and rejected of men; a man of sorrows". The meadows, whether of nature, or metaphorically of mankind, are happy to celebrate the coming of grace and have no reason to thank the Mower. The Mower's claim to "fellowship" with nature is itself ironic, since nature was not willingly subjected to "the bondage of corruption", but has awaited redemption. The symbolism of May-games and "trodden under feet" points to the allegory. "Gawdy" is a pun and includes the Latin meaning still current in the seventeenth century of "to rejoice".[4] Spring is the season of rebirth, renewal and resurrection. It is also the season when the created world will be destroyed and replaced by a new Heaven and earth.[5] May-games are pagan celebrations of seasonal rebirth, but May is Mary's month, and in Christian pastoral poetry Mary is the Queen of May. May is also the month of the Pentecost. Throughout the poem various Christian associations with spring are brought to mind. The traditional call of Whitsuntide is "come". The flowering meadows are symbolic of the Church assembling and rejoicing.[6]

"While I lay trodden under feet" significantly is the exact centre of the poem, and recalls the prediction in Genesis 3:15 that the seed of Eve will bruise the head of the serpent with his heel. Genesis 3:15 has traditionally been taken as a prophecy of the coming of Christ and of His conquest of sin. "Then *cometh* the end, when he shall have delivered up the kingdom to God, even the Father; when he shall have put down all rule and all authority and power. For he must reign, till he hath put all enemies under his feet" (I Corinthians 15:24-25). Winstanley, Marvell's contemporary, applied such millenarian expectations to the present:

> O rejoyce, rejoyce, for the time that the Lord God omnipotent wil raign in al the earth is beginning, and he wil be servant to the Dragon, Beast, and man of the flesh no longer, but wil tread down that murdering power, and make him his footstool.[7]

That the fate of the Mower should recall the conquest of sin and death is further suggested by the biblical word "trodden". In Malachi 4:3 the coming of the sun of justice is followed by the treading down of the wicked.[8]

But what you in Compassion ought,
Shall now by my Revenge be wrought:
And Flow'rs, and Grass, and I and all,
Will in one common Ruine fall.
For *Juliana* comes, and She
What I do to the Grass, does to my Thoughts and Me.

In the fourth stanza there is a shift in tense and perspective from the past to the present and future ("shall now . . . Will . . . *Juliana* comes"). The time of flowers and May-games ("*Juliana* came") has led to the moment when all created things will be destroyed ("*Juliana* comes"). The Apocalypse is a recapitulation of the original Fall, reversing its consequences, bringing an end to mutable, transitory things. The process of time which began with "one common Ruine" and "fall" has now come to its conclusion. But we see the events through the distorting perspective of the Mower; for him the moment of restoration is, ironically, a fall. We might see the Mower's lavish destructiveness here and in the other poems as recalling the Anti-Christ of Revelation.

The Mower claims to preside over a universal destruction. The world is under death's dominion until death is itself destroyed at the last moment before the appearance of "a new heaven and a new earth" (Revelation 21:1): "The last enemy *that* shall be destroyed *is* death" (I Corinthians 15:26). Marvell is here, as throughout the poem, making sophisticated use of traditional emblems and symbols. Sir Thomas More has Time saying "I shall in space destroy both see and lande . . . I shall in proces distroy the world and all".[9] "All", as in *The Mower's Song* and *The Garden* is "all that's made". Time, death and sin preside until "*Juliana* comes", when she brings an end to their reign, ending their hopes.

The Mower's complaint at the meadows' lack of dutiful "Compassion" has its ironies. "Compassion" reminds us of divine compassion. The Mower's harvest or revenge is a figure for the day of wrath: "And the angel thrust in his sickle into the earth, and gathered the vine of the earth, and cast *it* into the great winepress of the wrath of God" (Revelation 14:19). While "one common Ruine" puns on common land, the word "common" read in association with "fellowship" and "Companions" recalls that the Christian faith is held in common: "all that believed were together, and had all things common" (Acts 2:44). The common fields which in *The Mower against Gardens* "to all dispence / A wild and fragrant Innocence" have become a figure for the faithful. The "common Ruine" of all that is made occurs at the end of the world: "The field is the world . . . the harvest is the end of the world" (Matthew 13:38-39). "For the great day of his wrath is come; and who shall be able to stand?"

(Revelation 6:17).

Why should the flowers be cut along with the grass? Partly because flowers are used in the Bible, along with the grass, as a metaphor for the transitory, and partly because flowers are the faithful who must be harvested. Matthew Poole's commentary on Canticles 2:12 is interesting in connection with the harvesting of flowers. After interpreting "the flowers appear on the earth" as spring and the day of grace, he then says that the next phrase ("the time of the singing of birds") was anciently translated as "of *cutting* or *cropping*, not trees, which agrees not with that season, but the flowers".[10] Saints as well as sinners must die "in one common Ruine" before the appearance of the heavenly Jerusalem.

And thus, ye Meadows, which have been
Companions of my thoughts more green,
Shall now the Heraldry become
With which I shall adorn my Tomb;
For *Juliana* comes, and She
What I do to the Grass, does to my Thoughts and Me.

Heraldry points towards the figurative nature of the Mower's speech. The events depicted in the poem are heralds of things to come. The appearance of flowers among the grass, the coming of May and Juliana, announce the season of spring harvest and the beginning of a new year. The events depicted are signs of the multiplication of saints, the Annunciation, the Last Judgment and, finally, the new creation after this world has passed away. The Mower's making of a heraldic tomb for himself from the fallen world reminds us of death's reign over the world of time, and that the destruction of death occurs along with the destruction of the world. Thus the reaped meadows of the world are a fitting funeral monument for the Mower. The Mower's funeral pile would fulfil the prophecy in Jeremiah 51:49: "As Babylon *hath caused* the slain of Israel to fall, so at Babylon shall fall the slain of all the earth".

Within the varied significances brought to mind by the poem, the Mower's revenge also might suggest an imitation of Samson's destruction of the Temple (Judges 16:30). While Samson is a type of Christ because of various parallels between their lives — especially because of his voluntary death which destroyed the enemies of God — the Samson story was also treated typologically as the elect judging the world with Christ at the Last Day.[11] Thus by bringing to mind Samson's death, the Mower offers us a comic Apocalypse.

When the Mower speaks of the meadows as former "Companions of my thoughts more green", he is referring to less ripe thoughts (since his present thoughts are to be harvested by Juliana), and to his former hopes. But in fact the meadows were always unfaithful to the Mower;

awaiting the coming of spring, they were emblematic of the creation awaiting its redemption. The Mower's revenge on the meadows is humorous, since it is an attempt to gain some honour ("Heraldry") out of his destruction by Juliana. His attempt at dignity is amusing and meant to be so by Marvell. It provides the final touch to the witty reversal of perspectives upon which the Mower poems are based. Just as it is really Juliana who is victorious, not the Mower, so the end of death and the passing away of the natural world is due to the powers of Christ, not those of death. What the Mower sees as the ruin of his hopes is figurative of man's restoration. Commenting upon "O death, where *is* thy sting? O grave, where *is* thy victory?" (I Corinthians 15:55), Bernard says that death has no sting any longer but a song of praise and victory.[12]

The Mower poems show Marvell's imagination moving freely between symbol and meaning, playing with humorous incongruities between the Mower's point of view and the allegory. Humour, unlike irony, grows out of familiarity and affection rather than distaste. If my reading of the Mower poems is correct, they could only have been written by someone deeply read in allegorical interpretations of the Bible, and the seeking of types, signs and doctrinal truths in often unlikely places. Marvell has brought to such habits of mind a conscious delight in the fanciful and unexpected.

CHAPTER FOURTEEN

Musicks Empire

Praise ye the LORD. Sing unto the Lord a new song, and his praise in the congregation of saints. Let Israel rejoice in him that made him: let the children of Zion be joyful in their King. Let them praise his name in the dance: let them sing praises unto him with the timbrel and harp. (Psalm 149:1-3)

Musicks Empire offers an example of the problems in understanding Marvell's complex but subtle art; it has received little critical attention and it seems likely that even those who have written on Marvell do not realise that it requires close scrutiny and some scholarship to be understood properly. Indeed critics have usually assumed that the poem is a slight lyric in praise of music, which concludes with a glancing nod in the direction of either Lord Fairfax or possibly Cromwell. I know only of one instance where the poem has been correctly seen as religious and as alluding to Christ.[1] Properly read, *Musicks Empire* will be seen as a superb example of seventeenth century allegory in which the traditional Christian view of the history of the world is recalled by analogy to the creation and development of music. *Musicks Empire* is based upon several interlocking analogies. The progress of music throughout the poem recalls the history of the world, the rise of civilisation as recorded in the early books of the Old Testament, the increase and multiplication of mankind, the founding of the Davidic kingdom and other events which lead to the coming of Christ. Whereas the speaker in *The Mower against Gardens* sees the rise of civilisation as a fall from innocence into corruption, *Musicks Empire* recalls that the history of mankind has a divine purpose.

The Bible as read by biblical exegetes was an expanded metaphor. The Creation of the world in Genesis was seen as a sacrament of the future, and the seven days of Creation were seen as signs of the seven ages of the world. While there were various schemes for the seven ages, it was generally agreed that the first five ages were to be found recorded in the Old Testament, that the sixth age is from the coming of Christ to the present, and the seventh age is the Second Coming.[2]

The first stanza of the poem alludes to the Creation both of the world and of music. The next four stanzas bring to mind various Old Testament events. In stanza five music is described as the "Mosaique of the Air". Moses was the first historian, being the supposed author of the early books of the Old Testament. Moses is also a prophet of Christ. Music serves a similar function, symbolically showing that the history of the world is a preparation for the coming of Christ. The sixth, and last, stanza is analogous to the sixth age, the Christian centuries. Towards the end of the poem the implied typology is complex and subtle. The allegory is based on understanding the traditional meanings of the various types and forerunners of Christ. Moses prepares for Joshua; David prepares for Solomon; John the Baptist prepares for Christ. Joshua's conquest of Jericho is the overthrowing of sin; Solomon's Temple is a prophecy of the Church. Christ conquers sin and raises a new temple of believers. While Marvell does not directly allude to each of the forerunners, his words and phrases bring them to mind.

First was the World as one great Cymbal made,
Where Jarring Windes to infant Nature plaid.
All Musick was a solitary sound,
To hollow Rocks and murm'ring Fountains bound.

The first two lines of the poem refer directly to the Creation of the world rather than to music itself. "In the beginning" the world was made as a symbol. The pun points directly to the analogy between the development of music and biblical history. Marvell will continue to suggest a double narrative throughout the poem, since the harmony of divine art allows man to see all creation, including the development of music, as symbolic. If the Creation was a symbol (sacrament, sign) of the future of the world, the cymbal is an appropriate comparison since cymbals are used to praise God (Psalm 150:5) and are among the instruments which will later be used at the Temple service (II Samuel 6:5). If you make the world the way you make a cymbal you hammer or shape the raw material into a specific form; Marvell is alluding to the tradition that the world was first made as unformed matter which was subsequently given form.[3] The greatest sign at the Creation was the Word itself which looks forward to the coming of Christ (John 1:1). Christ is present at the Creation as part of the Trinity: "All things were made by him; and without him was not any thing made that was made" (John 1:3).

When "the earth was without form, and void; and darkness *was* upon the face of the deep" (Genesis 1:2), the only music was potentially in the symbol.[4] It existed in a confused form, not yet being tuned. "Where Jarring Windes to infant Nature plaid"[5] points to this immature state of Creation. The description brings to mind: "And the Spirit of God moved upon the face of the waters" (Genesis 1:2). The Spirit hovering over the waters was seen as a prophecy of the Annunciation; Mary will be "found with child of the Holy Ghost" (Matthew 1:18).

"All Musick was a solitary sound, / To hollow Rocks and murm'ring Fountains bound" means that the only music was the resonances and echoes found in the natural world. The world now has form. The events of the second day of Creation have taken place; however, the events of the sixth day have not yet occurred, and music is solitary, as "*there was* not a man to till the ground" (Genesis 2:5). But why was all music bound to nature? Why was there not heavenly music? The reason is that God has not yet completed the Creation; the angelic choirs have not yet broken out singing and the harmony of the spheres has not yet come into being.

Jubal first made the wilder Notes agree;
And *Jubal* tuned Musicks *Jubilee*:
He call'd the *Ecchoes* from their sullen Cell,
And built the Organs City where they dwell.

Jubal is "the father of all such as handle the harp and organ" (Genesis 4:21). During the Middle Ages commentators said that Jubal learned about intervals from watching his brother, Tubalcain, strike various resonances while hammering, and that Jubal similarly experimented with pitch before going on to make harps and organs.[6] Both brothers were seen as types of Christ during the Middle Ages.[7] Marvell imagines Jubal as discovering agreement between intervals and the tempering of the musical scale; also as having built the organ from the resonances found in nature. Jubal's role within the development of music is treated as analogous to the role of the Son in the Creation of the world. Commentators usually said that the Father's power created the world, the Son's shaping wisdom was responsible for the disposition of things, while the Holy Spirit perfected the work by vivifying or ornamenting things.[8] "*Jubal* tuned Musicks *Jubilee*" recalls the angelic choirs singing in praise of God's work at the Creation. Tuning alludes to the concord of harmony of the Creation. "Jubilee" is used in the sense of a time of rejoicing, exalting or praising. Jubilee is connected with the Sabbath (Leviticus 25:9ff); the Sabbath is a time of jubilation commemorating the Creation, especially the seventh day which is itself a figure of eternal peace. Music was first ordained for worship of God and took as its model the harmony of the sphere. Bartas describes the seventh day of Creation as "the grand *Iubile*, the Feast of Feasts,/Sabaoth of Sabaoths".[9] (The Bodleian manuscript of Marvell's poems reads "And Jubal tun'd Musick's first Jubilee").

"He call'd the *Ecchoes* from their sullen Cell" brings to mind the creation of man.[10] Man is formed in God's image from the dust of the ground (Genesis 2:7). "And built the Organs City where they dwell" might recall the creation of man's body, since the body was traditionally compared to a civic unit. It certainly alludes to Paradise (Genesis 2:8), since the city is described in stanza three as "that lovely place". Marvell also has in mind Amphion whose playing on the lyre was supposed to have caused the walls of Thebes to form themselves from scattered stones. Another founder of music who was supposed to have animated lifeless and motionless objects was Orpheus. In iconography Orpheus and Amphion are types of Christ. The Book of Psalms is called *Organum* or musical instrument in Latin.[11] The Psalms were traditionally supposed to have been written by David. They are hymns in praise of God, and prophetic of the coming of Christ. Augustine says that "David had great skill in songs, and loved music, not out of his private pleasure, but in his zealous faith: whereby, in the service of his (and the true) God, in diversity of harmonious and proportionate sounds, he mystically describes the concord and unity of the celestial city of God, composed of divers particulars. Almost all his prophecies are in his psalms".[12] Building the "Organs City" would be founding a type of David's city or Jerusalem. The earthly Jerusalem is itself a shadow of the heavenly city. Earthly music imitates divine harmony. The world is God's great organ, tuned by Christ to bring concord and harmony.[13] While both the earthly and heavenly cities have their origin in Adam and his descendants, Christ is the builder of the heavenly city.

> Each sought a consort in that lovely place;
> And Virgin Trebles wed the manly Base.
> From whence the Progeny of numbers new
> Into harmonious Colonies withdrew.

Each interval is joined in accord within the organ, as are the upper and lower registers. From the wedding of the sounds new harmonies are created, which in the next stanza will colonise various instruments. "Numbers" brings to mind the relationship of mathematical ratios to harmony and rhythm. They are "numbers new", having been derived from the one. Marvell's treatment of number and music here has similarities to Augustine's *De Musica* and the platonic tradition. Odd numbers are masculine, even numbers are feminine, and their union is a form of marriage, regarded as an emblem of generation.

The development of music recalls that mankind was supposed to have its origin in one couple and their progeny. "Each sought a consort in that lovely place" brings to mind Adam in the Garden of Paradise seeking a help meet. "And Virgin Trebles wed the manly Base" recalls the sacrament of matrimony: "In order that the conjugal society of man and woman might not be idle, after the sacrament of matrimony there was added the office which was to have been fulfilled in the mingling of flesh, so that those joined in matrimony might be exercised through obedience unto virtue and might bear fruit through the generation of progeny".[14] The sacrament of marriage is a sign that God willed marriage, so that man might "Be fruitful, and multiply, and replenish the earth" (Genesis 1:28); it is also a sacrament of the society which exists between Christ and His Church, and a promise of the heavenly marriage. The withdrawal of the "Progeny" from "that lovely place" reminds us of man's expulsion from Paradise.

Marvell's imagination is allegorical, not metaphorical. His phrases bring to mind a cluster of associations. If we are reminded of Adam and Eve, we are also led to think of such later biblical events as the Deluge and the recolonising of the world by Noah's children ("the Progeny of numbers new").[15] The "Progeny of numbers new" might be seen as an anticipation of the numbering of the Israelites: "Unto these the land shall be divided for an inheritance according to the number of names" (Numbers 26:53). The inheritance is read as a figure for the rewards of the elect. All history is brought to mind as unfolding in a harmonious plan from the Creation, when the world was made one great symbol.

Some to the Lute, some to the Viol went,
And others chose the Cornet eloquent.
These practising the Wind, and those the Wire,
To sing Mens Triumphs, or in Heavens quire.

In the fourth stanza sound has progressed to instrumental music. Marvell humorously imagines the sounds choosing appropriate instruments for themselves. Music divides into the secular and the religious. Marvell makes the traditional association of stringed instruments with religion and wind instruments with secular life. The development of the various instruments and kinds of music brings to mind the specialisation of labour by the progeny of Cain. The various kingdoms of music are analogous to the kingdoms founded by Noah's sons (Genesis 10:5),[16] the dispersal from Babel when humanity was scattered over the earth (Genesis 11:9), the parting of Abraham and Lot (Genesis 13:9), and the division of Canaan by the Israelites. These various events show the unity of mankind from Adam's seed which increased and multiplied and will subdue and conquer the earth, preparing for the spreading of the Gospel throughout the world. Some men will dedicate themselves to the earthly city; some to the heavenly city.[17]

Then Musick, the Mosaique of the Air,
Did of all these a solemn noise prepare:
With which She gain'd the Empire of the Ear,
Including all between the Earth and Sphear.

Music is the "Mosaique of the Air" in being made up of various notes which might be said to form a mosaic of song ("Ayres") and in being the Moses of the air. It was believed that Moses wrote the Old Testament, including books which record events after his death. He wrote them prophetically, having been given a vision of the future by God. The Old Testament story of Israel as told by Moses was allegorised as a prophecy of the coming of Christ.[18] Moses prepares for the coming of Christ: "The LORD thy God will raise up unto thee a Prophet from the midst of thee, of thy brethren, like unto me; unto him ye shall hearken" (Deuteronomy 18:15). The "Mosaique of the Air" also alludes to David, author of the Psalms, a forerunner of Christ. David, who was supposedly a great musician, added melody to prayer. Moses leads the Jews out of Egypt to the Holy Land. David completes the conquest of the Promised Land and unites the kingdom into an empire: "Thus David the son of Jesse reigned over all Israel" (I Chronicles 29:26). Moses is succeeded by Joshua who enters the Holy Land. David is succeeded by Solomon who builds the Temple. Both "prepare". Besides Moses and David we might think of Elijah (who "must first come" [Mark 9:11]) and of John the Baptist.

"Did of all these a solemn noise prepare". The various instruments come together for a religious service. "Solemn" brings to mind the Psalms and the Feast of the Tabernacles. The Psalms are solemn music. The Feast of the Tabernacles is known as a "solemn feast".[19] It is a Sabbath festival in praise of God's goodness; it is also a memorial of the seventh day of Creation. It is allegorised as a prophecy of Christ's Sacrifice and the joys of the Church at the Second Coming. It is prepared for by the solemn "blowing of trumpets" (Leviticus 23:24). The feast itself took place on the fifteenth day of the seventh month, and lasted seven days: "it *is* a solemn assembly" (Leviticus 23:36) of thanksgiving: "and ye shall rejoice before the LORD your God" (Leviticus 23:40). In John 7 the Feast is linked with the Lord's Day and Christ gives it apocalyptic associations. Methodius, after drawing a parallel between the seven days of Creation and the Feast of Tabernacles, says: "But when the days shall be accomplished and God shall cease to work in this creation of His in that Seventh Month, the great day of the resurrection, then will our Feast of Tabernacles be celebrated to the Lord. The things mentioned in Leviticus are merely types and figures of this Feast".[20] "Noise" has the sense of rejoicing: "Make a joyful noise unto God, all ye lands" (Psalm 66:1). Music's development into a "solemn noise" brings to mind David, who writes the Psalms and prophesies that Solomon will build the Temple — which is a figure for the Church (I Chronicles 22:5). Music has prepared a religious service which looks forward and does homage to Christ, the "gentler Conqueror" of stanza six.

"With which She gain'd the Empire of the Ear,/Including all between the Earth and Sphear". This music conquers the kingdom of the ear with its "solemn noise" or rejoicing; it is not, however, the heavenly music of the spheres since that is not heard by the ear. This music is heard by man — the harmony of the Bible or God's word being spread to all nations, originally by the Israelites, and then by the Church. The Jews first carry the divine message as the promise of a Messiah from the Davidic line. The Christians inherit the message and recognise the "gentler Conqueror".

Victorious sounds! yet here your Homage do
Unto a gentler Conqueror then you;
Who though He flies the Musick of his praise,
Would with you Heavens Hallelujahs raise.

The "victorious sounds" have increased and multiplied from their original solitary state until they have conquered the kingdom of the air. They are equivalent to the multiplication of mankind from Adam's stock. They recall the establishment of the Davidic kingdom and the spreading of the Gospel throughout the world. Historically, the "gentler Conqueror" who succeeds David is Solomon. The beginning of Solomon's reign was marked by peace, and he was known as the peaceful or peacemaker. "Raise" alludes to the Temple.[21] While David planned the Temple, God did not allow him to build it because he was a "man of war" (I Chronicles 28:3). David built the temple of psalmody, but the Temple was built by Solomon. "Homage" brings to mind Solomon's anointment: "Then Solomon sat on the throne of the LORD as king instead of David his father, and prospered; and all Israel obeyed him. And all the princes, and the mighty men, and all the sons likewise of king David, submitted themselves unto Solomon the king" (I Chronicles 29:23-24). God's promise of Solomon's reign is, however, read as a prophecy of the coming of Christ, the Church and the eternal kingdom (I Chronicles 22:9-10). That the Temple was built by Solomon rather than David was interpreted as showing that the Old Testament prepares for the New Testament, the Law prepares for the Gospel, and Old Testament prophecies of a Messiah apply to Christ.

Just as Genesis, according to commentators, reveals the coming of

Christ, so Chronicles is a prophecy of Christ. One relation between Genesis and Chronicles is that the latter begins with a recapitulation of Adam's descendants up to David and his children, thus showing that the history of the world was leading towards the establishment of David's lineage to the throne of Israel. Christ was supposed to have been born from David's line.[22] Another connection between Chronicles and the Christian interpretation of the divine scheme is that Second Chronicles ends with the destruction of Jerusalem and the Temple, thus showing that Israel's function had come to an end, and that the covenant had passed to Christians. Some writers said that the whole of history, from the Creation through the various events recorded in the Old Testament, led to the empire of Rome, so that Christ could be born into the universal peace of Augustus's reign, and the Gospel could be spread throughout the world.[23]

Christ then is the "gentler Conqueror" to Whom music pays homage; He is the "Prince of Peace" prophesied in Isaiah 9:6-7.[24] David and Solomon fulfil the promise of a kingdom, made to Abraham in Genesis 12:1-2; but the kingdom is only a shadow of the eternal kingdom prophesied in Genesis 12:3.[25] Whereas David conquers kingdoms through warfare, Christ conquers sin through His obedience and death. "He flies the Musick of his praise" alludes to Church music. Peter, thinking of David's prophecies concerning Solomon and the Davidic line, sees the fulfilment in Christ's Resurrection and Ascension. The Davidic kingdom becomes the heavenly kingdom (Acts 2:30-36). The Psalms are songs of praise in which Israel praises God, but they are also read as pertaining to Christ.

It is man's duty to praise or glorify God. In raising Hallelujahs you are raising a temple of believers and joining the angels who also sing Psalms.[26] Christ invites man to join in the glorification of God by joining the community of believers. Such hymns look forward to the elect taking their place in the heavenly choir:

> O may we soon again renew that Song,
> And keep in tune with Heav'n, till God ere long
> To his celestial consort us unite,
> To live with him, and sing in endles morn of light.[27]

Hallelujah means praise. Psalm 150 begins: "Praise ye the LORD. Praise God in his sanctuary". Sanctuary can be interpreted as His Temple. Psalm 150 continues:

> Praise him in the firmament of his power. Praise him for his mighty acts: praise him according to his excellent greatness. Praise him with the sound of the trumpet: praise him with the psaltery and harp. Praise him with the timbrel and dance: praise him with stringed instruments and organs. Praise him upon the

> loud cymbals: praise him upon the high sounding cymbals. Let every thing that hath breath praise the LORD. Praise ye the LORD.

"Trumpet" in verse three can be translated as "cornet". Here in Psalm 150 are the instruments which, in *Musicks Empire*, prepare a song of praise to God's work and Christ: the organ, the cymbal, the cornet, and stringed instruments.

Musicks Empire is in six stanzas, symbolic of the six days of Creation and the first six ages of the world. "So too it is clear that the entire creation of the world was achieved out of the harmony of the number 6: for *in six days the Lord made heaven and earth and all the things that are in them*, since the creative power of the Word contains the number 6 insofar as it produces bodies".[28] The sixth day witnessed the creation of man, the sixth age is the present era which will last until the Second Coming of Christ. The sixth day of Creation is symbolic of the period of the Church. God created man who is to be the temple of Christ. On the seventh day God rested, which is a figure of the seventh age of eternal repose, when the elect will celebrate the Feast of Tabernacles with Christ after the Resurrection.[29] It is fitting that Christ should be implicit in the beginning and end of the poem, since He is the Alpha and Omega, the first and the last:

> For the works of restoration are of much greater dignity than the works of foundation, because the latter were made for servitude, that they might be subject to man standing: the former, for salvation, that they might raise man fallen. Therefore, the works of foundation, as if of little importance, were accomplished in six days, but the works of restoration can not be completed except in six ages. Yet six are placed over against six that the Restorer may be proven to be the same as the Creator.[30]

CHAPTER FIFTEEN

The Garden

For the invisible things of him from the creation of the world are clearly seen, being understood by the things that are made, even his eternal power and Godhead. (Romans 1:20)

The Garden is the most completely imagined of Marvell's poems. While the garden and the emotions experienced through it are solidly realised within the poem, they are also felt to be symbols — not disembodied symbols, but concrete manifestations of spiritual realities. Each of the speaker's senses is engaged ("Upon my Mouth", "was ever seen", "Fair quiet", "Into my hands", "fragrant Zodiack"), but his pleasures lead him to see God mirrored in the world. His enjoyment is a simple, direct meditation on the Book of Creatures, which leads to contemplation of the idea of happiness and the source of the mind's knowledge and powers. This results in an ecstatic vision of God's "various Light". The progression of experiences in the poem is similar to the various steps by which Augustine, Bonaventura, Richard of Saint Victor and others have described the mind's ascent from the sensible world to mystical communion with God.

Marvell chooses a garden as a place for contemplation because of its associations with the greenness of the Creation, Paradise, the garden of the new Jerusalem, and because of various etymological links between "garden" and "Paradise".[1] In Christian symbolism the Church is a garden, the soul is a garden, the Virgin is an enclosed garden, while Adam, Christ and God are gardeners. Plants and herbs are emblems or signs. In the Dedication of his *Herball*, Gerard says:

> But the delights are in the outward senses: the principal delight is in his mind, singularly enriched with the knowledge of these visible things, setting forth to us the invisible wisdome and admirable workmanship of Almighty God.[2]

In the introduction, Gerard recalls the Creation of the world in Genesis and associates gardens with Paradise and "perfect happinesse". He says that Adam was the first herbalist and gardener. It is because Marvell can assume the reader's familiarity with such habits of imagining, that he is free to play sophisticated variations on the theme of the garden as a place of contemplation.

How vainly men themselves amaze
To win the Palm, the Oke, or Bayes;
And their uncessant Labours see
Crown'd from some single Herb or Tree,
Whose short and narrow verged Shade
Does prudently their Toyles upbraid;
While all Flow'rs and all Trees do close
To weave the Garlands of repose.

The poem begins with an ironic contrast between the peaceful shelter offered by the natural world, and the symbols of achievement earned by men in society. To labour to be crowned by "the Palm, the Oke, or Bayes" is useless, since "some single Herb or Tree" offers little protection in contrast to the abundant shade found in the garden. The natural world serves as an emblem, upbraiding man for his "uncessant Labours" and lack of prudence. He misuses God's creation to crown himself; and this is vanity. It is also a trap (a maze) created by human pride ("themselves amaze"), since achievement results in little protection ("Shade") or rest ("repose"), in contrast to the garden which is an enclosed or protected place. The garden upbraids man by reminding him of death and the vanity of his accomplishments. It is a place for contemplating the goodness of God's creation and the sin of man's disobedience.

Fair quiet, have I found thee here,
And Innocence thy Sister dear!
Mistaken long, I sought you then
In busie Companies of Men.
Your sacred Plants, if here below,
Only among the Plants will grow.
Society is all but rude,
To this delicious Solitude.

Silence and innocence are necessary to contemplation, because the mind must not be distracted by illicit desires. It must be separated from and purged of worldly temptations. Contemplation is best accomplished in solitude where the company of "Innocence thy Sister" is presumably more conducive to quiet than "in busie Companies of Men". As the garden is a place for meditation, providing emblems of the sacred plants of Heaven, no wonder "Society is all but rude, / To this delicious Solitude". It is delicious solitude not only in the sense of "enjoyable" and "exquisite", but also in the sense of "beloved", as in the Latin *dilectio*.[3] It is similar to the "am'rous . . . lovely green" of stanza three. It is a sign of God's love, and God should be loved through contemplation of it; just as Adam was set in Paradise to praise God's works through contemplation. "Here below" leads the mind towards Heaven, as quiet and innocence are said to be offshoots of their eternal realities.

No white nor red was ever seen
So am'rous as this lovely green.
Fond Lovers, cruel as their Flame,
Cut in these Trees their Mistress name.
Little, Alas, they know, or heed,
How far these Beauties Hers exceed!
Fair Trees! where s'eer your barkes I wound,
No Name shall but your own be found.

Red and white are used here as colours of secular love. Gardens of red and white flowers contrast to "this lovely green". The green is amorous and lovely because, like the greenness of creation, it is a sign of divine love. It is also a sign of hope and faith, emblematic of man's expectations and future Paradise.[4] Fond lovers are "cruel as their Flame" because they misuse affection; carving names in trees is an abuse of God's creation to celebrate erotic love. In parodying secular poetic imagery ("cruel", "Flame"), Marvell alludes to the difference in the nature of the object loved.

Besides referring to affection, "fond" can mean "credulous" or "naive". "Fond Lovers" are naive or foolish to prefer cruel mistresses instead of such "am'rous" green. Their naivety is shown by their not knowing or heeding "How far these Beauties Hers exceed". Marvell often makes use of the contrast between words in their biblical and erotic significances. "Know" can mean sexual knowledge; however, "know" and "heed" are both biblical words for a correct understanding of and attitude towards God's word. "Fond Lovers" lack spiritual understanding. In the joys of the garden they should seek to love God.[5]

When we have run our Passions heat,
Love hither makes his best retreat.
The *Gods*, that mortal Beauty chase,
Still in a Tree did end their race.
Apollo hunted *Daphne* so,
Only that She might Laurel grow.
And *Pan* did after *Syrinx* speed,
Not as a Nymph, but for a Reed.

A "retreat" is a period of retirement for meditation and contemplation. After vainly seeking happiness through worldly achievements (stanza one), friendship (stanza two) or erotic love (stanza three), we withdraw from the world to meditate. As in the previous stanzas, Marvell's imagination circles round various aspects of love. Love in the sense of desire or affection is in itself neither good nor bad; its use, or object, determines its value. Love directed towards the world and time is suggested by "run our Passions heat"; "run" and "heat" bringing to mind a race. Love of the world distracts the mind from the true object of its affection, God.

Marvell introduces a purposeful ambiguity. Is it our love, or the loved object that is pursued, which makes its retreat? Is the garden a place for purgation or a place where love is found? The justification of the ambiguity is that our love and the object of our love are the same, since our love, however used, is from God ("the Love which us doth bind"[6]). "Retreat" suggests repose or rest. Just as only the garden can give the shade, protection or crown mistakenly sought in winning "the Palm, the Oke, or Bayes", so the garden can best provide the unchanging love sought elsewhere.

The garden is not an object of love in itself; as a "retreat" it provides opportunities for meditation on divine love, and on the repose awaiting man in the heavenly garden. It is a place rather for the contemplative than the active life. Our "Passions heat" and love making "his best retreat" may remind us of Adam and Eve attempting to hide themselves from God after having eaten the apple. Although they were unsuccessful in hiding themselves, this event might be considered a type of the protection sought under the shade of Christ. Next we might reflect on the tradition that Ecclesiastes was written by Solomon in old age after having renounced the pleasures of the flesh, as represented by his love affair with the Queen of Sheba.[7] *The Garden* begins like Ecclesiastes (1:2-3) with a statement of the vanities of worldly endeavours. The contemplative pleasures of the garden are the love which Solomon wrongly sought elsewhere.

"The *Gods*, that Mortal Beauty chase, / Still in a Tree did end their race" has a similar ambiguity to that of the first two lines of the stanza. Do the Gods or "mortal Beauty" become Trees? The reference, of course, is to mythology, especially as told in Ovid's *Metamorphoses*; but we should remember that pagan mythology and Ovid were usually treated allegorically during the Renaissance. If we read "race" as "progeny" we might recall Adam and Eve, two immortal or God-like beings, who sought knowledge of good and evil ("mortal Beauty chase") in a "Tree", and brought death upon themselves and their progeny ("end their race"). Or we could see in the tree an allusion to Christ, the tree of life. The seed promised to Eve and symbolically carried by the Israelites ("race") is Christ, the fruit-bearing apple tree of Canticles, Isaiah and Revelation. Marvell's syntax is designed to lead the mind towards allegorisations. Christ, Who pursues the soul, ends on the tree of the Cross, and as the tree of life. He chases mortal beauty in the sense of lifting man's vision to the Cross and eternal life.

Double syntax is seen in Marvell's moralising of the pursuit of Daphne and Syrinx. Do the gods vainly chase them only to find that they have become laurel and reed, or do they purposely hunt them with such a metamorphosis in mind? If they chase them only to be themselves deceived, it would be emblematic of the vanity of worldly desires and an illustration of all flesh being grass. But if they hunt them intentionally to make them plants, they are similar to Christ Who hunts man's soul to plant him in Paradise. Apollo and Pan are common poetic images for Christ, while the laurel or bay tree and the reeds grow on the banks of the river of the heavenly garden.

In Golding's translation of Ovid's *Metamorphoses*, we are told that Daphne transformed into a laurel is a mirror of virginity, while Syrinx is an example of chastity.[8] It was common to see figures of Christ and the Virgin in the *Metamorphoses*. Under April in the gloss to Spenser's *Shepherd's Calender*, the story of Syrinx and Pan is explained as being among other things a figure for "Christ himselfe, who is the verye Pan and god of Sheepheardes". Thus, Pan chases Syrinx not as a mythological nymph, or a young girl; he is instead like the bridegroom wooing the spouse or Christ wooing the soul in Canticles.[9]

What wond'rous Life in this I lead!
Ripe Apples drop about my head;
The Luscious Clusters of the Vine
Upon my Mouth do crush their Wine;
The Nectaren, and curious Peach,
Into my hands themselves do reach;
Stumbling on Melons, as I pass,
Insnar'd with Flow'rs, I fall on Grass.

The garden is a place of signs. It is a window to eternity through which is glimpsed the Creation, man's first Paradise and Fall, prophecies of Christ, the Sacrifice, and the heavenly garden. A wonder is a sign or miracle. The works and days of God at the Creation are signs of His goodness, as will be shown throughout created time. The various fruits Marvell includes in stanza five can be found in medieval and Renaissance descriptions of Paradise. The speaker's happiness recalls man's innocence. It is the happy life (*vita beata*) sought by all men but only realised by those who live in Christ.

The nectarine is one of the fruits of Paradise. Its name suggests nectar; as a symbol of immortality it could be seen as a fruit of the tree of life. The nectarine is a kind of peach (*Persicum malum*) or Persian apple.[10] A "curious Peach" might be an emblem of curiosity, one of the causes of Eve's Fall.[11] But an exquisite "pêche" (péché) may refer to the paradox of the Fortunate Fall. Melon also involves a pun on the Greek for apple. Since to name is to understand and words are symbols, biblical commentators were as ingenious as any modern literary critic in finding significances in etymologies and aural similarities, even at the risk of being incorrect. The Latin word for apple (*malum*) can mean any variety of fruit, and because of its possible associations with malice was often replaced by the Greek *melum* in commentaries on Canticles 2:3:

> But lest the similarity between the words should lead some simpler folk to think an apple tree (*arbor mali*) an evil tree (*arbor mala*) and take its name as derived from malice, let us for our part call it the 'melum tree (*arborem meli*), using the Greek word which, as a matter of fact, is more familiar than *malum* to the simpler Latins. For it is better for us to offend the philologists than to put any difficulty in our readers' way when we expound the truth.[12]

As can be seen from Origen, it is not overly ingenious to see the nectarine, peach and melon as allusions to apples.

The sensuous imagery of stanza five has erotic resonances ("Luscious", "crush", "Peach", "themselves do reach"). If, remembering Isaiah 40:6 we substitute "flesh" for "grass" in "I fall on Grass", stanza five would conclude with a moment of sexual penetration, while the ecstatic emotions felt in the next two stanzas might be seen as the death or rapture following consummation.[13] The allusion to death fits, since the height of mystical rapture, when the mind is in repose, is often described as a kind of death, in some way analogous to the death of Christ. It is a passing over (Passover; "as I pass") the Jordan to the Promised Land; a passing over from the death of the flesh to eternal life. In stanza six the mind will create "other Seas".

Stanza five uses the well-known symbolism of Christ the vine, Whose blood is the wine crushed from grapes.[14] The Passion is seen in the bruising or crushing; and the blood of His wounds is the sacraments. It is significant that the allusion to Christ's Sacrifice ("Wine") occurs at line 36, the exact centre of the poem. If we have an allusion to the sacramental wine, where is the bread, symbolic of the flesh? In the fruits which at the Creation were given to man "for meat" (Genesis 1:29).

The passivity of the speaker is in keeping with his contemplative nature. We are reminded of traditional descriptions of Adam walking through Paradise, while nature pays homage to God's image by pressing delights upon him. The fruits are sacraments of God's blessings, especially the grace brought by Christ, which is necessary before fallen mankind can turn his affections from carnal things towards love of God. Contemplation of God is only possible through Christ.

While stumbling, insnared (snared), fall, and grass might bring to mind Eve who stumbles into the serpent's snares, the main associations have to do with Christ Whose death recapitulates mankind's first Fall. In Isaiah 8:14-15 the Messiah is prophesied as both a sanctuary and "a stone of stumbling". Poole says that such a prophecy was necessary as otherwise the rejection of the Messiah by the Jews would shake the faith of those who did believe in Him; "whereas now the accomplishment hereof was a notable confirmation of the faith, and an evidence that Christ was the true Messiah".[15] The speaker while lying on the grass undergoes a mystical experience, which can be described as a kind of sleep or death, since the mind withdraws itself and the soul is liberated.

> Mean while the Mind, from pleasure less,
> Withdraws into its happiness:
> The Mind, that Ocean where each kind
> Does streight its own resemblance find;
> Yet it creates, transcending these,
> Far other Worlds, and other Seas;
> Annihilating all that's made
> To a green Thought in a green Shade.

The speaker lying on the grass proceeds to contemplation of the divine image within the mind. Through meditation on the garden he has been purged of false affections and carnal desires. Now the mind purifies itself by withdrawing from the pleasures of the senses to find happiness within.

"Mean while" warns us that the steps up the contemplative ladder which follow occur almost simultaneously, in a flash of insight. The mind withdraws, creates, annihilates; it is God-like, being happy and having all ideas within itself. The variety of simultaneous activities also resembles the divine mind, in which all time is present. While the mind withdraws from lesser pleasures into its happiness, we would not be wrong to understand that lesser pleasures led the mind to seek the notion of happiness within itself. If the happiness of the mind is superior to the pleasures of the senses, the mind can only find concepts by first experiencing particulars. The movement is from lesser to greater, from multitude to oneness. The mind ascends from shadows to ideas to the source of ideas, the divine mind: "what exists in actuality is an image of what exists in the mind of man, and what exists in the mind of man is an image of what exists in the divine Mind".[16]

It was a medieval commonplace still current in the seventeenth century that oceans contain examples of all creatures found on dry land. The mind is like an ocean having all concepts or ideas ("resemblance") within it. "Kind" means species and recalls the various kinds created by God, Who, having all ideas within His mind, is often spoken of as a fountain or ocean. To find "streight" means at once and unfallen (upright). "Find" can mean recover. Augustine says that we cannot find what is lost without knowing what is lost. We cannot seek for happiness without having some remembrance of happiness. The kinds can only find their image within the mind because it has an image of their unfallen or original condition. For man to find his resemblance would be to recover the knowledge of his immortal soul created in God's image. Thus the contemplative mind, purged from sensual distractions, becomes introverted and recollects (pulls together) its diffuse notions of happiness. It finds within itself all ideas, remembers its original condition, and recovers the divine image. Its very activities (to create, annihilate) recall its source in God.

"Creates, transcending these, / Far other Worlds and other Seas" shows that the mind is not simply passive, collecting images from particulars; it is also creative. It makes images out of nothing, similar to God's Creation of the world from nothing. Augustine says that the mind's source of ideas does not solely come from the created world; its knowledge of what it has not seen must come from God by way of the soul which is made in His image. (Anselm and Bonaventura say the soul is a "creating essence" made in God's image.) The various activities of the mind are examples of how, seeking the sources of our knowledge, we come to God.

What are the "other Worlds and other Seas"? Since some writers claimed that in contemplation one was transported to unexplored regions of the universe, "Far other Worlds" might seem to be an allusion to the often discussed possibility that God created other, still unfallen, worlds. But if we read "transcending" in connection with the mind, it would suggest the mind's ideas of heavenly worlds. The mind, contemplating the divine image within itself, contemplates God's creation of the heavenly hierarchy, of which it has a "memory". Just as the oceans contain examples of all land creatures, so whatever is found in our world can also be found in the heavens:

> As the Earth hath beasts, the *Heavens* have their Lion and Beare, the great and lesse. Where the Sea hath fish, the *Heavens* have theirs, and waters enough, as wel above as under the Firmament. As the Ayre hath birds, the *Heavens* have Angels, as birds of Paradise. And if the upper Region of the Elements be of fire,

> the Seraphins are al of amourous fires of Devine love, and the highest order of the blessed Spirits.[17]

And if our eye falls on "annihilating" in the next line of the poem, we will recall the creation of a "new heaven and a new earth" at the end of time (Revelation 21:1). Such knowledge of future time is also found in the memory. We trace God in all our ideas, whether of the past, present, future, here or far above.

"Annihilating all that's made / To a green Thought in a green Shade" parallels "Stumbling on Melons, as I pass, / Insnar'd with Flow'rs, I fall on Grass". The various activities of the mind come to a halt, being replaced by a green thought, as the speaker lies under the shade of the plants and trees. While "green Thought" is no doubt appropriate to someone who has fallen on, or is resting on, grass, a literal reading of the two lines does not take us very far towards an understanding of what is implied. The mind annihilating "all that's made" recalls the passing away of the created world in Revelation 21:1: A key biblical passage is Isaiah 65:17: "For, behold, I create new heavens and a new earth: and the former shall not be remembered, nor come into mind". Poole interprets this as a promise of Christ's bringing a new church and "a new worship";[18] Augustine reads into it a promise of the saints' eternal bliss.[19] A green thought could be contemplation of the greenness of the Creation through the greenness of the garden, or it could be a thought of the heavenly garden in the midst of the new Jerusalem. Since the greenness of the Creation is a sign of the latter, the creation and destruction of the world merge into one thought, analogous to the simultaneity of all time in God's mind. Since green is, according to which emblem-book you consult, the colour of hope or faith, a green thought would be on God's promises.

As the mind ascends in its contemplation, it annihilates images of the world to a single all-embracing green thought. "Annihilate" is often used in mystical writings to describe the loss of conscious thought necessary for higher stages of contemplation. Richard of Saint Victor says:

> God can only be known by plunging the soul into the darkness of complete renunciation of the senses, of body and of mind. There it experiences the ray of divine light and becomes united to God by love in total 'unknowing'.[20]

As the word "annihilate" suggests, the mind has been emptied of all imagined forms or images. The mind being dead to the distractions of the world, the soul is ready to rise above itself and ascend towards illumination.[21]

The speaker has reached the stage of contemplation described in the *Ancrene Riwle* where true anchoresses are:

> birds of heaven, flying high up, or sitting and singing in happiness on the green boughs, that is, lifting their minds to the happiness of heaven, which never fades but is always green, and sitting in this greenness, singing happily, that is, remaining in such thoughts with gladness of heart, like people singing.[22]

Significantly the annihilating thoughts occur at the end of the sixth stanza. The world was made in six days and on the seventh God rested. The world will last for six ages at the end of which it will be destroyed and the faithful will repose in the new Jerusalem during the seventh age. It was common to draw an analogy between each day, or age, and seven steps of contemplative ascent.[23]

Here at the Fountains sliding foot,
Or at some Fruit-trees mossy root,
Casting the Bodies Vest aside,
My Soul into the boughs does glide:
There like a Bird it sits, and sings,
Then whets, and combs its silver Wings;
And, till prepar'd for longer flight,
Waves in its Plumes the various Light.

In stanza seven the speaker undergoes an instant of illumination and communion with the divine mind. This moment of ecstasy is the height of contemplation and only occurs to the soul which has been liberated from the senses and mind. It is an indescribable experience. Marvell wisely does not attempt to explain or describe it. A close examination of stanza seven would reveal it to be a skilful piece of *trompe-l'oeil*, in which, through traditional symbols, more is suggested than in fact is said.

The stanza begins with the Augustinian contrast between the world ("here") and eternity ("there"). The soul ascends from a knowledge of "here" to a moment of communion with, and vision of, "there". "Here" is a shadow of "there". The "Fountains" and "Fruit-trees" are signs of divine goodness from the Creation to the end of time. We recall the streams and trees of man's first Paradise and of the heavenly Paradise. The symbolism of the tree and fountain is well known. Christ is the tree and fountain of life. The boughs and root bring to mind the prophecy in Isaiah 11:1: "And there shall come forth a rod out of the stem of Jesse, and a Branch shall grow out of his roots". The rivers of Paradise (Genesis 2:10) are signs of the baptismal waters, while the tree of life is a sign of Christ on the Cross. "Some" points to the symbolism of the fruit-tree and the controversy over what kind of tree was originally meant, while "mossy" may be an allusion to Moses. In "Casting the Bodies Vest aside" we are reminded of the garment of skin God gives to fallen Adam in Genesis 3:21. If it helps to protect man, it also weighs down his soul with mortal, corruptible flesh. In achieving through contemplation the original nakedness of Adam, the speaker is like those who will put off the corruptible and enjoy eternal life. Marvell does not say that the body is cast aside; it is the body's "Vest" (skin, or clothing) which is put aside. The soul glides into the boughs from a body momentarily purified of carnality. It sings in contemplation of the various lights of God.

The speaker having entered through the gateway of Christ moves on to higher stages of contemplation. The soul ascends the tree of contemplation, feels liberated from its body, feels free to fly "like a Bird", finds peace ("it sits") and "sings" praises to God. It is now "there", momentarily elevated into a direct knowledge or communion with the divine. Its knowledge is different from the forms of knowledge it had before. It no longer sees signs; it is now in the presence of the "various Light" of God. Marvell wisely shifts the focus from the scene to the speaker. The soul sharpens ("whets") and purifies its desire to ascend closer to God. Does "Waves in its plumes the various Light" mean that it is basking in the light or still struggling to ascend further? Probably both. Union with the divine is impossible to mortal man. The apex of contemplation is knowledge or vision; it is only possible to approach God more closely after death. The soul is not yet "prepar'd for longer flight", although its moment of mystical vision is part of its preparation. The speaker will carry a remembrance of his visionary moment through the rest of his life, while preparing himself for death.

Marvell does not explain the "various Light". The soul's enjoyment is conveyed, not the meaning of the experience. For the latter Marvell relies on the tradition of the symbols he evokes. The tree of contemplation spreading upwards in love of God with a bird on each branch is a well-known theme of medieval literature, as is the figure of the soul as a bird vainly attempting to fly to God. The "various Light" should bring to mind the Trinity ("various") and the unity of God ("Light"). It is the light emanating from God which the soul undulates in its contemplative, grace-given wings.

While a knowledge of contemplative literature helps us to understand the kind of experience that stanza seven invokes, it would be a mistake to import a specific structure of ideas into the soul's ascent and vision. What the soul experiences is conveyed by allegorisation and symbol rather than the re-creation of emotions specific to exact stages of mystical contemplation. Notice Marvell does not say the light comes in waves; rather the soul "waves in its Plumes the various Light". The plumes are an aid to ascent, or longer flight. The soul is experiencing illumination, not an emanation. Its ecstasy is knowledge of, not oneness with, the divine mind.

The speaker began by meditating upon the significance of the created world, and progresses to a mystical contemplation of the creation with all its sacramental significance. He momentarily has a vision of the divine mind in which all time is eternally present. His vision prepares him for "longer flight". The soul, whetting and combing its wings, is preening its feathers in preparation for its final flight to everlasting bliss.[24]

> Such was that happy Garden-state,
> While Man there walk'd without a Mate:
> After a Place so pure, and sweet,
> What other Help could yet be meet!
> But 'twas beyond a Mortal's share
> To wander solitary there:
> Two Paradises 'twere in one
> To live in Paradise alone.

The intelligence resumes its interpretative powers after the moment of ecstasy, but it does so with a longing for the paradisial vision which the soul glimpsed. The change in mode of knowledge from direct to intellectual experience is implied by the change in tense and the emphasis on "there" in stanza eight. "Such was that happy Garden-state, / While Man there walk'd without a Mate" refers to Adam contemplating God's work in Paradise before the creation of Eve. The vision experienced in stanza seven is similar ("Such was") to Adam's direct apprehension of God. Stanza eight consists of thoughts about man's first condition. Life in the garden was happy; it was the true happiness shadowed by the "wond'rous Life" experienced in stanza five, and remembered by the mind in stanza six. It is only because man has a memory of such happiness, either implanted in his soul or inherited from Adam, that he knows what happiness can be. All his efforts, whether for accomplishments, company or erotic love, are vain attempts to find such happiness again.

The "Garden-state" is both the condition of Adam, and his empire or paradisial kingdom. ("State": Adam is given dominion over the creatures, is told to subdue the earth and to tend the garden.) Marvell says that such happiness existed before the creation of Eve ("While Man there walk'd without a Mate"). Adam walked in the garden contemplating God through His works, undistracted by any company. The place is free from sin ("pure") and a place for contemplation ("sweet"). Why then does God give man a help meet (Genesis 2:18)? Not being fallen he does not *yet* need help: "What other Help could yet be meet!" "Other" reminds us that Adam had God's help in contemplating God's goodness in the meats of the trees and plants of Paradise (Genesis 1:29). That man does now need help, through

Christ and His Church, is recalled in "yet". The shift in tense is significant of the purpose of the help-meet.

The marriage sacrament is read into Genesis 2:24: "they shall be one flesh".[25] It is the only sacrament of the Church specifically mentioned before the Fall, and is seen in relation to Genesis 1:27-28. In Genesis 1:27 God creates man; then we are told: "male and female created he them"; while in Genesis 1:28 He "blessed them, and God said unto them, Be fruitful and multiply, and replenish the earth". We need not become involved with some of the elaborate explanations which were once made to account for the seeming discrepancy between the two creations of woman (Genesis 1:27 and Genesis 2:22), since Marvell is explicit about why Eve was created: "But 'twas beyond a Mortal's share / To wander solitary there". A mortal is the opposite of an immortal, he will die. God knows man will fall and become subject to death. But God has commanded man to increase and multiply. God has also given the earth to mankind, "male and female". He has given it to them to "share". Thus the marriage sacrament.

Some readers have thought that in stanza eight Marvell is alluding to the tradition that Adam was androgynous or a hermaphrodite before the creation of Eve. This tradition, having roots in both Judaic and Greek Christian commentary, was still alive in Marvell's time. It was based on reading Genesis 1:27, where God "created man . . . created he him; male and female created he them" as referring solely to Adam. While Marvell wittily brings to mind the hermaphrodite Adam tradition, he seems to accept the more common reading of Genesis 1:27-28. Adam was created before Eve, but the blessing is given to both man and woman. A male Adam enjoys solitude in the garden, before the creation of a woman with whom he is expected to couple ("Mate", "be one flesh") to share God's blessings. Their marriage is a sign of the union of the Church with Christ, the heavenly bride with the divine bridegroom. From their union will result the lineage of the promised seed (Genesis 3:15), who will be the "Help" (assistance, saviour) that mortals need. Divine providence cannot allow man "to wander solitary there".

"Two Paradises 'twere in one/To live in Paradise alone" echoes "*It is* not good that the man should be alone" (Genesis 2:18) and "they shall be one flesh" (Genesis 2:24), "twain shall be one flesh" (Matthew 19:5). As in the preceding lines, the nostalgia for a paradise of solitariness is humorously undermined by recalling God's commands and promises. If the original Paradise is lost, another will replace it at the end of time. The first Paradise is a shadow of the second.

It might at first seem that the concern with marriage in stanza eight is in contrast to the rest of the poem; this is not so. Marvell's theme is solitude, not the life of the solitaire. The garden is a place isolated from the world, a place of spiritual retreat, a place for contemplation. By meditating upon God's works one will recall the Fall, and woman's role in it; but one will also remember the function of marriage and the mystical realities of which it is a sign. The speaker wandering in the garden may see in it signs of man's first Paradise, but he also recalls the Fall and expulsion. Man cannot return to Eden; but he has God's promises, as revealed in the Creation, that time is moving towards the coming of man's future Paradise. As the next stanza shows, we should hope and work for the fulfilment of man's destiny.

How well the skilful Gardner drew
Of flow'rs and herbes this Dial new;
Where from above the milder Sun
Does through a fragrant Zodiack run;
And, as it works, th' industrious Bee
Computes its time as well as we.
How could such sweet and wholsome Hours
Be reckon'd but with herbs and flow'rs!

Stanza nine begins with the speaker meditating upon a floral sundial. He sees in the dial and in the heavens signs of God's goodness throughout time. In Renaissance commentaries on Genesis, the work of the third day included a herbal.[26] The speaker is similar to Adam contemplating God's work through the plants of Paradise. God is the Gardener Who creates the flowers and herbs. God's goodness and care are recalled in "skilful". The flowers and herbs opening and closing, bending towards the sun, are symbols of God's order as revealed in nature. They mark the passing of time, and remind us that the mutable world is a shadow of the eternal. The sun and the Zodiac are also signs of the Creation (Psalm 19:1), and of the passing of time in the fallen world, where man must work while awaiting the Second Coming. Since the original perfection of the world was broken or corrupted by man's Fall, the dial has had to be made anew by Christ the Gardener (John 20:15).[27] Christ brings a new creation, redeeming man from his fallen state, and once again filling the world with signs of hope.

"Where from above the milder Sun / Does through a fragrant Zodiack run" presumably means that the rays of the passing sun move across the floral dial, in which some flowers have been planted to form zodiacal signs. The dial is a mirror of the seasons and the heavens, as well as recording the passing of the day. Floral sundials were common in the sixteenth and seventeenth centuries, and were emblematic of man's temporal stay on earth.[28] In measuring the motions of the sun they called to mind the progress of the heavens, the dying and reborn Saviour. They could be used for meditation, calling to mind that the world and time had a beginning and an end. God creates the Zodiac as a sign: "And God said, Let there be lights in the firmament of the heaven to divide the day from the night; and let them be for signs, and for seasons, and for days, and years" (Genesis 1:14). "Above" reminds us of the heavens and God, high above. "Above" is played against "here below" in stanza two, and directs the reader's mind towards seeing the things of this world as emblems of higher matters. The milder sun recalls Christ, the meek mild Son of charity, in contrast to the hot burning sun of justice, or noonday sun. If the heavens offer testimonies of God's work and glory (Psalm 19:1,7), the sun's motion particularly is a sign of Christ's life, death and Resurrection (Psalm 19:5,6). The new dial is an emblem for the passing of the present age, and looks forward to the end of time when the Redeemer will come again and Paradise will be regained.

Marvell's imagination creates upon all the levels of significance found in older Christian allegory; meditation and allegorisation are fused into a sacramental vision. The hours, the seasons, the sun, the stars, the flowers are all signs. The sun passing over the floral dial reminds man that created time is to be used to work towards salvation. The heavens, earth and man are all working towards one conclusion.

The bee, because of its industrious habits, is an emblem of work and of an orderly life. According to legend it never sleeps; it represents Christian vigilance and zeal in acquiring virtue. All creation therefore points to the moral that man must be active in his virtues and diligent in his purity, if he is to make proper use of time. That the bee "Computes its time" is a rather elaborate pun. "Compute" refers to "computation", an ecclesiastical term for calculating the Church calendar. The bee adds up its thyme; it can tell the time in the course of its work from the hours which the flowers of the dial open to the sun. The bee is morally an emblem of man's need to accumulate good works while awaiting his time of judgment. "Compute", however, is also a word connected with astrology and astronomy, and since the floral dial is also a Zodiac, the bee's computations remind us of the heavenly signs instituted by God at the Creation. Such signs have their place in Christian eschatology. Christ accuses his contemporaries "can ye not *discern* the signs of the times?" (Matthew 16:3). Paul says "knowing the time . . . *is* our salvation nearer than when we believed" (Romans 13:11). The bee computes the time with man, since creation fell and will be redeemed with man (Romans 8:19-23).

"How could such sweet and wholsome Hours / Be reckon'd but with herbs and flow'rs!" literally means that only the floral sundial is appropriate for determining the passing of time in the garden. "Reckon" is similar to "compute"; one determines the time or one adds up the time spent. The time is spent wholesomely in meditation and a holy life ("wholsome"), analogous to Adam in Paradise. One awaits the Second Coming. In reckoning the time one thinks of one's hope.

The time is also spent in holy hours.[29] A life of toil, recreation, prayer and meditation in harmony with the seasons is like a divine service, and recalls the hours and calendar of the Church. Holy hours would be the canonical hours — the times and services of daily prayer. The words "Zodiack", "Computes" and "reckon'd" remind us of the Church's calendar. Each month corresponds to events in the life of Christ and those of the saints. Each month is marked by an heroic act. The bee, because of its well-regulated communal life, is often a symbol for the Church. The bee working its way through the floral Zodiac thus brings to mind the Church keeping its memorial of the times in prayers, hymns, silence, lessons and other forms of devotion.[30] It is in keeping with the harmony of the poem that it should end with a meditation on the proper use of herbs and flowers, in contrast to the improper use found in the first stanza.

In the light of the above reading of *The Garden*, it is possible to make some suggestions about the nature of Marvell's art. It offers an impression of sensuous beauty without being sensual. It is both intellectual and devotional. It is profound in that it alludes to the deepest mysteries of the Christian faith, and complex in its multiplicity of implied analogies. It seems to me superior to the devotional poetry of other seventeenth century writers, both in its art and in its imaginative richness. No other poet seems to express such fullness of feeling in such complexity. Marvell's poetry fulfils the Augustinian demand that Christian art contain both eloquence and truth. In his use of secular poetic models, he is also within the Augustinian humanistic tradition. Pagan art can be made to serve a Christian purpose. Christian art improves upon its models by infusing them with divine truth.

The fusion of thought and feeling in Marvell's poetry would also seem to derive from the tradition of Augustinian meditation and allegorisation. Words give expression to ideas as they are felt; the emotions expressed exist simultaneously with the ideas. We do not dwell on a particular flower or tree and then consider its significance. Rather the beauty of flowers and trees is simultaneously present with our awareness of their emblematic significance. Although we move up a meditative ladder in *The Garden* by various stages, the doctrinal truths contained within the poem are present in each stanza. Each stanza is a partial expression of a unity. The unity of thought behind the poem is not derived from a sequential process and does not require a linear argument to be expressed. Any tree, any garden, any stanza of *The Garden* can contain within it signs of the whole of divine providence. Whether it is really possible to write poetry in this way is another question; but Marvell's verse comes as close to it as possible.

In reading Augustine one is aware of the unity between the devotional and theological, between the emotional and the intellectual. Intellect shades into meditation, philosophical arguments are supported by allegorisation of biblical passages. As the reader proceeds towards a certain conclusion, his mind also moves sideways, backward and leaps ahead as if each part contained the whole. This is not surprising, since each moment of time contains within it the whole of Christian history; each thing is a sign of the whole. The ideal is to achieve a oneness with the divine mind which comprehends everything within it. Marvell's poetry is a re-creation of such a mode of knowledge, during which the spiritual meaning of creation is revealed. Seldom has the Christian imagination been translated so finely and fully into lyric poetry as in *The Garden*.

CHAPTER SIXTEEN

Marvell's Universe

Marvell did not leave us a *Divine Comedy*, a *Paradise Lost* or a *Temple*. We have no finished body of work structured and ordered, offering us a completed vision or poetic universe. His poems have come to us in a haphazard fashion with an obscure history. Among the minor poems it is still impossible to say which are Marvell's and which have been mistakenly included among his work. Among the major poems, however, there are enough similarities to enable us to speak of Marvell's poetic universe. In trying to formulate the world of Marvell's imagination we should not look for originality of thought and doctrine. Marvell is not a philosopher; the theology of his poems is the orthodoxy of older Christianity.

Marvell's poetic universe is one of love; the world was created by divine love, and is held together by bonds of love. The whole of creation aspires towards union with divine, like a lover seeking to be joined with the object of his love: "Here disdaining, there in Love". The creation of the world, however, paradoxically resulted in a distance between the created and the divine: "For Fate with jealous Eye does see / Two perfect Loves; nor lets them close". Adam's Fall made matters worse. Instead of contemplating God directly through His works, man's mind became influenced by his senses. The divine image within the mind was clouded by a misdirected love of objects rather than a love of God: "O Who shall, from this Dungeon, raise / A Soul inslav'd so many wayes?"[1] Unable to rise to love of God through his own power, man would be left in hopeless despair if God's grace did not enable him to raise his vision from material things to an understanding of God's love, as revealed throughout all created time and space: "My Love . . . was begotten by despair / Upon Impossibility".

Man is at the centre of this drama of love. The world was created for man: "Loves whole World on us doth wheel", and even after the Fall the whole of history reveals how God's love works towards mankind's restoration. The Jews being led out of Egypt to the Holy

Land, the Pilgrims voyaging to the Bermudas, the Church sailing on the waves of time towards its eventual triumph are all acts and signs of divine love which will some day bring an end to the dominion of sin and death. The Mower, a figure of death, says "How happy might I still have mow'd, / Had not Love here his Thistles sow'd". Juliana's "scorching beams", figurative of the hot rays of the sun of justice, wither the grass of the Mower's dominion, but she does not esteem or love the Mower. It is the Mower's mistake to see the drama centring upon himself. Divine love, as figured by Juliana, has come to restore the world to its original fellowship and eternal spring. The May-games are reminders of the coming restoration of man. Even the glo-worms which appear at harvest time are natural signs that the world of death will pass. They are explicitly associated with the Exodus from Egypt, the journey to the Promised Land: "Ye Glo-worms whose officious Flame / To wandering Mowers shows the way". Sailing to the Bermudas, the Pilgrims affirm: "What should we do but sing his Praise / That led us through the watry Maze".

The central act in the drama of divine love working for mankind's redemption is the coming of Christ, the "milder Sun" which saves man from the burning rays of divine justice: "There is not such another in / The World, to offer for their Sin". Man must love God if he is to be saved. As a result of the Fall he is so weighed down with a sense of sin and guilt and has become so attached to created pleasures that he is unable to hope for salvation and fully love God any longer. To save man from his despair, divine love assumes the flesh and blood of humanity, undergoes the passions of the flesh and is willingly crucified on a Cross:

> And now, when angry Heaven wou'd
> Behold a spectacle of Blood,
> Fortune and He are call'd to play
> At sharp before it all the day:
> And Tyrant Love his brest does ply
> With all his wing'd Artillery.

The Unfortunate Lover not only atones for man's guilt, but also founds a Church of the faithful who through the example of His love have opened themselves to the grace of divine love. His love is expressed in the offering of His blood and flesh in the Eucharist:

> Torn into Flames, and ragg'd with Wounds.
> And all he saies, a Lover drest
> In his own Blood does relish best.

The Sacrifice is an act of love which resounds through all creation, showing man what true love is: "Thy Love was far more better then / The love of false and cruel men". Even the love of a Faun for a Nymph becomes a reminder of Christ's love for His Church and the human soul:

> . . . How could I less
> Than love it? O I cannot be
> Unkind, t' a Beast that loveth me.

The mind, having entered into contemplation through the gateway of love of Christ, sees that the universe is filled with signs of divine love. The grass, flowers and herbs of the garden are "am'rous . . . lovely green". After luxuriating in God's creation and contemplating the order and nature of the universe, the mind withdraws into itself from sensual temptations and finds all ideas and forms within its memory: "The Mind, that Ocean where each kind / Does streight its own resemblance find". It realises that its notions derive from its Creator. Having rediscovered that it was created in the divine image, the mind has glimpses of its original state in Paradise. "Remembring still its former height . . . And, recollecting its own Light" the soul discovers the divine image within itself: "The greater Heaven in an Heaven less". It travels back through time to the bliss of prelapsarian Adam: "Annihilating all that's made, / To a green Thought in a green Shade". Having recovered a semblance of its original bliss the soul, "Casting the Bodies Vest aside"

> . . . into the boughs does glide:
> There like a Bird it sits, and sings,
> Then whets, and combs its silver Wings;
> And, till prepar'd for longer flight,
> Waves in its Plumes the various Light.
> Such was that happy Garden-state.

Such spiritual illumination cannot long be sustained in this life. The soul returns from its ecstasy to the body. The mind has discovered that the world is made of love and the true "object strange and high" of its desires is God. But it also comes to realise the distance which separates the two, a distance which can be expressed by opposite poles of the universe, or by God and man belonging to two separate orders. Attracted to God through the force of Christ's love, the mind can achieve conjunction with God, but being weighed down by its body is physically separated from union with the object of its love:

> Therefore the Love which us doth bind,
> But Fate so enviously debarrs,
> Is the Conjunction of the Mind,
> And Opposition of the Stars.

The soul having glimpsed the pleasures of Paradise "Computes its time" on earth, happily preparing itself for its heavenly home. The soul now enlightened of the extent of divine charity realises that all other loves except the love of God or the love of Him through His creatures is vain and wanton, a misdirection of affection. All the fleshly beauties offered by Created Pleasure are nothing to the Resolved Soul if compared to the sight of Heaven:

Restless it roules and unsecure,
Trembling lest it grow impure:
Till the warm Sun pitty it's Pain,
And to the Skies exhale it back again.

Love of woman is love of an "object vain". It is the "wanton Love" or misdirection of affection from God to creatures which began with Adam's Fall.

The temptations of Created Pleasure and those offered by the speaker in *To his Coy Mistress* seems justifiable only if there is no future, no Heaven or after-life. The love of objects mistakes true happiness which is to be found in eternity, not in momentary satisfactions:

But at my back I alwaies hear
Times winged Charriot hurrying near:
And yonder all before us lye
Desarts of vast Eternity.

Divine love has offered us a promise of eternity and reminds us of this promise through signs and shadows. Platonism, although offering us timeless universals, mistakes the object of love, which is God, and cannot free man's soul from the confines of the fallen world of time and space:

But soon these Flames do lose their light,
Like Meteors of a Summers night:
Nor can they to that Region climb,
To make impression upon Time.

The world of Marvell's poetry is a mirror reflecting eternity: "And in the greenness of the Grass / Did see its Hopes as in a Glass". Time is not a mere sequence of events; it is a scheme of history as foreseen in the divine mind, stretching from the Creation to the last days of the created world. The important moments are signs and symbols looking forward and backward to the whole divine scheme. The individual moment that we know recapitulates the total pattern. Time is not to be wasted, as no moment is complete in itself. Each moment of time poses a choice between remembering man's hopes or being tempted into immediate but vain satisfactions:

Now therefore, while the youthful hew
Sits on thy skin like morning dew,
And while thy willing Soul transpires
At every pore with instant Fires,
Now let us sport us while we may.

The Resolved Soul must "now" learn to wield the armour of its faith.

The soul is "Creations Guest" and although given temporary dominion over the earth it is "Heavens Heir". The Resolved Soul knows that it "cannot stay" on earth, that its final "Rest" is in Heaven. The sensual allurements of the natural world "recall" the "Fall" and the soul knows that it has no "time to lose". It is not distracted by the beauties of the earth, but sees in them promises of greater beauties which it will see in the future in Heaven.

While aspiring to ascend to Heaven the soul learns that union with the divine is impossible in this world and can only come after death and the Last Judgment. The world of time and space can "prepare" the soul "for longer flight" and contribute towards that moment predicted in Revelation when "the giddy Heaven fall, / And Earth some new Convulsion tear". To hope to anticipate such joys is presumption. Man is "Heavens Heir" who has not yet inherited the heavenly kingdom. Eve fell from the wish to anticipate her destiny and be god-like. Traditionally one of the temptations offered by Satan to the Messiah is to assume His glory before His time. The voyagers in *Bermudas* who "kept the time" are living in obedience to the divine scheme. The speaker in *To his Coy Mistress* who complains at not having "World enough, and Time" is criminally misusing both. His attempt to "Time devour" contrasts with the steady fulfilment of time revealed in such images as "before the Flood", "Conversion of the *Jews*", "last Age" and "Eternity". A concentration on momentary pleasures without regard to promises of eternity turns man into an animal governed by carnal appetites, "like am'rous birds of prey", who forgets the eternal nature of his soul. The plea to "Seize the short Joyes then, ere they vade" might have formerly ("once") seemed a possible answer to the transitory nature of this world, but since the coming of Christ mankind has hopes for eternal salvation. The soul knows that its life on earth is a test, a preparation: "So Architects do square and hew, / Green Trees that in the Forest grew".[2] The Resolved Soul knowing this should courageously reject the temptations of created things:

Earth cannot shew so brave a Sight
As when a single Soul does fence
The Batteries of alluring Sense,
And Heaven views it with delight.

The slowness of time moving to fulfil its final destination of the last age (of which the speaker in *To his Coy Mistress* complains) is in itself a proof of the truth of the Christian vision of history. The Unfortunate Lover has been promised since the beginning of time: "And, e're brought forth, was cast away". Although dead He leaves the Gospel "Musick within every Ear". It is such a vision which rescues the soul from its despair at being imprisoned in a body influenced by the senses, subject to the dictates of fate, in a world of time. The Unfortunate Lover Himself must suffer in the flesh, but His Sacrifice offers the soul the hope of eternity.

Death which once saw the greenness of the grass as an emblem of its reign over the mutable world is now thwarted by the flowering of saved souls who "reform the errours of the Spring" and bring an end to its dominion. Time is drawing towards its conclusion:

And thus, ye Meadows, which have been
Companions of my thoughts more green,
Shall now the Heraldry become
With which I shall adorn my Tomb.

The Mower may see all of human history as a story of increasing corruption, but his perspective is incorrect. The Creation was a sacrament containing within it the whole of time: "First was the World as one great Cymbal made". The whole history of mankind, including the birth and progress of civilisation, contributes towards man's eventual salvation. The progress of history leads to that one moment in time when "a gentler Conqueror" came: "Who though He flies the Musick of his praise, / Would with you Heavens Hallelujahs raise". The present is the last age before the last days of the world. We may mistakenly try to "win the Palm, the Oke, or Bayes" "in busie Companies of Men"; or we can work like "th' industrious Bee" who "Computes its time as well as we" in understanding God through His creation: "How could such sweet and wholsome Hours / Be reckon'd but with herbs and flow'rs!"

The world is a place in which the soul undergoes temptation; according to the uses made of the world the soul will either be saved or damned. The soul can fall through pride like Eve in anticipating its promised divinity, or like Adam by loving something for itself rather than as part of God's creation. Or the soul can imitate Christ in resisting the temptations of the world. This essential choice is one of the main themes of Marvell's poetry. Each individual is confronted with it. It is a choice between "uncessant Labour" after an "object vain", a life of false carnal excitement "like am'rous birds of prey"; or a life free from the "self-deluding Sight"[3] of the senses, in which the soul can recover the divine image within itself, keep the time, and experience a tranquil happiness similar to prelapsarian Adam contemplating the works of God's Creation in Paradise. T.C. "begins her golden daies" in simple contemplation of nature. She is similar to unfallen Adam in knowing the right use of created things. She names and tames the flowers, as Adam did the animals. Soon, however, her knowledge will be tested by the possibilities of experience. Offered the beauties of the world she may gather flowers of more advanced spiritual knowledge and help regain man's Paradise; or, tempted by wanton love, she may pick the buds before they have blossomed. This seizing of the time criminally misuses nature and leads to spiritual death. Herbs and flowers can be misused as crowns for ambitious men, or they can be properly used as a means of recalling divine love. The garden can be a place for the fulfilment of lust and vanity, or a place to recall man's first innocence. Poetry may be written with a desire for worldly fame, interest and glory, or it can be written out of true humility, not caring for worldly rewards, as an acknowledgement of "Heavens Diadem".[4] The soul should be like the drop of dew, disdaining the temptations of the created world and in love with its Maker, excluding the world of fleshly pleasures below, bending upward ready to ascend to God.

The most direct statement of the theme of temptation is the *Dialogue between the Resolved Soul and Created Pleasure*. The soul is first offered temptations of the five senses. They are "Nature's banquet" which it is invited to share. Pleasure's address inadvertently and ironically reveals the essential situation, recalling the intoxication felt by Eve when she first ate the apple: "Where the Souls of fruits and flow'rs / Stand prepar'd to heighten yours". The pleasures of touch which might seem to bring rest to the Resolved Soul are contrasted to the spiritual satisfaction of being "Conscious of doing what I ought". The pleasures of smell "Such as oft the Gods appeas'd" are seen by the soul as presumption. The pleasures of sight are a form of self-love or cupidity: "In this Crystal view *thy* face". After the soul has overcome the allurements of the senses it is offered higher temptations of wealth, glory and forbidden knowledge. But the Resolved Soul imitates Christ in rejecting temptations of pride and vainglory. Having its spiritual eye firmly fixed on the promises of eternity, it knows that only by "Humility" can it "to Heaven climb". True pleasure lies not in this world but "beyond the Pole, / And is thine everlasting Store".

Because the resistance of temptation is an imitation of Christ and contributes towards man's redemption, chastity and virginity are among the ideals of Marvell's imaginative universe. Such poems as *Daphnis and Chloe*, *Mourning*, and, I think, *To his Coy Mistress* treat erotic love ironically. Secular love misdirects our attention from God, bringing moral corruption and sin in its train. It corrupts the mind and turns man into a sensual animal governed by his passions and no longer remembering the dignity of his immortal soul. The doctrine of chastity in Marvell's poetry, however, is not that of mere sexual virginity. Chastity and virginity are states of the mind and not technical terms for sexual inexperience. They stand for purity of motive, purpose and thought. The innocence sought is that of a mind conscious of divine love and untempted by created pleasures. As in other matters, sexuality may be an example of charity or cupidity; it may be properly or improperly used. The speaker in *To his Coy Mistress*, pleading for the indulgence of lust, misuses love.

Several of Marvell's poems seem to suggest that wedded sexuality for the purpose of producing children is noble and is to be prized. Marriage for the sake of progeny fulfils God's injunction to increase and multiply. While young ladies in Marvell's poetry are praised for not being carried away by amorous attentions, the poet looks forward to the future when the young girls will fulfil their parents' hopes in an approved marriage. T.C.'s "chaster Laws" may break Cupid's bow, but it is probable that "our hopes" include the prospect of her marrying. Both marriage and sexual virginity are morally good, providing they are based upon the love of God. The wedded life at Nun Appleton House is a "Domestick Heaven", and Mary Fairfax

> . . . like a *sprig of Misleto,*
> On the *Fairfacian Oak* does grow;
> Whence, for some universal good,
> The *Priest* shall cut the sacred Bud;
> While her *glad Parents* most rejoice,
> And make their *Destiny* their Choice.[5]

Mary is a symbol of wisdom, and her studies are part of her preparation for marriage. Such marriage, as in the sacrament itself, is a shadow of the wedding of the soul to God in Heaven and the wedding of the Church to Christ at the end of time.

Man is "mortal" and being subject to death must procreate and continue the work of time. Marriage is a sacrament and has its place in the divine scheme. That "Each sought a consort in that lovely place; / And Virgin Trebles wed the manly Base" prepares for the coming of the "gentler Conqueror" at the end of time. The individual's life is a microcosm of mankind; it can help "reform the errours of the Spring" by using love for its true purpose, love of God. The chaste mind will shun "the sweat leaves", regardless of the person's marital state, just as the chaste soul will make proper use of the created world.

A life of retirement from the corruptions of the active world does not, in Marvell's poetry, involve monastic life. The garden of contemplation can be that of Nun Appleton House just as easily as in a monastery. Indeed Nun Appleton House was once a nunnery, during which time it was a place of cupidity. It was not truly a "Religious House" until it came into the hands of the Fairfax family. We should not, then, make simplistic distinctions between activity and contemplation in Marvell's work. The contemplative life includes the need to labour for salvation. The most perfect state would be the solitary condition of Adam alone in the garden before the creation of

Eve, contemplating God's work while doing pleasant and useful labour; but as a result of Adam's Fall such a perfect condition of life is no longer possible.

The contemplative life involves society and civilisation, both of which contribute towards mankind's spiritual improvement. The country is the place where it is easier to study God's work without being distracted by vain desires and false titles, but such a life does not require one to live as a hermit or give up the arts and sciences of civilisation. The Mower complaining against gardens may see the development of civilisation as evidence of a progressing corruption of innocence, but he does not take into account the necessity for man to work towards redemption. The artificial sun dial in the garden carefully planted with various flowers and herbs can be used as a means of contemplating the divine scheme. The uses made of civilisation depend upon the attitude of mind, not upon things themselves.

The many allusions to art and science in Marvell's poetry reflect a belief that the progress of civilisation was instituted by God after the Fall as part of man's labour towards his salvation. The arts and sciences are both signs of the divine scheme, and have a moral significance. The Paradise lost by Adam's Fall cannot be regained through a radical rejection of civilisation. Just as Adam had to tend the plants of Paradise, so mankind must tame the wildness of the fallen world. While spiritual salvation is aided by the proper use of the arts and sciences, it is important that they be used properly. The speaker in *The Coronet* realises that poetry can be misused for worldly fame even when the writer purports to have a devotional purpose:

> Alas I find the Serpent old
> That, twining in his speckled breast,
> About the flow'rs disguis'd does fold,
> With wreaths of Fame and Interest.

The Resolved Soul knows that knowledge without humility is dangerous. In *The Garden* we are reminded of Eve's fatal curiosity ("curious Peach", *péché*, sin).

There is thus a distinction between the arts of nature and divine art. Art should imitate divine art. The desire for luxury corrupts art and helps transform the created world into a place of sensual indulgence: "Luxurious Man, to bring his Vice in use, / Did after him the World seduce". Gardening, mathematics, poetry, music should reflect divine art, the order and timeless scheme of the divine mind as expressed in the created world. Songs should be used to praise God, not to indulge the ear. Mathematics should reveal the original unity of things in the divine mind. The study of the stars should be used to recall their Maker and not for magical purposes.

Work and study can be part of the work of man's restoration: "How well the skilful Gardner drew / Of flow'rs and herbes this Dial new". The arts of nature cannot overcome the Resolved Soul which understands the proper use of things:

Now, if thou bee'st that thing Divine,
In this day's Combat let it shine:
And shew that Nature wants an Art
To conquer one resolved Heart.

The arts properly used are sacred. Marvell's imagination can find spiritual meanings in all intellectual endeavours, since products of the well-directed mind are shadows of religious truths. While attempting to square the circle may be an example of "vanity", or futility, the true study of mathematics leads the mind from the things of this world to a love of God:

As Lines so Loves *oblique* may well
Themselves in every Angle greet:
But ours so truly *Paralel*,
Though infinite can never meet.

The true arts imitate the "subtile Art" of divine love as expressed in the Bible and in the created world.

Music is the most important of all the arts found in Marvell's poetry. Misused it can "chain a mind" to created pleasures. Used properly it recalls the complete harmony of the divine scheme as expressed in the Creation, throughout history, and as seen in the harmony of the spheres. Music is the praise of God sung at the Creation, echoed in the song sung by the voyagers on their way to the Bermudas, and imitated in Clorinda's song since the coming of Christ: "But He ere since my Songs does fill: / And his Name swells my slender Oate". It is the song of the world in praise of God heard by Adam in Eden and still continuing although no longer accessible to the ears of fallen mankind. Marvell's poetry invites us to join in this divine harmony:

Of *Pan* the flowry Pastures sing,
Caves eccho, and the Fountains ring.
Sing then while he doth us inspire;
For all the World is our *Pan's* Quire.[6]

The song is the song of the Church: "Oh let our Voice his Praise exalt, / Till it arrive at Heavens Vault"; and of the soul in contemplation having recovered its original uncorrupted use of the senses, able to hear the eternal divine chord: "There like a Bird it sits, and sings".

The divine chord having all notes in it was first heard at the Creation. It is horizontally expressed in time through the agreement of the various notes of human history: "From whence the Progeny of numbers new / Into harmonious Colonies withdrew". The harmony of the world is shown by the fulfilment of biblical prophecy in both Testaments. The music heard at the Creation is shadowed in David's Psalms and in the music played at the Temple by the Israelites. It is heard again at the birth of Christ, imitated in the songs of the Church, and will be heard yet again at the end of time. It is this music in which Marvell's poetry invites our participation, and which the numbers and harmony of his verse reflect:

> Then Musick, the Mosaique of the Air,
> Did of all these a solemn noise prepare:
> With which She gain'd the Empire of the Ear,
> Including all between the Earth and Sphear.
>
> Victorious sounds! yet here your Homage do
> Unto a gentler Conqueror then you;
> Who though He flies the Musick of his praise
> Would with you Heavens Hallelujahs raise.

All the world and its history are filled with signs of the redemptive process. The Old Testament is filled with prophecies both of the coming of Christ and of the heavenly kingdom. Marvell's poems continually recall such relationships. The "Manna's sacred Dew" given to the Israelites in Exodus is a prophecy of the coming of Christ. Proclaiming "the Ambergris on shoar" and casting the "Gospels Pearl upon our Coast" bring to mind not only Christ's Gospel in the New Testament, but also the Old Testament prophets, especially Noah and Jonah. Similar associations with castaway prophets and Apostles are found in the second stanza of *The Unfortunate Lover*. The Faun tied with a silver chain and bell not only recalls the doctrine and preaching of the Church but also that of the Synagogue which foreshadowed it. The playing of the Nymph and Faun brings to mind the relation between Christ and His Church as traditionally allegorised in Canticles. The sun which does not stand still in *To his Coy Mistress* brings to mind Joshua leading the Jews to the Holy Land. The praises sung in *Bermudas* bring to mind the Psalms in which Israel praises God and which look forward to the hymns of the Church. The preparation of T.C. and Mary Fairfax for marriage recalls the allegorisations of Canticles as an apocalypse: the longed for marriage of the bride to the bridegroom symbolising the Second Coming when the faithful will enjoy a new heaven and a new earth under the leadership of the heavenly bridegroom.

Marvell's world is filled with signs. The particulars of reality are symbols which should be studied for the spiritual realities they recall.

Marvell's world points from itself towards higher truths. Grass is a glass, nightingales meditate, glo-worms are lights. The garden is a place of spiritual retreat. Solitude recalls Adam's condition before the creation of Eve. The greenness of grass may bring to mind the passing of time, man's hope of redemption, or Eden. The hot summer sun recalls the sun of justice. The shepherd with his flock brings to mind Christ with the faithful.

Such a world is a place for meditation, an aid to contemplation and a means towards higher forms of mystical union. It is because Marvell imagines the world in this way that his poetry suggests more than is said. All of creation seems infused with meaning: "What wond'rous Life in this I lead!" The Resolved Soul discovers in the pleasures offered the senses reminders of its journey towards Heaven. A drop of dew is the starting point for meditation upon the nature of the human soul and for signs of God's providence throughout history. The flowers gathered for a coronet lead to a meditation on the power of Christ and the sinful nature of man.

Contemplation and love, we are often reminded, are only through the grace of Christ and God and are not natural powers of fallen man. God's aid is necessary for the soul's progress. If Marvell's poetry speaks of hope and of the potential glory of the soul, it is also poetry of humility and man's limitations. It is only by humility that the Resolved Soul will ascend to Heaven. The journey to the Bermudas praises God's aid in mankind's salvation. The garden is not only a place for contemplating God's work and a means of the mind's ascent towards God, but it also reminds us of man's Fall from Paradise. In each of these poems the mind moves backward and forward through time, beginning with some present scene or situation and retracing the history of the race or looking forward to its future. Often the mind ascends vertically to a closer relationship with God. Some poems are meditations on traditional themes; other poems, such as *The Garden*, embody an elaborate process of contemplative ascent. Such poems as *To his Coy Mistress* and the Mower sequence have an unusually subtle relationship to devotional literature, in that the point of view of the speaker is not that of a Christian and the effects are often those of inverse irony. Yet the speakers in *To his Coy Mistress* and the Mower sequence bring to mind, without intending to do so, the sacramental nature of the world as a place of contemplating the divine scheme. *To his Coy Mistress* indeed is a kind of inverted contemplation, descending to carnal ecstasy instead of ascending towards spiritual ecstasy. The irony, however, forces us to think about the significance of the images and the arguments which the speaker offers.

The vision offered by Marvell's poetry is a rich poetic creation embracing the whole history of the world. In its ability to convey the feeling of a world charged with significance, Marvell's poetry is a supreme fiction in which the particularities of experience have coherence and meaning. In offering us a vision of the world's harmony, order, and purpose, Marvell temporarily redeems us from our sense of alienation. We may no longer believe in the doctrine behind Marvell's poetry, but we have need for art which reminds us what it like for life to have significance outside itself. Marvell's poetic vision is so finely, completely and profoundly imagined that it deserves to be recognised as one of the great achievements of English literature.

Appendix: *The Nymph* and Charles I

Some readers have the impression that *The Nymph* is figurative of the Anglican mourning for the destruction of his Church by the Parliamentary army. If so, like Richard Lovelace's *The Grassehopper*, it would refer to Parliament's decision in the 1640s to ban the celebration of the Anglican mass and to forbid the use of the altar. The rites and sacraments of the Church could not be performed, the Book of Common Prayer was forbidden, and the Parliamentary army destroyed "images". If the poem were to be read in this way, it would be necessary to see the Faun as both a figure for Christ and for His Church. It seems more likely that the contemporary relevance of the Faun's death is the execution of King Charles. The King was the "anointed" head of the Church and his trial and execution were often viewed in royalist writing on analogy to the Passion and death of Christ. He is the Royal Martyr.

Eikon Basiliké, supposedly written by Charles I before his death, begins with a poem — "Majesty in Misery" — clearly based upon the tradition of the Good Friday reproaches of Christ upon the Cross, of which George Herbert's *Sacrifice* is a well-known poetic example. The final chapters of *Eikon Basiliké*, especially the "Meditations upon Death", carry out this implied analogy. Since both the Faun's death in Marvell's poem and the King's meditations in *Eikon Basiliké* have strong analogies to Christ's death, it would be easy to show how passages in Marvell's poem *could* allude to the King. The following example may suffice. It may be compared to the first stanza of *The Nymph*:

> My next comfort is, that He give me not only the honour to imitate His example *in suffering for righteousness' sake* (though obscured by the foulest charges of tyranny and injustice), but also that charity, which is the noblest revenge upon and victory over my destroyers; by which, I thank God, I can both forgive them and pray for them, that God would not impute my blood to them, further than to convince them what need they have of Christ's blood to wash their souls from the guilt of shedding mine.[1]

If the King-Faun analogy is allowed, the demand that the Faun's killing be just alludes to the illegal execution of Charles I, which is seen as "murder". The typological meaning of the Nymph would thus include the faithful of the Anglican Church. The final section of the poem alludes to the Church statues and altars then being destroyed by the extreme Puritans; God forbids idols, not images.

I do not wish to argue strongly for the analogy between the death of the Faun and King Charles as I do not feel it can be proved. However, as can be seen from *The Mower against Gardens* and *Upon Appleton House*, Marvell's poetry sometimes had a contemporary topical relevance. Marvell's *Bermudas* and *The First Anniversary*, and Dryden's *Absalom and Achitophel* show that it was common during the seventeenth century to assign a contemporary significance to biblical typology.[2]

It is significant that in *An Horatian Ode* Marvell also portrays Charles's death on analogy to the Crucifixion. The death occupies the central portion of the poem and is presented as a kind of spiritual triumph. Biblical allusions abound:

> That thence the *Royal Actor* born,
> The *Tragick Scaffold* might adorn:
> While round the armed Bands
> Did clap their bloody hands.
> *He* nothing common did or mean
> Upon that memorable Scene:
> But with his keener Eye
> The Axes edge did try:
> Nor call'd the *Gods* with vulgar spight
> To vindicate his helpless Right,
> But bow'd his comely Head,
> Down as upon a Bed.

Even the next line, seemingly proclaiming Cromwell's triumph, mordantly brings to mind the Crucifixion: "This was that memorable Hour". Any mid-seventeenth century reader would recognise Marvell's description of the King's death as analogous to conventional poetic descriptions of the death of Christ. As D.C. Allen has shown, in his discussion of Robert Herrick's *Good Friday: Rex Tragicus, or Christ going to His Crosse*, it was traditional to see Christ as a royal actor in a divine drama.[3] I do not want to claim that *An Horatian Ode* is a royalist poem. It is Horatian and as in many of Horace's odes the exact sympathies of the author are difficult to discover. I think, however, that too much has been made recently of the view that it offers cautionary and discriminatory praise of Cromwell. For me the ironies outweigh the praise.

I have brought *An Horatian Ode* into this discussion at the risk of losing sight of *The Nymph*, partly because it may be additional evidence of the latter poem's topical relevance. Towards the end of *An Horatian Ode*, Cromwell is on the point of invading Scotland. It was exactly over this issue, the unjustified Parliamentary attack on the Scots, that Fairfax resigned his commission as leader of the Parliamentary army and retired to Nun Appleton House, taking Marvell with him as tutor for his daughter Mary. Although he was an extremely religious man, we know nothing of Fairfax's specific religious beliefs. Like Marvell, he appears to have been against the Roman Church and the Laudian high church faction and for religious toleration. From his interests and his distrust of the more radical Protestants, he was probably middle-of-the-road. Although he fought on the Parliamentary side, he was a well-known monarchist and was openly against putting the King on trial. Cromwell accused him of attempting to rescue the King, and at the time of the execution a guard was put around Fairfax's house. At the King's trial Lady Fairfax called Oliver Cromwell a traitor, and Fairfax appealed to the Council to spare the King's life. He wrote a poem on the King's death, *On the Fatal Day*: "Oh lett that Day from time be blotted quitt".[4] Fairfax remained a monarchist during Cromwell's rule, keeping in touch with the exiled King, and played a large part in his restoration.[5]

While these facts do not prove that *The Nymph complaining for the death of her Faun* necessarily alludes to King Charles's death, they do suggest that some critics have been too ready to assume that Marvell was a Puritan and a Cromwellian who could not have written poems favourably disposed towards the monarchy. His very presence in Fairfax's household as a tutor to the Lord's daughter suggests monarchist sympathies, or at least a willingness to write poetry which at the time was comfortable to those with such sympathies. If we keep such possibilities in mind it is not unlikely that *The Nymph* is a complex allegory evoking the life and death of Christ, while implying that the death of the King is a contemporary type of such sacrifice.

Notes

Chapter One

1. See G.W.H. Lampe and K.J. Woollcombe, *Essays on Typology* (London: SCM Press, 1957), p. 68. Also see John R. Mulder, *The Temple of the Mind* (New York: Pegasus, 1969), Chapter 6, pp. 130-150 for a discussion of seventeenth century typology.
2. "Sometimes, indeed, there were as many as seven. But the more normal number of senses was four". Robert M. Grant, *A Short History of the Interpretation of the Bible* (London: Adam and Charles Black, 1965), pp. 94-95. Useful studies of the development of Christian allegory and symbolism include Yrjö Hirn, *The Sacred Shrine: A Study of the Poetry and Art of the Catholic Church* (London: Macmillan, 1912); Herbert Musurillo, *Symbolism and the Christian Imagination* (Baltimore and Dublin: Helicon Press, 1962); Jean Daniélou, *From Shadows to Reality* (London: Burns and Oates, 1960).
3. William Durandus, *The Symbolism of Churches and Church Ornaments*, ed. J.M. Neal and B. Webb (London: Gibbings, 1906), pp. 4-6.
4. Alan Watts, *Myth and Ritual in Christianity* (London: Thames & Hudson, 1954), pp. 91-93. Also see Gilbert Cope, *Symbolism in the Bible and the Church* (London: SCM Press, 1959).
5. See D.W. Robertson, Jr., *A Preface to Chaucer* (Princeton University Press, 1963).
6. For the influence of Augustinian meditation on seventeenth century poetry see Louis L. Martz, *The Paradise Within* (New Haven: Yale University Press, 1964).
7. In *Studies in Seventeenth Century Poetic* (Madison: University of Wisconsin Press, 1965), pp. 50-51, Ruth Wallerstein appears to argue for a distinction between narrative allegory and allegory which focused upon the symbolism of words. She finds the latter within the Augustinian tradition and claims it distinguishes seventeenth century poetry from medieval allegory.
8. Saint Augustine, *On Christian Doctrine*, trans. D.W. Robertson, Jr. (Indianapolis: Library of Liberal Arts, 1958), p. 34.
9. *Ibid.*, pp. 88-89.
10. See Edward Bliss Reed, "The Poems of Thomas Third Lord Fairfax", *Transactions of the Connecticut Academy of Arts and Sciences*, Vol. XIV (1909), pp. 237-290.
11. Clements R. Markham, *A Life of the Great Lord Fairfax* (London: Macmillan, 1870), p. 368.

Chapter Two

1. *A Dialogue between the Resolved Soul and Created Pleasure*, lines 11-12.
2. *The Nymph complaining for the death of her Faun*, lines 18-19.
3. *The Mower against Gardens*, lines 1-2.
4. *Musicks Empire*, line 1.
5. *The Nymph*, lines 121-122.
6. *The Mower's Song*, line 4.
7. *The Mower's Song*, line 16.

8. *To his Coy Mistress*, line 1.
9. *Bermudas*, line 40.
10. *A Dialogue between the Resolved Soul and Created Pleasure*, line 17.
11. *The Picture of little T.C.*, lines 31-32.
12. *The Garden*, line 48.
13. *Clorinda and Damon*, lines 27-30.

Chapter Three

1. See George Herbert's *The Answer*: "As a young exhalation, newly waking, / Scorns his first bed of dirt, and means the sky". (lines 8-9).
2. An excellent study of this tradition in seventeenth century poetry is Louis L. Martz, *The Paradise Within*, (New Haven: Yale University Press, 1964).
3. See Saint Augustine, *Confessions*, trans. R.S. Pine-Coffin (Harmondsworth: Penguin, 1961), p. 226. Book X, Chapter 20.
4. *The Garden*, line 57.
5. *The Picture of little T.C.*, line 2.
6. See Saint Augustine, *Confessions*, pp. 218-219. Book X, Chapter 11.
7. For the classic statement of the progress from contemplation of the world to contemplation of self, and illumination see Saint Augustine, *Confessions*, p. 151. Book VII, Chapter 17.
8. Paul Oskar Kristeller, *The Philosophy of Marsilio Ficino*, trans. Virginia Conant (Gloucester, Mass.: Peter Smith, 1964), pp. 96-97.
9. *John Donne's Sermons on the Psalms and Gospels*, ed. Evelyn M. Simpson (University of California Press, 1963), p. 185.
10. Saint Bonaventura, *The Mind's Road to God*, trans. George Boas (Indianapolis: Library of Liberal Arts, 1953), p. 30.
11. Saint Augustine, *Confessions*, pp. 146-147. Book VII, Chapter 10.
12. Saint Augustine, *The City of God*, trans. John Healey (London: Dent, 1967), Vol. II, p. 300. Book XX, Chapter XXI.
13. See *A Dialogue between the Soul and Body*, lines 11-13:

    O who shall me deliver whole,
    From bonds of this Tyrannic Soul?
    Which, stretcht upright, impales me so.

    Also see *The Definition of Love*, lines 9-10:

    And yet I quickly might arrive
    Where my extended Soul is fixt.
14. See Donne's *A Valediction: forbidding mourning*, lines 1-4. The matter is discussed in Hugh of St. Victor, *On the Sacraments of the Christian Faith (De Sacramentis)* trans. Roy. J. Deferrari (Cambridge, Mass.: The Mediaeval Academy of America, 1951), p. 434.
15. Bonaventura, *op.cit.*, p. 44.
16. *Ibid.*, p. 4.
17. *Ibid.*, p. 28.
18. Christopher Ricks has pointed to a similar use of syntactical fluidity in Milton. See *Milton's Grand Style* (Oxford University Press, 1967), p. 138.
19. Saint Augustine, *The City of God*, Vol. II, p. 136. Book XVI, Chapter XXXVII.
20. Donne, *op.cit.*, p. 145.
21. *The Bunch of Grapes*, line 16. Herbert calls prayer "Exalted Manna" (*Prayer (I)*, line 10).
22. *Partheneia Sacra*, by H.A. (1633), intro. by Iain Fletcher (Aldington: Hand and Flower Press, 1950), pp. 64-65.
23. Thomas Traherne, *Meditations on the Six Days of the Creation* (1717), intro.

George Robert Cuffey (University of California Press: The Augustan Reprint Society, 1966), p. 18. The passage is based on Job 37 and 38. The dew of "correction" is hail. See Exodus 9:18 ff; Psalm 105:32; Psalm 148:8; Isaiah 28:2.

Chapter Four

1. In *The Church Militant* Herbert imagines religion as moving from east to west: "Religion, like a pilgrim, westward bent" (line 29). "Religion stands on tiptoe in our land/Ready to pass to the *American* strand" (*Ibid.*, lines 235-236). In *The Character of Holland* Marvell writes: "Sure when *Religion* did it self imbark, / And from the *East* would *Westward* steer its Ark" (lines 67-68).
2. Saint Augustine, *The City of God*, trans. John Healey (London: Dent, 1967), Vol. II, p. 18. Book XIII, Chapter XXI.
3. Numbers 13:23; Deuteronomy 8:8.
4. *Encyclopaedia Biblica*, ed. T.K. Cheyne and J. Sutherland Black (London: Adam and Charles Black, 1899), Vol. II, p. 1519.
5. Origen, *The Song of Songs, Commentary and Homilies*, trans. R.P. Lawson (London: Longmans, 1957), pp. 179-180.
6. See Psalm 118:22; Isaiah 28:14-16; Matthew 21:42; Mark 12:10; Acts 4:11; Romans 9:32-33; Ephesians 2:20; I Peter 2:7-8.
7. George Herbert, *The Sacrifice*, lines 202-203.
8. Matthew Poole, *A Commentary on the Holy Bible* (London: Banner of Truth Trust, 1962), Vol. II, p. 312. If the "tree" does "bear" "Apples plants", they could be the "sons" of Canticles 2:3. However Marvell may be thinking of the prophecy of Christ in Isaiah 11:1; "The stem of Jesse" was usually portrayed as a tree in medieval iconography. Thus the tree of Jesse bears Christ the apple tree of Canticles 2:3.
9. See Ernest Evans's note on charity in *Saint Augustine's Enchiridion* (London: S.P.C.K., 1953), p. 106.
10. The divine odour of Christ's Sacrifice, and His voice bringing the gospels, appear together in Herbert's *The Odour*:

    How sweetly doth *My Master* sound! *My Master!*
    As ambergris leaves a rich scent
    Unto the taster:
    So do these words a sweet content,
    An oriental fragrancy, *My Master.*

    (lines 1-5.) Also see Marvell's *The Unfortunate Lover*, lines 61-62.
11. Acts 7:48: "Howbeit the most High dwelleth not in temples made with hands; as saith the prophet".
12. *Paradise Regained*, Book III, lines 182-183.

Chapter Five

1. Sir John Edwin Sandys, *A History of Classical Scholarship*, Vol. I (New York: Hafner Publishing Co., 1958), p. 639.
2. For the medieval tradition of the grief and laments of the Virgin, see Rosemary Woolf, *The English Religious Lyric in the Middle Ages* (Oxford: Clarendon Press, 1968), pp. 239 ff. Also see Yrjö Hirn, *The Sacred Shrine: A Study of the Poetry and Art of the Catholic Church* (London: Macmillan, 1912), especially chapter 19, pp. 375-404.
3. During the Renaissance the bride in Canticles was often allegorised as the Virgin. The symbolism of the Church as the Virgin is well known. A history of interpretations of the Song of Songs can be found in Christian D. Ginsburg, *The Song of Songs and Coheleth*, 1857 (reprinted, New York: KTAV Publishing House, 1970), pp. 27-223. The presence of Canticles in *The Nymph* was first noted in M.C. Brad-

brook and M.G. Lloyd Thomas, *Andrew Marvell* (Cambridge University Press, 1940), and defended by Karina Williamson, "Marvell's *The Nymph Complaining*: A Reply", *Modern Philology* Vol. 51 (1954), pp. 268-271. The subject has often been discussed.

4. See Hirn, *op.cit.*, p. 440. For Fairfax's poems, see E.B. Reed, "The Poems of Thomas Third Lord Fairfax," *Transactions of the Connecticut Academy of Arts and Sciences*, Vol. XIV (1909), pp. 237-290, p. 250. For further discussion of Christian symbolism where the Annunciation is associated with Canticles, see Stanley Stewart, *The Enclosed Garden* (Madison: University of Wisconsin Press, 1966), pp. 36-39, & p. 45.
5. Alastair Fowler has shown that Renaissance elegies are often divided into eleven parts and contain 120 lines. (Marvell's poem consists of 122 lines.) See Fowler's *Triumphal Forms* (Cambridge University Press, 1970), pp. 198-199.
6. "For as the vnreasonable beest was slayne for clensynge of synnes, & the blode of it shedde vpon the awter, so cryst Ihesu the lambe vndefyled, moost innocent beest was put to dethe vpon a crosse & all his blode shedde for *the* remyssyon of synners. The people of Israell synned & were worthy to dye for it, those bruyte beestes dyd none euyl & yet were put to deth for thamendment of theyr synnes. Lyke wyse our sauyour cryst all though he was moost innocent, moost pure, neuer offended in ony condycyon, notwithstandinge he suffred deth moost pacyently for our offences". *The English Works of John Fisher*, ed. John E.B. Mayor (London: EETS, 1876), p. 129.
7. Origen, *The Song of Songs, Commentary and Homilies*, trans. R.P. Lawson (London: Longmans, 1957), p. 226. Also see Jeremiah 24:7: "And I will give them an heart to know me, that I *am* the LORD".
8. By the seventeenth century Anglican Bishop Thomas Ken. (No. 217 in the *English Hymnal*.) See A.M. Allchin, "Our Lady in Seventeenth Century Anglican Devotion and Theology," in *The Blessed Virgin Mary*, ed. E.L. Mascall and H.S. Box (London: Darton, Longman & Todd, 1963), pp. 53-76, p. 54. A useful source for Anglican attitudes towards Mary is George Herbert's *To All Angels and Saints*, lines 8-20.
9. *Meditations on the Life and Passion of Christ*, ed. Charlotte d'Evelyn (London: EETS, 1921; New York: Kraus Reprint Co., 1971), p. 5, line 149. I have modernised the quotation.
10. Jeremy Taylor, *The History of the Life and Death of the Holy Jesus*, Vols. II and III of *The Whole Works of The Right Reverend Jeremy Taylor* in 15 vols. (London, 1839), Vol. II, p. 27 & p. 26.
11. Origen, *op.cit.*, pp. 59-61.
12. I Corinthians 3:2; Hebrews 5:12; I Peter 2:2.
13. *Upon Appleton House*, stanza XXII, line 174. Cf. Exodus 30:30; Exodus 40:13; Leviticus 8:12.
14. Cf. under Le Cerf (lines 277-280) in Guillaume Clerc de Normandie, *Le Bestiaire Divin*, intro. C. Hippeau (Geneva: Slatkine Reprints, 1970), p. 112. Also see Origen, *op.cit.*, p. 300.
15. Thomas Robinson, *The Life and Death of Mary Magdalene* (London: EETS, 1899), p. 45 (Part II.13, line 991): "With milke-white hand, hee by y[e] hand her tooke".
16. *Meditations on the Life of Christ*, tr. Isa Ragusa (Princeton University Press, 1961), p. 89.
17. Origen, *op.cit.*, pp. 210-211.
18. Origen, *op.cit.*, p. 118.
19. *Ibid.*, p. 176.
20. *The Life and Works of Saint Bernard*, ed. John Mabillon, trans. Samuel J. Eales, Vol. IV, *Cantica Canticorum: Eighty-Six Sermons on the Song of Solomon* (London: Hodges, 1896), p. 430.

21. Matthew Poole, *A Commentary on the Holy Bible* (London: Banner of Truth Trust, 1962), Vol. II, p. 313.
22. Origen, *op.cit.*, p. 177.
23. Poole, *op.cit.*, Vol. II, p. 315.
24. *Ibid.*, Vol. II, p. 321.
25. Saint Bernard, *op.cit.*, p. 439.
26. *Meditations on the Life and Passion of Christ*, ed. Charlotte d'Evelyn, p. 46, line 1752. I have modernised the quotation.
27. Saint Bernard, *op.cit.*, p. 14.
28. Origen, *op.cit.*, p. 60.
29. Saint Bernard, *op.cit.*, p. 434.
30. *Partheneia Sacra*, by H.A. (1633), intro. Iain Fletcher (Aldington: Hand and Flower Press, 1950), p. 205.
31. George Herbert, *Dulness*, lines 11-12.
32. Rosemond Tuve, *A Reading of George Herbert* (London: Faber and Faber, 1952), p. 151.
33. *Meditations on the Life and Passion of Christ*, ed. Charlotte d'Evelyn, p. 11, lines 375-376. I have modernised the quotation.
34. Bernard says that roses are martyrs and lilies are virgins of the Church. Saint Bernard, *op.cit.*, p. 183.
35. A.G. Herbert, *Liturgy and Society* (London: Faber & Faber, 1961), p. 25.
36. *John Donne's Sermons on the Psalms and Gospels*, ed. Evelyn M. Simpson (University of California Press, 1963), p. 158.
37. Matthew Poole comments on Hebrews 5:7: "that which made him sweat through his flesh congealed clots of blood, squeezed by his agony out of his body, which made him weep and cry loudly; his voice as well as his soul was stretched out in prayer: the like was exercised by him in his conflict on the cross. Matth. xxvii.46. How bitter was his passion to him! How fervent, importunate, and loud his prayers!" (Poole, *op.cit.*, Vol. III, p. 828.)
38. The "Gumme" of line 96 almost certainly alludes to the biblical myrrh. See Origen, *op.cit.*, pp. 341-342.
39. Hugh of Saint Victor, *On the Sacraments of the Christian Faith* (*De Sacramentis*), trans. Roy J. Deferrari (Cambridge, Mass.: The Mediaeval Academy of America, 1951), p. 302.
40. See *Paradise Lost*, Book X, line 1100 — Book XI, line 27. For mixing tears, see Herbert, *Praise* (*III*), lines 25-26.
41. Hirn, *op.cit.*, pp. 188-190. Diana's shrine supposedly had a canopy and comparisons were drawn between it and the Christian altar. See Cyril E. Pocknee, *The Christian Altar* (London: A.R. Mowbray, 1963), p. 55.
42. Under Mosaic law, on the day of atonement, the High Priest alone enters the inner Tabernacle or Holy of Holies, to offer incense on the golden censer and to offer the sacrificial blood (Leviticus 16:2-27). "Which type, in all its parts, was perfectly fulfilled in Christ" (Poole, *op.cit.*, Vol. III, p. 847). See Hebrews 9:7 ff. Also see the comment on Hebrews 9:4 in Poole, Vol. III, p. 846.
43. Donne, *op.cit.*, p. 92.
44. Saint Augustine, *The City of God*, trans. John Healey (London: Dent, 1967), Vol. II, p. 123. Book XVI, Chapter XXIV. Saint Bernard, *op.cit.*, p. 358.
45. Poole, *op.cit.*, Vol. II, p. 326. Also see Job 19: 23-25.
46. Donne, *op.cit.*, p. 44.
47. Hirn, *op.cit.*, pp. 394-395.
48. *Partheneia Sacra*, p. 206.
49. While it is sometimes said that the altar of the Holy Church is Christ Himself, it is more common to speak of the altar as a shrine in which the Virgin encloses her Son. Thus a seventeenth century Anglican writes "here is the shrine and altar, the

glorious Virgin's lap". Allchin, *op.cit.*, p. 66.

50. Hirn, *op.cit.*, p. 72.
51. *Ibid.*, p. 24. Also see Revelation 6:9; and Pocknee, *op.cit.*, pp. 40-41.
52. Jeremy Taylor, *The Life of Our Blessed Lord and Saviour Jesus Christ*, *op.cit.*, Vol. II, p. lxxii.

Chapter Six

1. Saint Augustine, *On Christian Doctrine*, trans. D.W. Robertson, Jr. (Indianapolis: Library of Liberal Arts, 1958), pp. 103-104.
2. *Paradise Lost*, Book XII, lines 553-556.
3. Stanley Stewart shows how much *To his Coy Mistress* reflects Christian literature on the need to use this life as a preparation for death and final judgment. Stewart, however, sees the Christian doctrine as parodied, and reads the poem as making a case for the primacy of the body. Stanley Stewart, "Marvell and the *Ars Moriendi*", *Seventeenth-Century Imagery*, ed. Earl Miner (University of California Press, 1971), pp. 133-150.
4. Commenting upon the tension between religious and secular usage of words in medieval Latin literature, Wilhelm says that "*iamiam* or the alternate word *nunc* . . . is interesting. Albertus Magnus pronounced the final judgment upon such seemingly innocent adverbs when he called the inferior, fleeting, illusory goods of this world *bona et nunc*, 'goods for here and now'." James J. Wilhelm, *The Cruelest Month* (New Haven: Yale University Press, 1965), pp. 108-109.
5. The rhyme words of lines 33-34 present a textual problem. The Folio has "hew" and "glew". The latter is usually amended to "dew". The Bodleian copy (M.S. English poet d. 49) changes "hew" (line 33) to "glew" and "glew" (line 34) to "dew". While the Bodleian version is now commonly accepted, it is probable that "hew" and "glew" are instances of Neo-Platonic jargon and that "hew" refers to the soul's assumption of its mortal form. (See Spenser, *The Faerie Queene*, Book 3, Canto 6, lines 33, 35, 38, and *Amoretti*, 79, 80.) Even "ewe" in the older sense of appearance would fit.
6. Saint Augustine, *The City of God*, trans. John Healey (London: Dent, 1967), Vol. II, pp. 174-175. Book XVII, Chapter XX.
7. *The Ruines of Time*, line 372. See Matthew 16:18.
8. As Samson bore the doors away,
Christ's hands, though nailed, wrought our salvation,
    And did unhinge that day.
George Herbert, *Sunday*, lines 47-49. Christ's victory is prophesied in Isaiah 45:2.
9. For Mary as "the gate of life" see *The Ancrene Riwle*, trans. M.B. Salu (London: Burns and Oates, 1955), p. 17; Stephen Manning, *Wisdom and Number* (University of Nebraska Press, 1962), p. 87; and Saint Bonaventura, *The Mirror of the Blessed Virgin Mary* and *The Psaltyr of Our Lady*, trans. Sr. Mary Emmanuel (St. Louis and London: B. Herder, 1932), p. 228.
10. It would not affect my interpretation if "glew" is the correct reading. Hirn, however, shows that "dew" was often a symbol of the Incarnation. Yrjö Hirn, *The Sacred Shrine: A Study of the Poetry and Art of the Catholic Church* (London: Macmillan, 1912), p. 363. Also see the conclusion of Marvell's *On a Drop of Dew*.
11. See Hirn, *op.cit.*, p. 293.
12. *The Whole Works of the Right Rev. Jeremy Taylor*, Vol. II (London, 1839), *The Life of Our Blessed Lord and Saviour Jesus Christ*, p. 21.
13. *Ibid.*, p. 23.
14. *On a Drop of Dew*, lines 25-26.
15. Saint Francis de Sales, *The Love of God*, trans. Vincent Kerns (London: Burns and Oates, 1962), Book I, Chapter X, p. 26. For contemplation as a kind of death, see

John Donne's Sermons on the Psalms and Gospels, ed. Evelyn M. Simpson (University of California Press, 1963), pp. 42-44.

Chapter Seven

1. Bartas in the *Devine Weekes* uses the figure of a shipwreck for Adam's Fall and the traditional figure of God as a rock:

   But mortall *Adam*, Monarch heere beneath,
   Erring, drawes all into the pathes of death;
   And on rough Seas, as a blind Pylot rash,
   Against the rock of Heau'ns iust wrath doth dash
   The Worlds great Vessell.

   Bartas: *His Devine Weekes and Workes* (1605), trans. Joshua Sylvester (Gainesville, Florida: Scholars' Facsimiles & Reprints, 1965), p. 330. Also see *Paradise Lost*, Book X, lines 665-718. In Vaughan's *Man's Fall and Recovery*, the Fall is similarly portrayed:

   Farewell you Everlasting hills! I'm Cast
   Here under Clouds, where stormes and tempests blast.

   Henry Vaughan, *Poems*, ed. L.C. Martin (Oxford University Press, 1963), p. 241.
2. *Incarnationis Profundum Mysterium*, *The Sonnets of William Alabaster*, ed. G.M. Story and Helen Gardner (Oxford University Press, 1959), p. 31. See *Early Christian Writings*, trans. Maxwell Staniforth (Harmondsworth: Penguin, 1968), *The Epistle to Diognetus* (anon), p. 182: "Though He has existed since the beginning, He came as one appearing newly; though we know Him to be from old, He is born ever anew in the hearts of His Saints. This is He who is from everlasting". An interesting discussion of the symbolic association between Mary and the waters of Creation over which the Spirit moved is in Alan Watts, *Myth and Ritual in Christianity* (London: Thames and Hudson, 1954), p. 107.
3. Luke 17:25-26: "But first must he suffer many things, and be rejected of this generation. And as it was in the days of Noe, so shall it be also in the days of the Son of man". "Now Jonah prophesied Christ rather in suffering than in speaking and that most manifestly considering the passion and resurrection". Saint Augustine, *The City of God*, trans. John Healey (London: Dent. 1967), Vol. II, p. 203. Book XVIII, Chapter XXX.
4. *A Hymn on the Nativity of My Saviour. The Works of Ben Jonson*, ed. Francis Cunningham (London: Chatto and Windus, 1903), Vol. III, p. 279. See Matthew 26:39.
5. See Ephesians 2:20-21: "And are built upon the foundation of the apostles and prophets, Jesus Christ himself being the chief corner *stone*; In whom all the building fitly framed together groweth unto an holy temple in the Lord". I Corinthians 10:4: "And did all drink the same spiritual drink: for they drank of that spiritual Rock that followed them: and that Rock was Christ".
6. The "Covenant of theirs was smashed to pieces, so that the seal of the Covenant of Jesus the Beloved might be stamped on our own hearts". *The Epistle of Barnabas*, in *Early Christian Writings*, p. 197.
7. Lapide says of Luke 1:5 that Christ was born in the days of Herod "to show that the sceptre had now departed from Judah, and had passed over to an alien, and therefore that the time for the advent of the Messiah was at hand according to the prophecy of Jacob, Gen. xlix. 10." (The prophecy is the "Shiloh come" symbolism alluded to in Marvell's Mower poems.) *The Great Commentary of Cornelius A Lapide*, trans. Thomas W. Mossman. *S. Luke's Gospel* (Catholic Standard Library, Vol. IV. Edinburgh: John Grant, 1908), p. 5.
8. Isaiah 42:13: "he shall cry, yea, roar; he shall prevail against his enemies".
9. For the threatening clouds and the thunder, see Vaughan's *The Law and the Gos-*

pel. Paul says "all our fathers were under the cloud, and all passed through the sea" (I Corinthians 10:1).

10. See Rosemond Tuve, *A Reading of George Herbert* (London: Faber & Faber, 1952), p. 35.
11. See Hebrews: 1:2: "Hath in these last days spoken unto us by *his* Son, whom he hath appointed heir of all things, by whom also he made the worlds".
12. See *Paradise Lost*, Book IV, line 196.
13. See *Paradise Regained*, Book IV, lines 409-421.
14. Saint Bonaventura, *Breviloquium*, trans. Edwin Esser Nemmers (St. Louis and London: Herder Book Co., 1947), p. 129.
15. *Paradise Regained*, Book II, lines 252-259.
16. *Ibid*., Book I, lines 159-161.
17. Isaiah 9:6-7: "For unto us a Child is born . . . Of the increase of *his* government and peace *there shall be* no end". Luke 17:5: "And the apostles said unto the Lord, Increase our faith".
18. Psalm 44:22: "For thy sake are we killed all the day long; we are counted as sheep for the slaughter". The sufferings of the apostles are also a "spectacle": "For I think that God hath set forth us the apostles last, as it were appointed to death: for we are made a spectacle unto the world, and to angels, and to men" (I Corinthians 4:9).
19. A similar theme can be found in Crashaw's *Vexilla Regis*:

    But though great LOVE, greedy of such sad gain
    Usurp't the Portion of THY pain,
        And from the nailes & spear
        Turn'd the steel point of fear,
    Their use is chang'd, not lost; and now they move
    Not stings of wrath, but wounds of love.

    The Poems of Richard Crashaw, ed. L.C. Martin (Oxford University Press, 1927), p. 278, stanza III, lines 13-18.
20. The image of the lover "Cuffing the Thunder with one hand" has its parallel in Christ's description of Himself in Herbert's *Sacrifice*: "Who grasps the earth and heaven with his fist" (line 130).
21. But there were Rocks would not relent at This.
    Lo, for their own hearts, they rend his.

    Crashaw, *Evensong — The Hymn*, *op.cit.*, p. 273. In *Emblems*, Book V, *The Farewell*, Quarles writes "break this fleshly rock in sunder, / That from this heart, this hell of grief, / May spring a Heav'n of love and wonder". Francis Quarles, *Emblems Divine and Moral* (London, 1866), p. 233. For "stubborn Rock" we might also recall Peter's conduct in Matthew 16:22-23.
22. In *The Sacrifice* Herbert brings together allusions to the Last Supper, flagellation, Sacrifice, and Eucharist:

    Then with a scarlet robe they me array;
    Which shows my blood to be the only way
    And cordial left to repair man's decay.

    (lines 157-159). In *The Invitation* Herbert also expresses communion imagery in terms of feasting:

    God is here prepared and drest,
                    And the feast,
    God, in whom all dainties are.

    (lines 4-6).
23. The sacrificial offerings in Leviticus 1, types of Christ's Sacrifice, are "a sweet savour unto the LORD". According to Dom Gregory Dix, relishes were offered at Jewish eve of Sabbath or holy day suppers before the meal began. For the relation of such relishes to the Last Supper, see Dix's *The Shape of the Liturgy* (London:

Dacre Press, second edition, 1945), pp. 50-51.

24. For a discussion of the perfume of grace, see Jean Daniélou, *The Bible and the Liturgy* (Notre Dame University Press, 1956), p. 125. Images of smell and sound are used in Herbert's *The Odour* as symbols of Christ, lines 1-5.
25. An early Christian hymn quoted by Ignatius of Antioch: *The Epistle to the Ephesians*, in *Early Christian Writings*, pp. 77-78.

Chapter Eight

1. An interesting but controversial study is: Andars Nygren, *Agape and Eros* (London: S.P.C.K., 1954). For Augustine's theory of love, see John Burnaby, *Amor Dei* (London: Hodder and Stoughton, 1938).
2. Saint Augustine, *Confessions*, trans. R.S. Pine-Coffin (Harmondsworth: Penguin, 1961), p. 251. Book X, Chapter 43.
3. *The Life and Works of Saint Bernard*, ed. John Mabillon, trans. Samuel J. Eales, Vol. IV, *Cantica Canticorum: Eighty-Six Sermons on the Song of Solomon* (London: Hodges, 1896), p. 239. Taylor says: "despair is opposed to hope, and hope relies upon the Divine promises; and where there is no promise, there the despair is not a sin, but a mere impossibility". *The Whole Works of the Right Rev. Jeremy Taylor*, Vol. III (London, 1839), *The History of the Life and Death of the Holy Jesus*, p. 356.
4. Matthew 19:26; Luke 18:26-27.
5. Also see Jeremiah 32:17; Zechariah 8:6; and especially Hebrews 6:18. "A birth as rare" would bring to mind Christ's Virgin Birth.
6. Magnanimity is, of course, one of the Aristotelian virtues. Herbert says "Pitch . . . thy projects high . . . magnanimous be . . . who aimeth at the sky . . . a grain of glory . . . cures . . . lethargicness". *The Church-Porch*, lines 332-336.
7. Saint Bernard, *op.cit.*, p. 489.
8. *Ibid.*, p. 243.
9. Marvell's *On a Drop of Dew*, line 26.
10. The humour of depicting hope as feeble and unable to fly towards the divine object is enhanced if we remember the famous passage in *Phaedrus* where the soul contemplates the beauty of the earth and is transported into a recollection of the true beauty:

    > he would like to fly away, but he cannot; he is like a bird fluttering and looking upward and careless of the world below; and he is therefore thought to be mad. And I have shown this of all inspirations to be the noblest and highest and the offspring of the highest to him who has or shares in it; and that he who loves the beautiful is called a lover because he partakes of it.

    The Dialogues of Plato, trans. B. Jowett, third ed. (Oxford, 1892), Vol. I, p. 156.
11. Saint Bernard, *op.cit.*, p. 15.
12. See Marvell's *A Dialogue between the Soul and Body*, lines 12-13: "this Tyrannic Soul / Which, stretcht upright".
13. Saint Bernard, *op.cit.*, p. 174.
14. Boethius, *The Consolation of Philosophy*, trans. V.E. Watts (Harmondsworth: Penguin, 1969), p. 135.
15. *Symposium*, *op. cit.*, p. 534.
16. See Matthew 5:48: "Be ye therefore perfect, even as your Father which is in heaven is perfect"; and I John 2:5 and 4:17.
17. *Partheneia Sacra*, by H.A. (1633), intro. Iain Fletcher (Aldington, Hand and Flower Press, 1950), p. 85.
18. "Then takes he th'Astrelabe, where-in the Sphere Is flat reduced". Bartas: *His Devine Weekes and Workes* (1605), trans. Joshua Sylvester (Gainesville, Florida: Scholars' Facsimiles & Reprints, 1965), p. 490.

19. Earl J. Schulze, "The Reach of Wit: Marvell's 'The Definition of Love'," *Papers of the Michigan Academy of Science, Arts, and Letters*, Vol. L (1965), pp. 563-574, p. 572.
20. See the first two stanzas of Marvell's poem, *Upon the Hill and Grove at Bill-borow*.
21. The tradition is reflected in *Paradise Lost*, Book II, lines 753 ff.
22. "Corner-hunting Lust". See Francis Quarles, *Emblems* (London, 1866), Book V, 14, p. 227.
23. See Robert B. Prentice, *The Psychology of Love According to St. Bonaventura* (New York: The Franciscan Institute of St. Bonaventura, 1951), p. 63.
24. Paul Oskar Kristeller, *The Philosophy of Marsilio Ficino*, trans. Virginia Conant (Gloucester, Mass: Peter Smith, 1964), p. 97.
25. *The Works of Edmund Spenser*, Variorum Edition (Baltimore: Johns Hopkins Press, 1933). *The Faerie Queene*, Book Two, ed. Edwin Greenlaw, *et al.*, p. 473.
26. *John Donne's Sermons on the Psalms and Gospels*, ed. Evelyn M. Simpson (University of California Press, 1963), p. 185.
27. Robert Bellarmin, *The Mind's Ascent to God*, trans. Monialis (London: A.R. Mowbray, 1925), p. 108.
28. See Etienne Gilson, *The Mystical Theology of St. Bernard*, trans, A.H.C. Downes (London: Sheed and Ward, 1940), p. 104 and p. 239.
29. Saint Bernard, *op.cit.*, p. 246.
30. *Partheneia Sacra*, p. 119.
31. Abraham Cowley, *Poems*, ed. A.R. Waller (Cambridge: English Classics, 1905). *Impossibilities*, p. 130, stanza 3.

Chapter Nine

1. "Simplicity" might suggest singleness and unity as opposed to "duplicity" — twoness and a fall into multiplicity. The soul is like God in its simplicity of being, i.e. to exist is the same thing as to live.
2. *A Dialogue between the Resolved Soul and Created Pleasure*, line 1, line 11.
3. Sister Mary Irma Corcoran, *Milton's Paradise with Reference to the Hexameral Background* (Washington, D.C.: Catholic University of America Press, 1945), pp. 56-57.
4. *John Donne's Sermons on the Psalms and Gospels*, ed. Evelyn M. Simpson (University of California Press, 1963), p. 193. See *Partheneia Sacra* by H.A. (1633), intro. Iain Fletcher (Aldington: Hand and Flower Press, 1950), pp. 237-238. In Isaiah 7:14 it is prophesied that a virgin will conceive and call her son Immanuel. "Emmanuel, which being interpreted is, God with us" (Matthew 1:23). See Matthew Poole, *A Commentary on the Holy Bible* (London: Banner of Truth Trust, 1962), Vol. II, p. 341.
5. *The Life and Works of Saint Bernard*, ed. John Mabillon, trans. Samuel J. Eales, Vol. IV, *Cantica Canticorum: Eighty-Six Sermons on the Song of Solomon* (London: Hodges, 1896), p. 385.
6. J.W. Blench, *Preaching in England in the Late Fifteenth and Sixteenth Centuries* (Oxford: Blackwell, 1964), p. 163.
7. *The Ancrene Riwle*, trans. M.B. Salu (London: Burns and Oates, 1955), p. 110.
8. See *Paradise Lost*, Book VI, lines 750ff; and Dante's *Purgatory*, Canto XXIX, lines 106ff. Alastair Fowler shows that *The Picture of little T.C.* is in part modelled on Petrarch's *Triumph of Chastity*, and discusses the central accent. See *Triumphal Forms* (Cambridge University Press, 1970), p. 78. I have discussed the relationship of *T.C.* to Petrarch's *Triumphs* in "Lovelace's *Lucasta* and Marvell's *T.C.*: Petrarch (and Dante?) in Seventeenth England", *Complit — Litcomp*, Vol. I, No. 1 (1973), pp. 70-86. Petrarch's *Triumphs*, I think, explain the pictorialism of Marvell's poem and lend support to my reading of *T.C.* as about chastity and eternity. The biblical

motifs I find in Marvell's poem can also be found in Petrarch and Dante associated with similar ideas and symbols.

9. Emile Mâle, *L'art religieux du xiiie siècle en France* (Paris: Librairie Armand Colin, Livre de Poche, 1958), Vol. II, pp. 75-76.
10. "Some Fruit-trees mossy root", *The Garden*, line 50.
11. Saint Bernard, *op.cit.*, p. 296. Also see Canticles 2:17 and 4:6; both passages are linked to the prophetic meaning of 8:14, allegorised as the Second Coming.
12. See under Dead in *Encyclopaedia Biblica*, ed. T.K. Cheyne and J. Sutherland Black (London: Adam and Charles Black, 1899), Vol. I, p. 1042. Where the AV translates dead or death, the RV often translates shades, or the shades. Also see under Eschatology, *Encyclopaedia Biblica*, Vol. II, p. 1341.
13. See Geoffrey H. Hartman, "Marvell, St. Paul, and the Body of Hope," *ELH*, Vol. XXXI (1964), pp. 175-194.
14. *Verse Letter to Sir Edward Herbert*, line 33-34. *The Poems of John Donne*, ed. H.J.C. Grierson (Oxford University Press, 1942), p. 171. Also see Marvell's *First Anniversary*, lines 153-156.
15. Bruce King, "Marvell's Tulip", *Notes and Queries*, N.S. Vol. XVI, No. 3 (March, 1969), p. 100. Also see the editor's note to Saint Bernard, *op.cit.*, p. 290, where it is suggested that the biblical lily may be a lotus or tulip.
16. *The Works of Gerrard Winstanley*, ed. George Sabine (Cornell University Press, 1941), p. 212.
17. *Paradise Lost*, Book IV, lines 269-271.
18. See Dante's *Purgatory*, Canto XXVIII, line 50.
19. *A Maske Presented at Ludlow Castle*, lines 453-469.

Chapter Ten

1. Geoffrey Hartman was the first to explain the relevance of Romans for the Mower poems. Geoffrey H. Hartman, "Marvell, St. Paul and the Body of Hope", *ELH*, Vol. XXXI (1964), pp. 175-194.
2. The relationship between man and nature is made explicit in Milton and Bartas.

   Earth felt the wound, and Nature from her seat
   Sighing through all her Works gave signs of woe,
   That all was lost.

   (*Paradise Lost*, Book IX, lines 782-784).

   The World's transform'd from that it was at first:
   For Adams Sinne, all Creatures else accurst:
   Their Harmonie dis-tuned by His iarre:
   Yet all againe concent, to make Him warre;
   As th' Elements, and aboue all, the Earth.

   (Bartas: *His Devine Weekes and Workes* (1605), trans. Joshua Sylvester [Gainesville, Florida: Scholars' Facsimiles & Reprints, 1965], p. 327).
3. *The Garden of Cyrus*, *The Prose of Sir Thomas Browne*, ed. Norman Endicott (Garden City, N.Y.: Doubleday & Co., 1967), p. 295 and p. 306.
4. See Bruce King, "Marvell's Tulip," *Notes and Queries*, N.S. Vol. XVI, No. 3 (March, 1969), p. 100.
5. See Arnold Williams, *The Common Expositor* (Chapel Hill: University of North Carolina Press, 1948), p. 159-173.
6. Cain's name was usually glossed as meaning possession. See Bernard F. Huppé, *Doctrine and Poetry* (New York: State University of New York Press, 1959), pp. 155-156.
7. *Paradise Lost*, Book IV, lines 1013-1026.
8. *The English Works of Sir Thomas More*, Vol. I, ed. W.E. Campbell (London: Eyre and Spottiswoode, 1930), pp. 493 ff. Also see *The English Works of John Fisher*,

ed. John E.B. Mayor (London: EETS, 1876), p. 36.
9. Francis Quarles, *Emblems* (London, 1866), Book I, Embleme II, p. 8.
10. See James 1:8: "A double minded man *is* unstable in all his ways."
11. Ah, what a thing is man devoid of grace,
Adoring garlic . . .
Who makes a root his god.
George Herbert, *The Church Militant*, lines 111-112, 115.
12. Acts 13:26; Philippians 3:5.
13. See Rosemond Tuve, *Allegorical Imagery* (Princeton University Press, 1966), p. 24; and Stanley Stewart, *The Enclosed Garden* (Madison: University of Wisconsin Press, 1966), p. 122.
14. See Marvell's Latin poem, *Upon an Eunuch*. The cherry was sometimes called the fruit of Paradise. See George Ferguson, *Signs and Symbols in Christian Art* (New York: Oxford University Press Galaxy Book, 1966), p. 29. There may be an allusion to Christ's Virgin Birth in the creation of the cherry. Stones can mean testicles.
15. *The Life and Works of Saint Bernard*, ed. John Mabillon, trans. Samuel J. Eales, Vol. IV, *Cantica Canticorum*: *Eighty-Six Sermons on the Song of Solomon* (London: Hodges, 1896), p. 76. For other contrasts between art/grace/enclosed and nature/wild see Stanley Stewart, *The Enclosed Garden,* pp. 52-58.
16. Marvell's *The Picture of little T.C.*, line 27.
17. I have discussed the relation of the Mower's complaint to Digger polemics in "'The Mower against Gardens' and the Levellers," *Huntington Library Quarterly*, Vol. XXXIII, No. 3 (May, 1970), pp. 237-242.

Chapter Eleven

1. Such as Aurelian Townshend's *A Dialogue betwixt Time and a Pilgrime*; *Paradise Lost*, Book X, line 606: "The Sithe of Time mowes down"; and Spenser's *Faerie Queene*:
   . . . wicked *Time*, who with his scyth addrest,
   Does mow the flowering herbes and goodly things,
   And all their glory to the ground downe flings.
   (Book III, Canto 6, xxxix). It should be remembered that death is spoken of as a leveller.
2. See Robert Herrick's "To Doctor Alabaster" (lines 17-20), and "Master Herrick's Farewell unto Poetry" (lines 33-35), and see Richard F. Giles, "A Note on April", *T.S. Eliot Newsletter*, Vol. I, No. 1 (1974), p. 3.
3. J.D. Rosenberg was the first to see this parabolic meaning of Juliana. See "Marvell and the Christian Idiom", *Boston University Studies in English*, Vol. 4 (1960), pp. 152-161.
4. See Matthew Poole, *A Commentary on the Holy Bible* (London: Banner of Truth Trust, 1962), Vol. III, p. 980; Alastair Fowler, *Spenser and the Numbers of Time* (London: Routledge and Kegan Paul, 1964), pp. 66-67; Revelation 16:8; and Dante's *Purgatory*, Canto 29, lines 117-120.
5. See Jeremiah 29:26; Hosea 9:7; and *Encyclopaedia Biblica*, ed. T.K. Cheyne and J. Sutherland Black (London: Adam and Charles Black, 1899), Vol. III, p. 2892.
6. Francis Quarles, *Emblems, Divine and Moral* (London, 1866), Book IV, Embleme XIV, p. 182.
7. *Encyclopaedia Biblica*, Vol. I, p. 6.
8. For the harvest of corn as an allegory of the soul, see John MacQueen, *Allegory* (London: Methuen, 1970), pp. 1-4.
9. Pierre Legouis, *Andrew Marvell: Poet, Puritan, Patriot* (Oxford University Press, 1965), p. 26.
10. *Three Middle English Sermons*, ed. D.M. Grisdale (Leeds School of English

Language, Texts and Monographs, 1939), p. 11. See Stanley J. Kahrl, "Allegory in Practice: A Study of Narrative Styles in Medieval Exempla", *Modern Philology*, Vol. LXIII, No. 2 (November, 1965), pp. 105-110.

11. For the contrast also see *Paradise Lost*, Book IV, lines 266-268.
12. See Richard Bernheimer, *Wild Men in the Middle Ages* (Harvard University Press, 1952), p. 96.
13. Bernard's Fourteenth Sermon on Canticles speaks of the Synagogue murmuring, recalling "her merits, her labours and the burden and heat of the day which she has borne" in contrast to the delights received by the Church. *The Life and Works of Saint Bernard*, ed. John Mabillon, trans, Samuel J. Eales, Vol. IV, *Cantica Canticorum: Eighty-Six Sermons on the Song of Solomon* (London: Hodges, 1896), p. 78.
14. Also see Isaiah 53:12 and the refrain in George Herbert's *Sacrifice*: "was ever grief like mine". For Abel, see Bernard F. Huppé, *Doctrine and Poetry* (New York: State University of New York Press, 1959), pp. 155-156.
15. See Poole's comments on Jonah 4:6; Poole, *op.cit.*, Vol. II, p. 933. Also see *Encyclopaedia Biblica*, Vol. II, p. 1899 and Vol. III, p. 3551.
16. MacQueen, *op.cit.*, pp. 23-28.
17. In Revelation it is the Beast who is "wounded to death; and his deadly wound was healed" (Revelation 13:3; 13:12). The Mower's healing of himself is based on a story found in Gerard's *Herball*. See the notes in H.M. Margoliouth's edition of Marvell's poems (Oxford University Press, revised edition, 1971).
18. The word "saviour" in the Bible can have both a medical and a religious significance. See *A Theological Word Book of the Bible*, ed. Alan Richardson (London: SCM Press, 1957), p. 103.
19. Jean Daniélou, *The Bible and the Liturgy* (Notre Dame University Press, 1956), pp. 54-55.
20. Pseudo-Chrysostom, quoted in Daniélou, *op.cit.*, p. 166. Also see Saint Methodius, *The Symposium*, trans. Herbert Musurillo (London: Longmans, 1958), pp. 133-134.
21. Poole, *op.cit.*, Vol. II, p. 585.

Chapter Twelve

1. See J.D. Rosenberg, "Marvell and the Christian Idiom", *Boston University Studies in English*, Vol. 4 (1960), pp. 152-161.
2. J.B. Leishman, *The Art of Marvell's Poetry* (London: Hutchinson, 1966), p. 144.
3. See Holland's translation of *The Historie of the World*, ed. of 1635, I, 326 and I, 593. Quoted by Leishman, p. 152.
4. In *The Tretyse of Love* we are told that the nightingale sings all night waiting for the sunrise. This signifies the holy soul in the dark night of this life awaiting The Lord. When she feels His coming, she sings with great joy. *The Tretyse of Love*, ed. John M. Fisher (London: EETS, 1951), p. 114. See *The Garden*, stanza eleven.
5. *The Whole Works of the Right Rev. Jeremy Taylor*, Vol. II (London, 1839). *The Life of Our Blessed Lord and Saviour Jesus Christ*, p. 47.
6. "Courteous" is also ironic in that it points beyond the glo-worms to the spiritual. "The very typically North French word *courtois* (*cortois*) . . . was applied to Christ and the Virgin Mary". James J. Wilhelm, *The Cruelest Month* (New Haven: Yale University Press, 1965), p. 244.
7. *The Mower's Song*, lines 21-22.
8. In the famous fourteenth century meditations on the life of Christ it is said of the time before the Incarnation: "For a very long time . . . because of the sin of the first man, no one was able to rise to his Home". *Meditations on the Life of Christ*,

trans. Isa Ragusa (Princeton University Press, 1961), p. 5.

9. See *The Garden*, stanza six, and *On a Drop of Dew*.
10. *Clorinda and Damon*, lines 17-23.

Chapter Thirteen

1. *The Life and Works of Saint Bernard*, ed. John Mabillon, trans. Samuel J. Eales, Vol. IV, *Cantica Canticorum*: *Eighty-Six Sermons on the Song of Solomon* (London: Hodges, 1896), p. 352.
2. *Ibid*., p. 352. Matthew Poole interprets the flowers as "evidence of the spring time, which . . . signify the day of grace, or the glad tidings of salvation". *A Commentary on the Holy Bible* (London: Banner of Truth Trust, 1962), Vol. II, p. 313.
3. Christopher Ricks discusses Milton's use of "luxurious" and "luxuriant" in *Milton's Grand Style* (Oxford University Press, 1967), pp. 111-112.
4. For the relationship of *gaude* with the *ave* as celebrating the Virgin in direct address, see Rosemary Woolf, *The English Religious Lyric in the Middle Ages* (Oxford: Clarendon Press, 1968), pp. 135-136.
5. See Robert Herrick, "To Doctor Alabaster" and "Master Herrick's Farewell unto Poetry". See Richard F. Giles, "A Note on April," *T.S. Eliot Newletter*, Vol. I, No. 1 (Spring, 1974), p. 3.
6. "Thus the prophetic Word can compare the Church with a meadow full of gay-coloured flowers, adorned and garlanded not only with the blossoms of chastity, but also with those of continence and motherhood: for *on the right hand* of the Bridegroom *stands the queen ornate in a gold-embroidered gown*". Saint Methodius, *The Symposium*, trans. Herbert Musurillo (London: Longmans, 1958), p. 57.
7. *The Works of Gerrard Winstanley*, ed. George Sabine (Cornell University Press, 1941), p. 208.
8. Also relevant are Psalm 110:1; Acts 2:34-35; Psalm 8:6; Romans 16:20; Revelation 14:20.
9. *The English Works of Sir Thomas More*, Vol. I, ed. W.E. Campbell (London: Eyre and Spottiswoode, 1931), p. 334.
10. Poole, *op.cit*., Vol. II, p. 313. The Douay version is "The time of pruning is come".
11. For Samson and the Apocalypse, see Barbara K. Lewalski, "*Samson Agonistes* and the 'Tragedy' of the Apocalypse," *PMLA*, Vol. 85 (1970), pp. 1050-1062.
12. Saint Bernard, *op.cit*., p. 164.

Chapter Fourteen

1. Jonathan S. Goldberg, "The Typology of 'Musicks Empire'," *Texas Studies in Literature and Language*, Vol. 13, pp. 421-430. In her recent edition of Marvell's poems, Elizabeth Story Donno also assumes that the poem is praise of either Fairfax or Cromwell. (Andrew Marvell, *The Complete Poems*, Harmondsworth: Penguin, 1972, pp. 262-263).
2. Hugh of Saint Victor, *On the Sacraments of the Christian Faith* (*De Sacramentis*), trans. Roy J. Deferrari (Cambridge, Mass.: the Mediaeval Academy of America, 1951), pp. 295-297. Also see: Saint Bonaventura, *Breviloquium*, trans. Edwin Esser Nemmers (St. Louis & London: Herder Book Co., 1947), p. 8; and Jean Daniélou, *The Bible and the Liturgy* (Notre Dame University Press, 1956), p. 278.
3. Bartas: *His Devine Weekes and Workes* (1605), trans. Joshua Sylvester (Gainesville, Florida: Scholars' Facsimiles & Reprints, 1965), pp. 9-10:

   That first World (yet) was a most forme-lesse *Forme*,
   A confus'd Heape, a *Chaos* most diforme,
   A Gulph of Gulphes, a Body ill compact,
   An ugly medly, where all difference lackt:

Where th' Elements lay iumbled all together,
Where hot and colde were iarring each with either.

Also see *Paradise Lost*, Book VII, lines 213-234.

4. Hugh of Saint Victor, *On the Sacraments*, pp. 9-10: "Matter was first made unformed and then formed, to show by this very fact that things not existing had first received their essence from that mode without which in a confused state they could not have form and order . . . Therefore, before form, matter was in a broken state, yet in form — in a form of confusion, before a form of disposition. In the first form, that of confusion, all corporeal things were first created as matter simultaneously and once; in the second form, that of disposition, they were afterwards arranged through the intervals of the six days".
5. Bartas, *op.cit.*, p. 11:

   This was not then the World, 'twas but the matter,
   The Nurcerie whence it should issue after:
   Or rather th' *Embryon* that within a *Weeke*
   Was to be borne: for that huge lumpe was like
   The shape-lesse burthen in the Mothers wombe.
6. Paul E. Beichner, *The Medieval Representative of Music, Jubal or Tubalcain* (Notre Dame: The Mediaeval Institute, University of Notre Dame, 1954), pp. 10-11.
7. *The Life and Works of Saint Bernard*, ed. John Mabillon, trans, Samuel J. Eales, Vol. IV, *Cantica Canticorum*: *Eighty-Six Sermons on the Song of Solomon* (London: Hodges, 1896), p. 42.
8. Bernard F. Huppé, *Doctrine and Poetry* (New York: State University of New York Press, 1959), p. 111. For Christ's presence at the Creation see Luke 1:78-79; John 1:1-3; Colossians 1:15-18.
9. Bartas, *op.cit.*, p. 246.
10. The verbs "made . . . tuned . . . call'd . . . built" are reminiscent of God's work at the Creation: "God created . . . blessed . . . said", etc.
11. *The Didascalicon of Hugh of Saint Victor*, trans. Jerome Taylor (New York: Columbia University Press, 1961), p. 109.
12. Saint Augustine, *The City of God*, trans. John Healey (London: Dent, 1967), Vol. II, p. 166. Book XVII, Chapter XIV.
13. Rosemond Tuve, *A Reading of George Herbert* (London: Faber & Faber, 1952), p. 146. See *John Donne's Sermons on the Psalms and Gospels*, ed. Evelyn M. Simpson (University of California Press, 1963), p. 115: "But nothing is more properly the word of God to us, than that which God himself speakes in those Organs and Instruments, which himself hath assumed for his chiefest worke, our redemption. For in creation God spoke, but in redemption he did; and more, he suffered".
14. Hugh of Saint Victor, *On the Sacraments*, p. 152.
15. In Bartas, the Progeny of Cain are described in the third part of the second day of the "second Week" under the heading "The Colonies".
16. Bartas, *op.cit.*, p. 437:

   To stop Ambition, Strife, and Auarice,
   Into Three Parts the Earth deuided is:
   To Sem the East, to Cham the South, the West
   To Iapheth falls; their seueral scopes exprest:
   Their fruitfull Spawne did all the World supply.
17. Saint Augustine, *The City of God*, Vol. II, p. 62. Book XV Chapter II: "Thus then we find this earthly city in two forms; the one presenting itself, and the other prefiguring the celestial city and serving it".
18. John 5:46: "For had ye believed Moses, ye would have believed me: for he wrote of me".

19. Deuteronomy 16:15; Daniélou, *op.cit.*, p. 344. Psalm 118:27 (Douay version): "Appoint a solemn day, with shady boughs". For the Feast of the Tabernacles (also known as the Feast of the Booths) see Exodus 23:16; Leviticus 23:43; Numbers 29:12; Nehemiah 8.
20. Saint Methodius, *The Symposium*, trans. Herbert Musurillo (London: Longmans, 1958), p. 133. See pp. 131-140 for an elaborate interpretation of the Feast which throws light on the associations Marvell has in mind.
21. "Raise" also has associations with the Resurrection and Ascension. Cf. Luke 1:69; John 6:40; Romans 4:25; Romans 6:4; I Corinthians 6:14, II Corinthians 14:14; Ephesians 2:6.
22. Matthew Poole, *A Commentary on the Holy Bible* (London: Banner of Truth Trust, 1962), Vol. I, pp. 774-775: "The chief design of these books is, to complete the history of the kings of Judah . . . which (though ignorant or inconsiderate persons may think trivial and useless) was a work of great necessity, to preserve the distinction of the tribes and families, that so it might appear that Christ came of that nation, and tribe, and family, of which he was to be born. And this account having been hitherto neglected, is most seasonably mentioned in these books, because this was to be in a manner the last part of the sacred and canonical history of the Old Testament, and therefore the fittest place to record those genealogies, upon which the truth and authority of the New Testament in some sort depends".
23. *Continuations and Beginnings*, ed. E.G. Stanley (London: Nelson, 1963), p. 90.
24. Poole (*op.cit.*, Vol. I, p. 806) says that God's unwillingness to let David build the temple (I Chronicles 22:8) shows that "the church (whereof the temple was a manifest and illustrious type) should be built by Christ, the *Prince of peace*, Isa. ix.6".
25. See Saint Augustine, *The City of God*, Vol. II, p. 117. Book XVI, Chapter XVI; and Vol. II, p. 145. Book XVII, Chapter II.
26. Saint Bernard, *op.cit.*, p. 35.
27. Milton's *At a solemn Musick*, lines 25-28.
28. Saint Methodius, *op.cit.*, p.118.
29. Methodius believed the first five days of the Creation were signs of the Temple while the sixth day was a sign of the Church. See Methodius, *op.cit.*, p. 35. Also see pp. 18-21.
30. Hugh of Saint Victor, *On the Sacraments*, p. 4.

Chapter Fifteen

1. The Semitic word for garden derives from a root meaning cover or protect. Hebrew also used *Pardés* from old Persian, meaning an enclosure or a walled-in place. A paradise is a garden or an orchard.
2. John Gerard, *Gerard's Herball*, the Essence therof distilled by Marcus Woodward, from the Edition of Th. Johnson 1636 (London: Spring Books, 1964), p. 1.
3. See *Saint Augustine's Enchiridion*, trans. Ernest Evans (London: S.P.C.K., 1953), p. 106.
4. "Was ever seen" recalls "but hope that is seen is not hope" (Romans 8:24). See *The Mower's Song*, lines 3-4.
5. "The cross taught all wood to resound his name". George Herbert, *Easter.* line 9.
6. Marvell's *The Definition of Love*, line 29.
7. Stanley Stewart, *The Enclosed Garden* (Madison: University of Wisconsin Press, 1966), pp. 34-35.
8. *Shakespeare's Ovid: Being Arthur Golding's Translation of the Metamorphoses*, ed. W.H.D. Rouse (London: Centaur Press, 1961), p. 2, 66-70; pp. 37-38, 857-864.
9. For laurel and reed, also see George Ferguson, *Signs and Symbols in Christian Art* (New York: Oxford University Press Galaxy Book, 1966), p. 33 and p. 37. Marvell

is making use of the usual pun on reed for pipe. Christ's voice is the Gospel Word.

10. See John McChesney, "Marvell's *The Garden*", *The Explicator*, Vol. 10 (1951), item 4. Also see William Empson, *Some Versions of Pastoral Poetry* (London: Chatto and Windus, 1968), pp. 99-109, and p. 132.
11. Ferguson (*op.cit.*, p. 36) says that the peach is sometimes used in painting in place of the apple to symbolise the fruit of salvation.
12. Origen, *The Song of Songs, Commentary and Homilies*, trans. R.P. Lawson (London: Longmans, 1957), pp. 179-180.
13. See Don A. Keister, "Marvell's *The Garden*", *The Explicator*, Vol. 10 (1952), item 24.
14. See Herbert's *The Bunch of Grapes*. In John 15:1 Christ is "the true vine". Christ is read into the grapes of Numbers 13: 23.
15. Matthew Poole, *A Commentary on the Holy Bible* (London: Banner of Truth Trust, 1962), Vol. II, p. 344. See Matthew 21:42-44; Romans 9:32-33; I Peter 2:6-8.
16. *The Didascalicon of Hugh of Saint Victor*, trans. Jerome Taylor (New York: Columbia University Press, 1961), p. 156.
17. *Partheneia Sacra*, by H.A. (1633), intro. Iain Fletcher (Aldington: Hand and Flower Press, 1950), p. 82.
18. Poole, *op.cit.,* Vol. II, p. 485.
19. Saint Augustine, *The City of God*, trans. John Healey (London: Dent, 1967), Vol. II, p. 360. Book XXII, Chapter III.
20. *Richard of Saint-Victor: Selected Writings on Contemplation*, intro. Clare Kirchberger (London: Faber & Faber, 1957), p. 51.
21. In mystical theology the annihilation is an imitation of the death of Christ, Who at the hour of His death felt annihilated. It is common to allegorise Psalm 72:22 (Douay translation and numbering) as referring to Christ: "I am brought to nothing, and I knew not". Sir Thomas Browne says: "And if any have been so happy as truly to understand Christian annihilation, extasis, exolution, liquefaction, transformation, the kisse of the Spouse, gustation of God, and ingression into the divine shadow, they have already had an handsome anticipation of heaven; the glory of the world is surely over, and the earth in ashes unto them". *Hydriotaphia or Urne Buriall, The Prose of Sir Thomas Browne*, ed. Norman Endicott (Garden City, N.Y.: Doubleday & Co., 1967), p. 285. Also see Browne's *Christian Morals*, Section 30, *op.cit.*, p. 422.
22. *The Ancrene Riwle*, trans. M.B. Salu (London: Burns and Oates, 1955), p. 59. See *Times Literary Supplement*, 11 August, 1950, p. 508, letter from Katharine Gavin.
23. See Saint Bonaventura, *The Mind's Road to God*, trans. George Boas (Indianapolis: The Library of Liberal Arts, 1953), p. 42.
24. "For why no thynge that is foule & corrupte by synne may entre in to *the* euerlastynge kyngdome, we must proyne and ordre all our feders, all our actes in euery condycyon that we may be the more apte to flee vp̄ vnto *the* place of euerlastynge blysse". *The English Works of John Fisher*, ed. John E.B. Mayor (London: EETS, 1876), p. 154.
25. The blessing on marriage to increase and multiply is given before sin, so that man will know that the procreation of children belongs to the glory of marriage and not the punishment of sin. Cf. Saint Augustine, *The City of God*, Vol. II, p. 51. Book XIV, Chapter XXI.
26. Arnold Williams, *The Common Expositor* (Chapel Hill: University of North Carolina Press, 1948), pp. 57-58.
27. The dial in Rome was dedicated to Jupiter. Pliny reports that a dial on the Campus Martius for thirty years did not agree with the sun. Preachers drew an analogy between the dial and Christ's earthly life. See J.W. Blench, *Preaching in England in the Late Fifteenth and Sixteenth Centuries* (Oxford: Blackwells, 1964), p. 225.
28. Stewart, *op.cit.*, p. 100.

29. "Wholesome" and "holy" have the same root. See Christopher Ricks, *Milton's Grand Style* (Oxford University Press, 1967), p. 62.
30. See Saint Francis de Sales, *The Love of God*, trans. Vincent Kerns (London: Burns and Oates, 1962), Book V, Chapter VIII, p. 200: "We search, like bees, here and there among the flowers of God's perfections, God's creative wonders; from these we gather the nectar of so many motives for gratification; from those we produce the heavenly honey of glory, praise and honour with which, to the best of our ability, we magnify and extol his name".

Chapter Sixteen

1. *A Dialogue between the Soul and Body*, lines 1-2. As the poem appears to be unfinished, I have not discussed it.
2. *Ibid.*, lines 43-44.
3. *Eyes and Tears*, line 3, line 5.
4. *The Coronet*, line 18. See Bruce King, "A Reading of Marvell's 'The Coronet'," *Modern Language Review*, Vol. 68 (1973), pp. 741-749.
5. *Upon Appleton House*, lines 739-744.
6. *Clorinda and Damon*, lines 27-30.

Appendix

1. *Eikon Basiliké: The Portraiture of His Majesty King Charles 1st* (London: D. Stewart, 1879), pp. 213-214.
2. See Bruce King, "'The Mower against Gardens' and the Levellers," *Huntington Library Quarterly*, Vol. XXXIII, No. 3 (May, 1970), pp. 237-242; and see Steven N. Zwicker, *Dryden's Political Poetry: The Typology of King and Nation* (Providence: Brown University Press, 1972).
3. Don Cameron Allen, *Image and Meaning* (Baltimore: Johns Hopkins Press, revised edition, 1968), pp. 138-151.
4. E.B. Reed, "The Poems of Thomas Third Lord Fairfax," *Transactions of the Connecticut Academy of Arts and Sciences*, Vol. XIV (1909), pp. 237-290, p. 281.
5. For Fairfax, see Clements R. Markham, *A Life of the Great Lord Fairfax* (London: Macmillan, 1870); and M.A. Gibb, *The Lord General: A Life of Thomas Fairfax* (London: Lindsay Drummond Ltd., 1938).

Index